26 Febru

Mum,

Under the circumstances rather apt don't you think!

Love Al xx

MANHUNT

MANHUNT

THE SEARCH FOR MR RIGHT

COLETTE SINCLAIR

SIDGWICK & JACKSON
LONDON

To Dave Hill

Your help and
encouragement made this
book a reality. Thank you.

First published in Great Britain in 1989 by Sidgwick & Jackson Limited

ISBN 0–283–99725–7

Typeset by Rowland Phototypesetting Limited
Bury St Edmunds, Suffolk
Printed in Great Britain by
Mackays of Chatham PLC, Chatham, Kent
for Sidgwick & Jackson Limited
1 Tavistock Chambers, Bloomsbury Way
London WC1A 2SG

CONTENTS

1

Wogan

As I stood in the wings of the television studio, waiting, I felt sick with terror and excitement. I tried to remember that it was my big moment, that not every girl gets a chance to appear on *Wogan* – in fact, I am one of the few unknowns to have been asked – and that, after the Make-up Department at the BBC had finished, I at least looked pretty good. I had imagined what it would be like, what I would say, what I would feel. I knew I would be nervous, but I hadn't been prepared for the blind panic – the butterflies that grew into moths and then large seagulls, beating their wings. I could see the audience, and a very small stage, with a sofa, a chair and a small table, right near a drop that looked about 10 feet *deep*.

The green sign, saying 'On Air', was formidable. I had passed it on my way down the stairs to the Hospitality Room. There I had been told that I was the first on, information that had done nothing to calm my nerves, overriding the couple of glasses of wine and the tablet I had taken to relax me. I had been given an idea of the questions Sue Lawley would ask, and I went over them again to try to remember the best answer, the one I had worked out in the safety of the little dressing-room with my name on the door. My mind felt like soggy blotting paper, and my legs shook. At least my walking on was not to be filmed. I was to sit down on the sofa, and Sue Lawley, the presenter while Terry Wogan was on holiday, would walk over to greet me, allowing me the choice of whether to stand or sit while I shook her hand. 'Only stand if your legs will take it,' I had been warned.

Sue started to talk to the audience, telling them that the theme today was love and marriage. I began to say something to the girl standing next to me, but was told firmly to 'Ssssh'. The music started, the 'On Air' sign lit up and I almost walked on myself, but she grabbed my arm and held on to it like a vice.

The lights were very bright out there, the audience expectant. Sue was talking: the show was about 'the eternal topic of love and marriage. . . . But let us begin at the beginning, with a woman who is looking for a man. My first guest knows even more about lonely hearts and blind dates than Cilla Black. She's given herself two years to find Mr Right. She's advertised, and out of the 400 replies she's received, she's been on twenty-four dates (including two trips to the States) and six second dates. She's had three serious proposals of marriage, none of which so far she's accepted. Ladies and gentlemen, please welcome – Colette Sinclair.'

A hand pushed me forward, and on I went, across a floor that seemed to grow as I put one foot in front of the other. Suddenly Sue Lawley was walking towards me, and I stood, as I had hoped I would, and shook her hand. The first thing I noticed was that she was wearing a black suit, a white shirt, and a bow at the waist of her jacket. Just like mine. I had searched high and low for the right clothes to wear, eventually finding what I'd thought was the perfect thing: a black velvet Frank Usher suit, with a mid-calf length, straight skirt, a jacket with a peplum, trimmed with bronze, and a bronze bow at the waist.

As I sat down, I had no control over whether I crossed my legs, smoothed my skirt or lay on the floor, for that matter.

'We look like the ladies in black sitting here,' said Sue, beaming at me. 'Do you think we're in mourning?'

All I could think of to say was, 'This isn't planned.' Luckily she backed me up.

'Certainly isn't planned. It must be the fashion.'

Her skirt was much shorter than mine. Perhaps I had been too careful not to come across as tarty, desperate, unladylike. But I wore sheer black stockings, and high patent leather black shoes, to make up for it.

'What sort of man are you looking for, Colette?' asked Sue. I had had plenty of time to prepare this question, as it was constantly in my mind.

'A successful businessman.' She nodded encouragingly. 'Tall, attractive, handsome, exciting, vivacious, who wants a happy family lifestyle.'

'You're advertising for the perfect man, really.'

'Absolutely. I want someone who's fun and successful.'

'What do you say for yourself in your advertisements?'

'I try and tell the truth in as short a space as possible. That I'm thirty-one, brunette, with a daughter aged 2½.' No point in trying to hide it.

'Does love come into it, though?' she wanted to know. I smiled, the memory of bitter-sweet moments still strong. I had fallen in love with 2½ of them.

'But Colette, how can you fall in love with half a man?' The audience laughed and so did I.

'Well, let's say that the two and a half men weren't as interested in me as I was in them, and the half was because we had had only one date, and maybe I wouldn't have liked *him* the second time.'

I have had passionate affairs in America, in Monaco, in Paris and London, but they haven't come to anything in the end.

'Yes, love definitely comes into it. Absolutely. To fall in love is the ultimate. I want to be passionately in love.'

'But how much does money matter? Would you marry a good-looking pauper, or would you rather have a sort of rich Frank-enstein?' she wanted to know and so, it seemed, did everyone else.

'If I receive a letter, and it indicates they don't have the income I'm looking for, I discount it,' I told her. The audience gasped, obviously thinking me too mercenary, and certainly too frank.

'But occasionally I bump into people who are gorgeous, but don't have any money. What can I say? Unfortunately, the heart takes over.'

The audience were with me now. Sue leant forward, woman to woman. 'What I want to ask you, Colette, is, why do you do it? You don't look like a desperate woman.'

I joined in the laughter that followed. 'Thank you – I hope that's a compliment. The problem is, you can go to singles bars, but there I meet the single yuppy type, who doesn't appeal to me. They're not looking to settle down, and it's most important I find a father for my daughter, as well as a husband for myself. We're a couple. There's no point in me falling madly passionately in love and travelling all over the world. I've got a daughter, and she's important.'

'Can you spot a fraud?'

'At first, no, but after two years, definitely. You learn to read between the lines.'

'Do they tell fibs?'

'Well, let's say misrepresentations. Or they want to portray themselves in a good light. They say they're dark; when I meet them, they're bald, with a couple of dark hairs sprouting from their scalp. They say they're tall, which means anything from 5 feet 2 inches up.'

'Do they boast about their jobs?'

'Definitely. They're all company directors, which means that they've got together with a couple of chums and set up a company that does odd jobs painting and decorating.'

I didn't say that they lie about their age, their background, their weight, their finances, but by now I didn't have to. I didn't need to tell her that attractive means that they have two eyes, a nose and a mouth, and sometimes not even that. I swear one of them had a glass eye. That when they say house on the ocean, it means they borrow a beach hut. Not all of them, admittedly, but plenty.

'How do you feel when you fly to the States?' Sue asked me, crossing one slim leg over the other, and resting her chin on her hand. Her diamante earrings glinted in the lights. 'Full of optimism, and anticipation, or do you feel vaguely ridiculous?'

'Initially, you're all excited. And then it's halfway across the Atlantic, and you're into the champagne and you start to wonder what it's going to be like. Is he what he said he was? And the doubts get deeper and deeper.'

'What happens when you walk in? Are you carrying the *FT* or wearing a rose? I suppose you have some kind of a marker buoy?'

'Once someone was half an hour late, so none of that would have made any difference,' but she wanted to pursue the question.

'What happens at the moment when you see him, and you think, Oh my God . . .?'

'I did, I did,' I said, with feeling, remembering the awfulness of the time it happened. 'What can you say? He must have lied a foot on his height and twenty years on his age, so what can you do but be nice and escape as soon as you can?'

'Have they all been gentlemen?'

I was emphatic. 'Absolutely. All of them. But they are all genuinely looking to meet a sincere wife. I hold myself correctly, and I don't give them any leeway . . .'

'You don't give them the wrong impression,' she finished for me. 'Quite right, and you haven't met a cad yet. You never know. There may be someone out there who's going ping at this very moment. It all depends if you can go pong in return.'

Amid the gales of laughter, she thanked me and asked me to stay with her when the next guest came on to join her.

She had been wonderful. She looked at me with those big eyes, and led me through it so that for most of it I didn't realize that there was anyone but me and her there. I'm sure with anyone else I would have cracked. As it was I was so relieved not to be talking that I sank back on to the cushions like Joan Collins on to her shoulderpads.

The next guest was Christina Rhodes, who runs the English

Rose agency, and I almost stopped listening. By now, I was feeling totally drunk, intoxicated perhaps by the wine I had drunk before coming on, and the little pill the doctor had given me to relax my nerves, perhaps by adrenalin. I just concentrated very hard on not making a fool of myself, and when she produced some photographs of American men for me to choose from, I just said the first things that came into my head, and tried to be polite.

The next thing I knew, a man from the Marriage Guidance Council was on, telling me that I should try to be more realistic, and, instead of disagreeing, I found myself nodding like a dog on the back shelf of a Mini, and smiling like the Cheshire Cat. When the whole thing was over, and after Cliff Michelmore and Jean Metcalfe had appeared as a shining example of a long and happy marriage, I was *so* relieved. I went straight up to the Hospitality Bar, where I downed a stiff g&t and felt a bit stronger.

I had genuinely thought that the response would have been amazing. But no. Despite the perfect BBC make-up that made my skin look quite flawless, Sue Lawley's help and the gaze of the television cameras on such a popular show, I received only three letters, none of which was any good at all.

One came from a hotelkeeper in Devon, who told me with pride that he was 'Thirty-five to thirty-six years of age, 6 feet 5 inches tall, dark hair balding, and a member of the Official Monster Raving Loony Party, and during the General Election polled a record 747 votes.' His other charms included three cars, one sprayed as a Union Jack, and 'a great sense of humour'. It wasn't going to be the same as mine, I felt sure, so I gave that one a miss. Another forty-seven-year-old wrote to the 'very brave lady who appeared on television in front of all those viewers to say you are looking for a husband'. I didn't feel like being patronized for the rest of my life, and anyway, he was too old.

The other one was from a man in Blackpool, who said he was '5 feet 10 inches, 11¾ stone, with a good head of hair and quite fit and active. A young forty-four with a lively mind and a good sense of humour.' I phoned him, but he didn't inspire me either. So that was that.

Still, I was the eighth wonder of the world (our world, anyway – Littlehampton is exactly like its name) for a week after the show, and people fell over themselves to be friendly. I still get recognized in the street every so often, months later, but none of this brings home the bacon, or the husband.

I waited and waited for the flood of responses to come pouring through the letter box. I accepted a date, without bothering much about it, convinced that it didn't matter whether it worked out or not, because there would be plenty of others to choose from.

The last date I had had before this came as a result of an article in the *Sunday Express* with the headline 'Queen of the Lonely Hearts'.

Someone, who I'll call Mr Gambler, had read the article, and wrote to the journalist Philippa Kennedy. She called me, very over-excited and said, 'I've found him, I've found him. I just had to call you. He's the one.' I was dying to see the post, and was really hopping by the time his forwarded letter arrived, three days later.

Attached to the three large sheets of rather nice, thick grey paper was a photograph of two men standing in the doorway of what I later learned was Crockford's Casino, all white and gold and rococo. Mr Gambler was holding a glass of champagne and wearing a dinner jacket, with a red carnation pinned to his lapel. He looked a bit fat to me, and perhaps too old, but what did it matter, I thought; I'd get plenty of letters from *Wogan* so, if he worked out, great, and if not, then I'd move on to one of the others. And his letter impressed me. He covered only one side of the paper, which I thought stylish and generous, like his handwriting, which was large, without spelling mistakes.

'Like yourself, I am a single parent,' he said. A good sign. He wouldn't think Moya was a problem and I would welcome his two children. 'No matter how many holidays and how busy my social life may appear to others [good – I liked the idea of travelling] I just feel that my life is rather empty and meaningless, apart from the love I have for my little girls.' Better and better.

He expanded on his business interests, which indicated that he was more than solvent: 'They include an electronic components company, various property investments, including factories and offices, and partnership in a small fourteen-bedroom hotel, a fast food restaurant and a recently formed sports promotion company.'

He made it clear that he wanted a good and stable home life 'to spend far more time at home with a family I can love and feel protective and loving towards', which pleased me too. He said that he didn't want to meet very young girls, which indicated that he meant what he said, and he ended the letter by suggesting dinner one evening. Could I ring him?

I did. He hadn't seen *Wogan*, which I thought wasn't such a bad thing, and we talked for an hour. His voice was just a tad common, and he admitted that he was overweight and would like to be fitter. I heard him light a cigarette, and that made me feel better, because he wouldn't mind about my smoking, although he did say that he must cut down, like we all do. He told me he had a house in Marbella, and had bought another plot of land, which he wanted to build on immediately. He didn't say how his wife had died, and I didn't bring it up, but talked a bit about his little girls, aged six and eight.

He invited me to London, which I said was fine, but that I'd have to leave early to get the last train home. So he extended the invitation for the night. He suggested Crockford's for dinner, then the Claremont and on to Annabel's. It sounded fine. I told him that I had been to Stringfellows, Tramp and Tokyo Joe's and he kept saying, 'You are a girl, you are a girl, I'm dying to meet you!'

We talked about casinos, and how I'd worked at the Metropole in Brighton. He'd been there, and told me some more about gambling. It was a pleasant conversation, he was friendly, and the date was something to look forward to.

At 1.15 on the day before I was to go up to town he rang again to finalize the arrangements.

This time he told me that he had considered marriage bureaux but didn't like their connotations. He said his daughter had seen me on *Wogan* and thought I'd looked like Mr Spock. 'But my ears weren't even showing,' I said, and he wouldn't tell me what she'd really thought.

I explained about writing my book and going on the television and the radio, which seemed to bring him up a bit short.

'What happened to the girl who wanted to stay at home?' he asked, in a jocular way, but with a little challenge in his voice.

'I wouldn't be the same girl you want to see if I stayed at home all the time.'

'True. I've often wondered about my sudden trips to Monte Carlo or Spain or whatever. If I had a wife, I wouldn't be able to make them as often as I do. And I've been thinking about my little girls – perhaps my lifestyle isn't fair on them. When I telephoned you, I expect you noticed I was a bit puffed. That was because I had been jumping on the bed with them.'

I thought that was very sweet. He talked about giving them riding lessons, and said that he would give them a pony a bit later on.

Moya went past at that moment and said hello to him. He said hello back, without being silly or self-conscious about it, which I thought was very sweet.

We agreed to meet at the Rooftop Bar at the Hilton. At first he suggested I wait there until he arrived.

'No. I don't like the idea of hanging about alone,' I told him firmly. 'Why don't you ring me on the courtesy phone and I'll come and join you there?'

'Fine. I'll take care of everything. All the financial arrangements too. Don't worry about a thing. Something I wondered – I hope you don't think it too much of an imposition for me to ask you up for the night like this?'

'Not at all. I assume you will be a gentleman and there will be a single room.'

'If that's the way you'd like it,' he replied, not nastily. There was no doubt that he completely understood the position, and I felt no pressure at all. I began to look forward to the date a lot. He had done all the right things. Sent a photograph. Called when he said he would. The area he lived in sounded nice. He seemed serious, and keener than ever to meet me.

That evening I spent watching myself on *Wogan*. It seemed so long ago, and yet it had only been yesterday. I had a bit of shock, seeing myself on the television. I had honestly thought I was more attractive than that. I looked so nice and well brought up, but I looked much better two years previously. Stresses of motherhood and all that, I suppose. I decided to wear my hair straight to make my face look thinner, and lots more eye make-up, turning up at the edges, to draw attention to my eyes.

That night, I checked to see if he had really booked the room, and all was as he had said it would be. I had quite a shock when the Hilton confirmed that a booking was indeed made, for a late arrival, about 6 p.m., in the name of Mr Gambler, held by an American Express Card. I have been let down so many times by these guys that I could hardly believe it.

The next day I went up on the train to London, and arrived at the hotel. I went up to the desk and asked for my room. Immediately his lack of style began to show.

'The booking is in the name of Gambler, M. Gambler. I checked last night. It should have been held and paid for on Amex,' I told the snooty clerk, who looked at me quite approvingly. I was looking quite good, in my cream dress, with my small, neat overnight bag. I smiled at him, as nicely as I knew how. The smile was wiped off my face soon enough when he looked it up in the book.

'It's been booked in that name, and held, but it hasn't been paid for, Miss . . . er . . .'

He looked at me more coldly now, clearly thinking I was a prostitute or something similarly unsavoury. Oh God, I thought, it's happening again. These guys are all the same. All talk.

'There must be some mistake.' I tried to speak calmly, to look as though I was in complete control, and that I could pay any bill I ran up. I don't think it impressed him. Funny how money talks.

I kept going. 'Look, I have an important meeting, and I have to get myself ready.' Oh yeah, I could see him thinking.

'Would it be possible to go to the room that's been booked and freshen up? I won't take long, so if there is a hitch . . .' I paused, and looked him in the eye, willing him to agree. The Arabs on the banquettes by the news-stand were really interested now, practically on the edge of their seats. I imagined I could hear the chink of money, the rustle of tenners as they prepared for action. Please, I thought, you little squirt. Please, don't be so pompous and believe me. Please.

'All right, Miss er . . . Sinclair. The room is yours until 9 p.m. After that, it will be the full rate – £157, plus VAT.'

'Thank you,' I breathed, and forced myself to smile regally as I tottered across the tiles, my heels clicking sharply as I walked past the disappointed pair of men on the sofa, taking care not to catch their eyes.

I was seething. OK Mr Gambler, I thought, you're just like the rest – another wasted evening. I was incredibly careful with the room, not dropping ash or rumpling the covers. The £157 repeated itself like the wheels of a train, and there was no way I was shelling out that much. It was weeks and weeks of child benefit money, for God's sake. Still, I made myself look good, in the same Frank Usher black velvet, sheer black stockings, patent shoes and a cloud of Opium.

When I was satisfied with my appearance, the telephone by the double bed chirruped, and his voice told me that he had arrived and was waiting in the Rooftop Bar. I went upstairs to meet him, and was pleased to see his eyes widen with appreciation as I walked in. Mine didn't. I thought, 'oh', and not much more. He was older than in his photograph, fatter, greyer than I had imagined, but his smile was warm and friendly, and he greeted me politely. We sat down and ordered drinks, on my room bill, which was a bit alarming.

As I sat there sipping my champagne, I quickly decided that this one was a non-starter. Even without the *faux pas* with the Amex card, he really was not my type. He was too old, not attractive enough and certainly didn't look after himself. His voice had a lower-class twang, which sat oddly with his dinner jacket, and he certainly wasn't someone I wanted to be seen with regularly. For tonight, it was okay, but even then, Annabel's was more seductive than he was. At the thought I cheered up, and began to make him feel pleased to be with me – I bubbled like the golden liquid in my glass, and was charming and friendly, going into neutral and settling into the same old charming routine, which I can do now without thinking about the questions: 'Did you have a nice trip? How are you feeling? How are your children?' etc. etc.

When we had finished the bottle, he went down to pay the bill. I freshened up in my room and then joined him in reception. We went out of the hotel and into the NCP car park. There my hopes rose. Among several shiny Rolls Royces, Daimlers, Mercedes, I expected something pretty flash. But no – my hopes sank as fast as they had risen. We walked over to a grubby motor, in the corner, Jaguar admittedly, but so filthy you could hardly see the colour. A small corner showed that it was maroon, and not that old. I got in, hoping that nobody I knew would be passing, and we drove off swiftly to Crockford's.

Crockford's is a gambling club in Carlton House Terrace, in one of those tall white buildings that overlook the Mall. From the moment we arrived, it was clear that I was on show. He had told everyone that I was coming, and I felt great pressure on me to act like a queen. I was cross about that too because it's always a strain, and I really didn't think he was worth the trouble. But I obliged and did my bit – I knew I looked good, he obviously thought I did, and I had been to plenty of these places before.

It was very smart, in a nouveau sort of a way. We decided to have dinner first – it was by now 10 p.m., and I walked down the steps to the restaurant feeling thankful, because by then I needed something to soak up all the drink.

The room was pretty, and we had a good table, with a good view of everything around. I think these things matter – I hate being stuck in a corner, not able to see anybody. There was a lot of gilt, rather new and shiny, and curved, high ceilings, lots of ornate cornicing and large dark painting around the walls. An enormous fireplace was at one end, and comfortable chairs were covered with tapestry and leather.

I ordered lobster, and he made a big fuss about the chef being a mate and rustling him up something that wasn't on the menu. I expected a roast boar's head with an apple in its mouth, the way he went on about it, but he got prawns done with some sort of sauce, and looked to see if I was impressed. I wasn't, but pretended a bit. The food was quite good, as these places go. The wine was delicious, and, again with much flourish and bother, he ordered more and kept it coming.

Around us were young and attractive Arabs, who looked a lot more interested in me than in their dates; the same went for me, but, of course, I couldn't be encouraging. To the far right were two women, probably Middle Eastern, beautifully dressed, but even they didn't intimidate me. I felt classy, certainly classier than Mr Gambler, who, quite honestly, didn't fit the bill even though he was paying it. At least, I hoped he was – the Hilton still remained in the back of my mind!

We talked, or rather, he did, non-stop. I'm good at listening by now, or looking as though I am, when men go on and on and on. He even brought a lump to my throat, I must confess, when he told me about his wife's death of lung cancer (which didn't stop the two of us from puffing away), and how his children wanted a new mummy, and how his mother was ill.

Before we got too maudlin, and began to sniff into our Chateauneuf du Pape, we were joined by a director of the club, who he had invited, clearly to impress me. Failed again. I know the type from old, but I quite liked her – someone who had been around, knew all the tricks and, although past her prime, still made people look at her and had done all right for herself. About forty-five, with a face that was still attractive, she had been Miss Penthouse, I think, or a *Playboy* centrefold, quite a long time ago. She told us about her twenty-five-year-old daughter, and we were supposed to ooh and aah and say she looked young. I didn't do any of this, but I admired her presentation, and her guts. Hard as nails, and a peroxide blonde, she obviously used to ooze sex appeal.

After one drink she went back to her other guests and Mr Gambler turned all his attention back to me. Which wasn't as good as one might think. I don't think that man listened to one word I said all evening. After a fair amount to drink all he was interested in was gambling, gambling and gambling. He hadn't mentioned it in his letter, but, boy, was he making up for it now. He had forgotten already that I had once worked as a croupier and I had to listen to the whole boring process. He was very proud of his success at the tables, at the races, the cards, the wheel. . . . He sometimes lost £10,000 in one evening, and dropped over half a million a year which of course was the reason he got into all these smart places. He wasn't a member of any of them, but he got in, and was given tickets for the best boxes at Ascot, for charity balls, all that sort of thing. One minute he went on and on about all the smart places he went to, and all the smart friends he had, and then the next minute he said how he enjoyed beating the rich at their own game.

After telling me interminably about his foolproof system, which he got from a book a friend had given him, he went on to give me a running commentary downstairs at the table. He played and played and played, but it didn't occur to him to give me any chips of my own. He joined a table with only one person at it, and cashed some money, rather a lot, in £50 notes, although I pretended to look the other way. By now, there was no chance that I was going to show this horrid little man that I was one bit interested in his money or his system or anything else about him. I honestly couldn't see that he was doing anything I wouldn't have done, without even having set eyes on his wretched book. I was bored out of my brains, and itching to go to Annabel's, but, no, he was going to make £1000, 'because it's such a special night, Colette'.

He almost did it. He was just £75 short, and I hoped desperately it might all be over, but then he lost the lot. I sat miserably while he went off to cash a cheque for £2000, wondering how much longer it would take. Miraculously, he made another £2000 in twenty minutes, and at last we could go.

He'd been paged by the friends who were waiting to sign him in to Annabel's, so we went along to the Claremont to meet them. That place oozed class. Real class. Old money. Old aristocrats dozing off in front of the fire in palatial surroundings. There were good paintings, and comfortable, authentic old furniture, and the coffee came in bone china cups, brought by a waiter with a nice voice.

His friends were great, much nicer than he was. Particularly one old chap, who made me laugh and didn't make me feel I was out with a used car sales manager any more. They knew that Bill was trying to impress them, and they knew that I outclassed him, and that they outclassed me, and they giggled nicely at us both. But we still had to get to the nightclub, and I was now on to Diet Coke, my head spinning.

Annabel's closes at 4 a.m., and we arrived at 3.30. All I wanted to do was go to bed and rest my drink-soaked head, but he kept on drinking, throwing it back non-stop, and going on about himself and what a good time he was having, and how he did this sort of thing all the time.

There was hardly anyone in the place by now, perhaps eight people, who all looked like frightful young snobs, something in the City, probably crashing bores, but certainly the real McCoy, no more interested in me than I in them. It was very dark, as you would expect, all emerald greens and maroons, with a tiny parquet dance floor. Nothing to write home about, quite honestly. I've seen some places in the States that knock it into a cocked hat. By now, I was beginning to get a bit worried. His behaviour had changed slightly. He wasn't shouting or singing or anything like that, he was just a bit more dogmatic, more boring, if it were possible, droning on more and more about himself. He was paying, and he was going to have a good time.

He had won something like £3000 and, with a grand gesture, gave me £50 (to cover my train fare and taxis), and then, overflowing with generosity, another £50 – 'buy something for Moya'.

At 4.00, we finally drove back to the hotel, with me clinging to the seat belt across me, hoping he wasn't going to hit anything. I could be forgiven for thinking that by now I had paid my dues.

But no. Instead of leaving me in the lobby, he came up in the lift to my room, and stood at the door, saying that he really wanted another drink. Oh Lord, I thought, now I'm in trouble. I've more or less managed to avoid trouble so far, although I must say that there have been some near misses, and I certainly wasn't going to have any funny business from Mr Gambler. But I could see I would have to be careful.

I let him in, and he undid his tie, took off his jacket and lay down on the double bed, in a very definite sort of way.

'Look, Bill, I really have a bad headache, and I'm exhausted, so I really need my sleep. You're welcome to have a cup of tea, but after that, I'd like to go to bed – alone.'

'Listen, Colette. Why don't you come over here and give me a kiss?' He had already poured himself a drink.

'No, Bill, I don't think so.'

'Don't be nasty. Come over here and give me a little kiss,' and he pulled me towards him, and made me sit beside him on the bed.

'I've really enjoyed tonight, honey. You're just perfect, did you know that? Just perfect. I really enjoyed playing the table in Crockford's. You brought me luck, you really did. It's such a good system, don't you think? A friend told me about it, and I think . . .'

While he rambled on into his glass, I went to the loo. When I came back, he had taken his trousers off, and I was faced with the sight of Bill Gambler, all 15 stone or so of him, in his dress shirt, socks and Y-fronts, with his huge fat stomach flopping over the top of them. This was a complete fiasco.

'Now look, Bill,' I began. 'This wasn't the arrangement. You know that. You're not staying, I don't want you to.' I was panicking a bit, but kept my voice firm.

'I'm not staying, Colette, just come and kiss me.'

I sat gingerly on the edge of the bed, wondering if this might be enough to get rid of him. He pulled me over again, and kissed me. Then he put his hand on my breast, trying to get inside my bra, rubbing like Aladdin trying to get the genie to materialize. It might have worked for Aladdin; it wasn't going to work for Bill Gambler.

'Look Bill,' I said suddenly. 'I think I'm going to be sick. All that drink's making me feel awful.'

He looked up blearily. 'Let's have another drink. It'll settle your stomach. I want another one too,' he added, as an afterthought.

'OK. Just one. And then you must go, like you agreed. If you don't I'll just sleep in the station and catch the first train back home. I mean it.'

Grudgingly, I poured him another drink, and, feeling really cross now, but still a bit scared, I turned to get him his shoes.

At this point, it all got too much for me. He caught my arm, pulled it, and forced me down on to the bed, heaving himself on top. Ugh. I lay there, completely winded, and I could feel an erection between his legs, getting rather too close for comfort. With one last shove, I pushed him off me and stood up.

'Please Bill.'

'OK. OK. I'll go.'

He pulled his trousers on again, and I felt much more secure.

'Look Colette, I'm sorry, but you do this to me. I haven't had a date in four months. I think you're great, you've got a really good figure, you really turn me on. When can we see each other again?'

I was just alert enough to think of a different excuse to squash every suggestion he made – Moya's birthday party, badminton, Mummie. Eventually we left it that he would ring.

As he tidied himself up, I inched him towards the door, with some cautious kisses, patting myself on the back for having escaped at last, and I told him that he was sweet so he wouldn't feel too rejected or too cross. Finally, he reached down to do up his flies, and I gave a sigh of relief. It was a little premature, however. Instead of pulling up the zip in one fluid movement, he whipped out his prick and held it proudly for me to see.

'Colette – see what you've done. It's not been like that since my wife died. My last girlfriend could never do that to me. You're so sexy and beautiful. I want to . . .'

Now I was really fed up, and I sounded like it. 'Put that thing away, and get out of the room. I've seen one before, you know, Bill. For God's sake, that's enough. I really feel sick and tired and I want to go to bed.'

He could see that his rather direct tactics had misfired. His prick got floppier and floppier, but he didn't give up. 'I've been having a problem ejaculating, Colette. It's been terrible. You . . .'

'Oh really.' He shifted uncomfortably, and put it away, trying to tell me a dirty joke to lighten the atmosphere.

'I'm really not interested, Bill. Don't bother. I'm not that sort of girl.'

Crestfallen, he looked around for his cigarettes, took another, slightly defiant, sip of his drink, and went towards the door. On the way, he looked as though he was about to change his mind again, but the look on my face put him off.

'OK, I'll go. Goodnight. It was a wonderful evening. I'll call you.'

We both knew he wouldn't.

'Fine. Do that. Thank you very much. I had a lovely time. Goodbye, Bill.'

I kissed him lightly on the cheek. I closed the door after him with a sharp click, and leant against the wall beside it, almost slipping on the carpet in my stockinged feet. I suddenly felt very cold. I washed and got into bed, and pulled the covers safely around me. It was good to be alone again.

The next morning I slunk past the hotel reception, in case he hadn't paid the bill and got a taxi to the station. On the train, I felt disheartened, disillusioned, angry and miserable, but I promised myself that something was going to change, very soon, and change for the better. There was no way I was going to give up, no way, and if I had to meet a lot more toads before one of them turned into Prince Charming, then so be it.

2

Early Years

I was born in Dorset in 1956 to middle-class parents living in a large delapidated cottage on my father's parents' family estate, miles from anywhere. I was the only daughter. My brother, Richard, was three years older. We now know he is mildly retarded. At the time this was not something people thought about, and we just thought he was a bit slow. We used to play together – I liked him well enough, and am now very fond of him – but he worried me, because I couldn't understand why I was always the leader.

My parents' marriage was extremely unhappy. My mother was clearly quite miserable about my father's behaviour towards her although she did try, unsuccessfully, to cover it up, and was as nice to us as she could be. My father was far more than just a difficult man – he used to indulge us one minute, playing merrily in the garden, and then switch to a really nasty mood. I was uneasy about him. His moods changed without warning. He was capable of being very cruel, and he frightened me. I still hear from him occasionally, as he wishes to contribute to my daughter's upbringing, but his conditions are ludicrous and I find them ridiculous. He says he has set up a trust for her (not that I believe a word of it), but if I miss out on the monthly letter telling of her progress (length and content stipulated) which I've never written, she loses one month's contribution. I told him to go to hell and that I was not interested in this sort of blackmailing relationship, feeling somewhat bad as I did so, because I do want the very best for Moya. But I feel in my bones that I would be foolish to get too involved with him – even for her sake.

He was a research chemist by profession with an average income. The family moved to Essex to be closer to his job. But from the time I was old enough to remember, I was aware of extreme tension, brutality and financial problems. He was extremely mean to my mother, giving her as little housekeeping money as possible. He was constantly in and out of work, never able to hold a job because of his awful mood changes. Mother was very concerned for us all.

'If you want money so much, go out and earn it, if you can,' he would say to her aggressively.

So she was forced, by total absence of money to do something. Since she had no professional training she used what she had – her looks, which were quite something. On my father's insistence she went to London and worked as a hostess in a very smart club, where men would come and have a drink or several. No topless shimmying or suspenders, just conversation and flirtation and another drink or two.

I do not resent it in retrospect, but at the time I missed her badly. Being at home alone with my father could be disconcerting to say the least. He would really enjoy tormenting us when he had us all to himself. He would shut us in our rooms if we had been only slightly naughty, and then later he would act as if nothing had happened and play happily with us. It was impossible to gauge his moods and we never knew what behaviour would get us a reward or solitary confinement. It seemed to have nothing to do with 'goodness' or 'naughtiness' – just his whim.

We had a succession of German au pairs, some of whom I liked because they were kind, and some who were neither particularly kind nor efficient. They were supposed to look after us, but I couldn't have been a very appealing charge for them, a nervous, withdrawn child, angry at being deserted, as I saw it, and scared of being bullied too.

Predictably, my mother started drinking. It was an occupational hazard, and one that helped her when she started thinking about the unpleasant side of her life. I'm sure she felt guilty about constantly leaving us.

Soon she found a sugar daddy, Philip, some thirty-three years older than her, with lots of money. She instantly gave up working at the club. Most of her new-found money was for living expenses, though he bought her presents – minks, diamonds and a Jaguar. I watched from the sidelines, gratefully clutching the Sindy doll he had brought me and realized that while some men caused unhappiness, others provided the wherewithal to escape from it.

Mummie looked glamorous but was unhappy although she loved her affluence. She showered us with things too, but I wanted more love from her and for her to stop drinking and leaning on me when things went wrong. I think she has always loved me, but has never known how to show it. And it is a bit too late now although we're trying to make up for the large gaps of affection in my childhood which have left large scars on my battered little psyche. I don't want to sound either self-pitying or phonily erudite. I have spent the rest of my life doing something about it, and I am nearer now to succeeding than I ever have been before. There is only one thing missing – a partner for me, and a father for Moya.

We later moved to Cheshunt, and into a beautiful Georgian house – mother's man was still footing the bills. My father was just as abusive towards her and she drank for strength. I was something like six or seven years old, and had developed a nervous shudder. I was sent off to school, where I was the youngest boarder. My mother thought it best for me but she never had the time to come and visit me, or take me out to tea, or have me and a friend home for weekends, like the other girls' parents did. I longed for some kind of normality, to be like everyone else. My mother was glamorous, knocking spots off most of the other mothers, but I would willingly have traded her mink coat for yards and yards of rough, hairy tweed, every huge and flashy diamond for a comfortable rope of undistinguished pearls, every purr of the Jaguar for the grumble of an old Rover. Over one holiday, I had to stay at school, and hated every moment of it. I felt unwanted and desperately alone. I was spreading out in all directions, eating and eating and eating in the time-honoured fashion of unhappy children. I nearly always came top of the class, because there was all the time in the world to study, and it got me a bit of praise from the teachers. Not much of a substitute for a smiling mother at the school sports day, waiting encouragingly at the finishing line for me to flop over it in a sack, but it was a good deal better than nothing. I had little outside contact, even with my brother, as he had been sent to a special school.

I loved my mother. I never felt angry with her, just miserable, wondering what I could have done wrong. She was all I had and I was all she had too. When things would get on top of her, and she had no one else to talk to she would forget my age and tell me about her problems with men, her sugar daddy, and her guilt. She wanted to leave her sugar daddy, she told me, but how could she? She hadn't any money and my father refused to work. Eventually she decided to leave him and on the day she did she got a call from a man whom she had fancied for some time and asked him along to give her courage. He collected Richard and me from our respective schools and we all left for a flat in Shoreham. At first it looked a better bet than before. He was a pilot, rather glamorous, and very good looking.

Philip continued to keep us even knowing about Bob, the new man. Mummie was in such a state by this time that she couldn't cope with me at home, watching her finish bottle after bottle, and I was packed off to another boarding school, this time in Haywards Heath, to be out of harm's way. When I came home for the holidays, knowing that it would not be very much fun, but longing to be away from school and with her again, she told me that she was pregnant. I was thrilled; Bob was pleased as far as I could tell, and Philip was also strangely pleased and bought Mummie a larger house in the country. Bob was becoming less of a good bet by the minute, although mother was crazy about him. He never had a proper job, spent a lot of money, his when he had it, and Mummie's, or rather Philip's, when he didn't, which was most of the time. Sometimes he would do something decidedly illegal like running arms to trouble spots around the world. He wasn't particular about who they were for, just as long as he got the cash. He wasn't very good for Mummie much as she loved him. I would find her plastered and in floods of tears at any time of the day or night, when she would pour out her worries, and a double gin at the same time. I tried to comfort her and cheer her up. I had a sister, Amy, soon enough, and loved her to pieces. We all did. Mummie called her the princess, and I lavished all the affection I had to spare, which was plenty.

I went to a new day school, a convent, and despite the drinking bouts, Mummie looked as glamorous as she always did, putting me in the shade. Which wasn't hard. She was still pretty and always needed to be the centre of attention, and I was now a very fat little piggy-eyed child, hanging around her, wanting and waiting to be loved.

I had horses and spent most of my time with them, winning plenty of rosettes, and wishing Mummie would be there to watch me. She hardly ever was – Philip, Bob and Amy plus her addiction saw to that, but I was only jealous of the men. Soon we were in dire financial straits, Philip was cutting back and I was blamed for much of it. My horses cost too much, and so did my education, she told me. I was sent to state school at my request but that was a dismal failure. I was too refined to cope with the rough kids and when the other pupils bullied me and mimicked my accent it reduced me to tears. Back I went to the convent. Despite all this yoyoing about, I was still doing very well academically, although I could never have been described as a well-balanced child.

By then I hated Bob with a passion. I couldn't wait to get away from home, telling myself that he was the whole problem, which of course was partly true. He did cause a lot of trouble and was extravagant with the income provided by Philip.

Like the ugly duckling, I suddenly bloomed when I was about thirteen years old. The rows grew more intense between me and my mother. Mainly over my indulgence in clothes and spending her hard earned money. Rather than put up with all that, I begged to be allowed to live with a friend and her parents. Mummie put up some resistance but eventually agreed, glad to have me out of her hair, I think, and I went to stay with the Hamptons in their house in a small town. I was, for the first time in my life, really quite happy.

It wasn't all perfect, of course. My mother would ring late every night, at least for the first few weeks, drunk and often hysterical, calling me a wicked child. I cried endlessly over the phone and in the morning she apologized and I felt close to her once more. The family really seemed to care about my happiness, and for a while it felt that in that atmosphere nothing could really hurt me. I felt sorry for my mother rather than angry, and when I put the telephone down, I would be cuddled and told that it didn't matter, my mother did love me, they were kind about my mother. I found their way of life very strange. It was normal, there were no rows, no empty bottles, no men who spent money and made me unhappy. However, normality was also unsettling for me, I wasn't used to it. But it was not to last long. Philip's wife died and Mummie married him and we moved to his Hertfordshire mansion, and me to another school. I hated leaving Sussex, but I had no choice. Mother persuaded Philip to give me another horse to make me happy, but even that didn't make me hate the old man less.

Parties started happening, and I began to find out that I wasn't so bad-looking after all. I had learnt enough from my mother to know that boys were useful, and their admiration made you feel good and got you places. When I got a glimmer of what life could be like, I made the most of it. As usual, in my life, things got out of hand. I got my first pocket money job – a pretty menial one in a hotel washing up, although it had a fancier name. I was sexually assaulted by one of the men I had met there, and gone out with a couple of times. It was horrible, but I was quite tough by now, and didn't tell anybody about it, tucking it firmly into the back of my mind where no doubt psychologists could have a field day with it, and with all the other debris that has been piling up there over the years. Shortly afterwards mother separated from Philip and we returned to our Sussex house.

As a child people were always feeling sorry for me, because I always looked so serious and worried. Now I was looking less serious and much less worried, and I preferred it that way. I had plenty of boyfriends – one with a red Ferrari. It should have been red roses, but I made the mistake early on of trying to take them home to meet my mother. She would offer them a pint of whisky, swaying about the room or bursting into tears. I felt so sorry for her – she didn't do it deliberately – she was after all an alcoholic. Of course, it did nothing for my relationships. I would never see them again, and so I soon learnt to keep them out of her sight and in so doing was always out a lot, a rebellious teenager.

I began to go out with the head boy of Lancing College, the public school on the hill. He took me to parties, there was laughing and kissing and lots of champagne. All quite smart and a lot of fun, and it gave me an early taste of what socializing well felt like. A taste I would like Moya to have and to enjoy.

Home was still as bad as ever, and suddenly I had had enough. I packed my bags one day and left for London. Just like that. I looked great at just sixteen, tall and slim, with long shining hair, smooth skin and outrageously sexy clothes which made the most of my figure. It did not take me long to find a job with a property company who wanted my looks and my 'O' levels in that order. I enjoyed the work and did it well for almost a year. Things went wrong again and I went home. I had split up with my boyfriend, Rashid, and had decided to make another attempt to make up with Mummie and see if we could somehow forge some kind of normal relationship. But this wasn't to be. I had little idea of what was normal myself, and she was still in an alcoholic haze. Suicide was a way out of everything. I tried it and failed.

I went to Brighton, trained as a croupier, for the glamour, and got very good at it, working at the Hotel Metropole for a couple of years. Boyfriends came and went. I had an affair with a married man twenty-two years older than me, who was great fun (I know, I know). Mark was wealthy and getting wealthier. I enjoyed his company, his attentions and his money. I looked good, had a ball and bought myself an MGB-GT.

Then I left him and went to Jersey where I got a good job. I met a man – this is a phrase you will get used to – and fell for him. We moved in together. I managed a wholesale food operation and had a great time. My man loved me, I felt special and really cared for.

After two years the island began to feel very small. We went on holiday to somewhere much larger – California. Even before our holiday we were arguing a lot and when we returned we decided to have a trial separation – one of those that means I had had enough of him but didn't have the courage to say so. I returned permanently to the States and soon learned that Los Angeles is fast, furious and not very kind to spoilt pretty girls from England, unless they move as fast and furiously as it does. I worked in Beverly Hills as a very English receptionist, and then got a job as a nanny, but it wasn't great. Feeling lonely, I contacted my ex-boyfriend, Norman, from Jersey, (he could refuse me very little) and soon he came to join me. For Norman and I to remain permanently in the States we needed citizenship so I married for the first time.

I am older now, and wiser, learning very late the lessons I should have absorbed as a child in the comfort and protection of my family. I don't blame my mother. She had fifteen years of living hell at the hands of my father, finally winning a divorce on the grounds of extreme mental and physical cruelty with no access granted to him for me or my brother which gives you some idea of her problems.

Most of our early troubles were caused by her alcohol dependency. It was only when relieved of the pressures placed on her that she was able to become teetotal and I admire her for it.

She and I have a pretty good relationship now, and live together with very few rows and more respect, laughs and affection than ever before. She is a wonderful Grandmother to my daughter, Moya, and loves her dearly. Together we are trying to give Moya the upbringing neither of us had.

I love my daughter very much, and I hope I shall be able to make a good, affectionate, balanced and comfortable home for her, now and more especially in the future, and thus help her avoid all the mistakes I have made. That is why I want a husband to start building the family life I never had.

3

Marriages and First Dates

It has been said that someone who has met as many men as I have over the past couple of years (and before for that matter), and someone who has been married three times, should surely have found Mr Right by now. Well, I couldn't agree more, but although I have said yes to the all-important question three times, I have never had a real married life.

My madcap scheme to marry an American in order to stay in the States worked, believe it or not. My then best-friend Sarah found a husband for me, among her six brothers, and later she agreed to marry my boyfriend from Jersey, Norman. The contract for both was identical – just for the immigration papers, no questions asked, no commitments, no demands.

It was all very embarrassing when it happened. Off we went to Vegas, arriving two hours before the ceremony was booked. We had a hilarious double ceremony, with a nervous minister officiating for four rather hysterical and wild-eyed people. He felt that I at least did the right thing when tears started to pour down my cheeks, but they were tears of hysteria, not emotion. Back we came to the flat in California, and both of us got through immigration, although it was no easy matter.

Norman and I were happy together. I loved him, or thought I did for another two years. He was a good, honest, upright man, really my best friend. But there had always been some fundamental problems. He was from Yorkshire, and was thirteen years older than me, and although he did truly love me, I wasn't charmed for ever by his reliability, although it's something I always look for in men now. I look for other things too, though, and Norman did not have the panache, the money or the lifestyle that I had been used to before I had met him. Not having treated him very well (in my defence, it was a long time ago), I moved out, and found someone else in that sun-soaked state, where everyone is slim and brown and your next Ferrari is only a real-estate deal away.

I met my second husband at a private and very exclusive disco on Newport Beach. He knew that I was with someone else, but wouldn't take no for an answer. One day, my resistance was low and I accepted his invitation for a drink. He was not the most beautiful of men, small, dark, Arabic and not at all handsome, but what he lacked in looks he made up for in intelligence, fun and his sense of humour, and of course in hard cash. I was always being given presents, taken out for wonderful expensive meals and was the only woman in a male entourage (he was closely connected to a Middle Eastern royal family). He was very patient. He worked on me slowly, remorselessly, and soon we became friends, and eventually lovers. He worshipped me, pure and simple – not that I was either of those things. He paid my expenses at my separate apartment. I lived with him only when he was in the States, which I enjoyed because I wasn't in love with him, and didn't want to get that involved. I liked him very much, though, and looked forward to his company.

For a while, I just sat back and forgot all about England, loving the attention, the fun, all of my life's rich pattern – and I mean rich. Then one day I went to my hairdressers, a smart Beverly Hills salon, and looked across the dryers straight into the eyes of this devastatingly handsome Mexican/American man – brown and strong and tall and gleaming. That was it. We met, he was to do my hair, we talked, we went out, without telling Abdullah, of course, who was out of town anyway. We made love again and again, in the separate apartment that had been so conveniently supplied for me. I couldn't help it. I was wild about Alfredo. This had never happened before. I owned up to Abdullah that I had a new passion, and that this was the 'real thing'. He was too obsessed by me to let me go that easily, and I was rushed to Vegas for the second time against my better judgement. I had had a divorce from the first travesty of a marriage, and so Abdullah saw his chance. We married, but it was hardly something that was meant to last. I sought an annulment quickly, and Abdullah by this time was getting into trouble with his princely masters who were quite happy to have me around as a decorative appendage, but not so thrilled to have me as the wife of their right-hand man.

So I said that I would not bring up my children in the Moslem faith, and the rest was easy, for me, but not for him. He minded terribly, but he could do nothing with me or I about myself.

Alfredo and I lived for each other. Our passion was intense, and all powerful; all the overblown words that have been invented for wild emotional attachments could have been invented for us. I felt completely clean and new, and I thought that I had learnt that money is not the be all and end all of life. Nor, I found out, is love. Not on its own anyway. Ours began to fray at the edges when I found out, even before our rushed marriage in Tijuana (by this time signing my name in registers was becoming a regular occurrence), that he was ultra possessive, jealous and a heavy user of cocaine. The latter meant that he spent a lot of money, money he didn't have. He would drink, and so would I and there would be ugly scenes, resulting in black eyes for me, or I would walk out and go and stay with my friend Marian, who helped me through the whole thing.

I ran away to my old flat that Abdullah was still keeping for me, but went back. I ran away all over the place, until all the running became too unbearable and I ran back to England for a holiday. There I met Moya's father. I had become a glutton for punishment, believing that each romantic encounter was the answer to my prayers, and all I can say is that, although I was wrong, I was sincere at the time. My childhood had taught me that men could be the best thing in my life, and also the worst. I didn't care until the worst happened, because I had also learnt to live for the moment, if it was good. There hadn't been that many of those.

Michael and I were crazy about each other and I came back from the States a month later to live with him, and I got a job in London.

That's when the disillusionment began. He was great looking, 6 feet 4 inches, brown and with a wonderful smile and great in bed but he was an emotional wimp, who would not make any kind of decision and depended on me for everything. I couldn't stand it, so went off to America, moving back to LA from Houston. With a girlfriend, I rented a terrific apartment, one of the most expensive on Newport Beach, for six months. I got a job, this time as a real-estate negotiator and was doing perfectly well, until I began to get fat. My stomach grew and grew and I began to get worried. One doctor diagnosed a tumour, but luckily he was wrong. I was five months pregnant! I was thrilled, ecstatic. A baby was something I'd always wanted. I intended to bring her up in the States.

I had had very little to do with my mother over the past years, but recently she had become teetotal and now offered me a home with my new baby. I had sobered up too. I had decided that returning to England to devote my life to my child, and becoming the world's best mother would be a good idea. For a while I did just that. She was and is a wonderful little girl and both Mummie and I love her to pieces, more than words can say here. I began to view life differently. I was more fulfilled, happier, and content to be with my mother, my brother (who stayed at weekends) and with Moya, who was all I wanted her to be. I never got as depressed as I used to, and I no longer felt an emotional wreck. I didn't want to live on the edge any more, I no longer craved excitement, I had had my fill of that.

It wasn't all roses though. I was totally dependent on my mother for a roof over my head. She paid for everything, for me and for Moya, and to begin with she was trying her hardest to show that she too had changed. She paid for warm coats and jumpers for me, because, of course, I didn't have any clothes for the cold. She bought all Moya's clothes, so I wasn't able to choose what she wore (although I have to admit I loved most of the clothes Mummie bought for her). When we went out shopping she would see me try on the clothes in the shop and buy the ones she thought best, which was also pretty humiliating. All in all, it didn't do my self-image very much good which was fragile anyway. I would protest at times, saying, 'I am able to look after myself, you know.'

'No, you're not,' she would answer. 'Otherwise you wouldn't be here would you?' There was no answer to that. She 'mummied' me constantly, trying to make up for the home life she had never been able to give me.

I had learned young that I was attractive, and that men were vulnerable. I suppose if I had had a father I respected, I would have had a clearer picture of men, but now everything is rather muddled. Nevertheless, in general I like men. I see them as protectors, providers, and lovers, and I do, really and truly, believe that there is one man out there, somewhere, who will be all I want and we will be all he wants. I may not find him, I may have to settle for Mr Almost Right, but it doesn't shake my faith. All that matters at the moment is that I need a good father for Moya, and someone I love, like, admire and find sexually attractive to be a husband for me. I enjoy being in love and miss the warmth of being loved in return.

I was very grateful to my mother for taking me in. I was fed up with California in many ways. Just before I left, there had been a baby snatching case, which had earned itself a lot of publicity and frightened me to death. I had just got myself a wonderful baby, who I promised myself I would cherish and look after and love, as I never had felt loved, and I was terrified that she would be whisked away from me. Mummie jokingly pointed out that in this country you would be more likely to worry about the pram being pinched!

I was also sick of the constant pressure to be beautiful, to spend hours in front of a mirror trying to look natural. The concrete jungle of Los Angeles was not where I wanted to stay, and I certainly didn't want my daughter to be subjected to it, or to the American educational system. One of the things children seemed to learn best was how to take every possible drug on the market. It was difficult to avoid drugs in the States. Every party, every dinner, every meeting with other people was a time for a 'snort', a 'toke', a 'hit'. The language completely bewildered me.

I was happy to be in England and was fascinated by all the things that are different from America. I have always loved the countryside, and had sorely missed it. I looked at the woods and the sea and the country lanes as if I'd never seen them before, and my soul felt refreshed. California is an essentially unrefreshing place. It teaches you how to be efficient, how to survive, how to worship the making of money, so of course I found the slowness of England a trial at first. But I can tell you that after years of high-tech, high-finance, high-achieving living, I was ready for a rest.

Trying to bring Moya up as I would have liked didn't last long at Mummie's. All too soon, Moya was hideously spoilt. I tried not to give her sugar in her diet, but Mummie and Richard, my brother, would always be slipping her sweets, which of course she preferred, so I was the wicked mother trying to deprive my child.

I had to hide my feelings towards my mother as much as I could. When she is angry, she frightens me, and I don't like the feeling. I was scared of being kicked out, and so, because she wanted everything her way – it was her house – I tried not to thwart her.

When I moved in, and she was being extra sweet, she could see I had been through a lot and needed tender loving care. She told me that there were only a couple of rules of the house: not to wear high heels and ruin the carpet, and always to use cups with saucers to avoid rings on the furniture. If only that had been all. There were hundreds of rules, of complaints.

I have learned to adjust now and, as I said, we enjoy each other's company for the most part and have a lot of fun, but on bad days it was, 'I don't know how you can watch that rubbish. Turn it off,' or 'you are obsessed with that washing machine. You don't pay for the electricity to run it' or 'the shopping I have to do is far too much for me to carry' or 'you are constantly on the phone. You could write a letter, couldn't you?' and so on. It was very depressing and, however hard I tried, I couldn't always avoid talking back, and if I hit a nerve, she would suddenly become the old, frail, pathetic provider, who was only trying to help her daughter and granddaughter. I couldn't win, so in the end I stopped trying. I'm no angel, and I know after many years of living my own, crazy, independent life, I was not easy to have around the house either. I certainly wasn't used to trying to survive on such a low budget, and my mother wasn't used to having two new dependants.

When I arrived in Littlehampton, all my friends gave me a barbecue and welcomed me like a celebrity, which made me feel very much at home and wanted, and happy about myself. Six months later, after the occasional row with Mummie and when my novelty had worn off a bit, and Mr Right hadn't appeared, I was less contented, more anxious, and much more worried about the future for us all. All this made me more desperate than ever to get out.

But what could I do? I could hardly go out to work with a small baby, and a mother who categorically refused to look after her singlehanded. I would never earn enough to support us and pay for a nanny for her, and I'm sure that Mummie would not have looked that kindly on a nanny in the house – her house. It was already too small for all of us. We sat down and thought about the future. The starting point was that Moya needed an ordinary family life with a father figure, and I needed someone to love, be loved by and to support us.

I am attractive for my age, now thirty-one, but not a dolly bird, so not in the running for fast cars and fast men any more. I am not skinny, not fat, a size twelve, and I have long brown hair which I take care of, keeping it shiny and soft. I am 5 feet 8 inches, although I look taller, and I have been brought up to know how to behave. I am outgoing, a bit crazy perhaps, but I've never once been called boring. I possibly talk too much, but that's because I have a brain that moves even faster than my tongue. I like fun and excitement, but more often than not I am quiet and enjoy painting, drawing, crafts and art in general. I cry at movies, I am sentimental, but I can also be hard-headed, and feel that people would do better if they would get off their backsides and get on with it. I am many different things, a mass of contradictions, but the sum of the parts is not unpleasant.

In short, Mummie and I decided that somewhere out there, there was a suitably attractive, kind, comfortably off, dependable, family-minded man who would be only too happy to have me as his wife, and Moya as his daughter. The question was – where on earth to find him?

One thing we were certain of was that he definitely exists. It was the finding that would be a problem, but by the end of this consideration, we knew that we were prepared to have a go. We worked out the qualities that we needed in Mr Right.

He should be an entrepreneurial type, independent of mind and means. He should be taller than me, ideally 6 feet 4 inches, but 5 feet 11 inches would be fine. If he were madly attractive it would be a bonus, but as I'm not fabulous looking we were prepared to drop the madly. He should not be bald, and I would prefer him to wear contact lenses (I do) if he needed help with his eyesight. He should have a good physique, neither skinny nor fat – I couldn't cope with sparrows' legs. Ideally, he should have nice hands, with long slim fingers – I am particularly attracted to hands. It would be better if he could enjoy socializing and have an active social life, but we would also enjoy staying at home. He should want to spend time with Moya, his children if he has any, and me, being a family at home, or going on outings. Alone together we might go to the theatre, cinema, discos, concerts. If he had his own interests like a boat somewhere it would be good, but he should not expect me to paint the hull every weekend. We should enjoy each other's company and there should be chemistry between us. Naturally we would have to fancy one another before anything could gel and lastly he should want to have more children in the future. Asking a lot, I know, but I thought, encouraged by Mummie and the pressing overdraft, that it was worth a concerted effort.

In Sussex, the sports clubs are full of retired people or women. I had no job and couldn't have one so that way of meeting people was out. My friends and I weren't into propping up bars so it seemed that advertising was the only way to get to meet this paragon.

Mummie went out and unexpectedly found *Singles*, a magazine specializing in advertisements for Lonely Hearts. Initially, they all sounded wonderful, so I rushed to put pen to paper (and so did Mummie to hurry the process along) and sent out ten letters in reply to the ads. I also put in my own ads in some other papers and waited excitedly. From *Singles* came nine responses, of which I chose two. I arranged to meet both; one had sent a photo, one had not. The first meeting was outside a coffee shop in Brighton. I was completely petrified, as you can imagine. Would he be weird? Revolting? A maniac? Divine? Would he hate me? Love me? Paw me? It is a lot easier now, after years of practice, but it still is exciting and nervous-making at the same time.

My very first date was with a man called Richard, Richard Warner. He was thirty, 5 feet 10 inches, blond, well-spoken and obviously well-educated. His mother was American and his father English so we had much in common, as we had both spent a lot of time in America. It is rather unfortunate that he was the first man I met, because it gave me an *entirely* unrealistic impression of the dating game. I thought everyone would be like him. How wrong I was!

Because he was so keen to meet immediately, I agreed to do so without seeing a photograph, something I wasn't going to do, and rarely do now. We arranged to meet outside Browns in Brighton, and I recognized him at once.

Determined to look my best, restrained yet attractive, I wore my cream wool suit and a camel coat. He was conservatively but well dressed, in a dark suit, a blue shirt, red tie, well-cut dark blue overcoat. Rather straight, but nevertheless smart, and it suited him. I was pleasantly surprised.

We had lunch and then walked together, and then I took him to meet my friend Georgie who lives with her parents in a beautiful house near Brighton. She has been rather disapproving of this whole thing, but was intrigued by my progress at the same time, although I know she feels I should work and have a career, and not do something that is a little degrading in her eyes. Her parents were even more disapproving but I respected their judgement and used them this first time as a barometer. We drove to the house in his natty red souped-up Lancia, with all sorts of extras to make it even flashier. It wasn't a Ferrari, but I was impressed. I was less impressed with his not paying when I went to buy a cake for tea, but anyway, off we went. He liked the manor, as I knew he would, and was very polite. Later they told me that they thought he was too conventional for me, but they liked him.

After that we tried to go out to dinner, but after trying six restaurants, all full, we settled on a pub. He said he had forgotten his wallet, so I bought the first round of drinks. On top of the cake business, this was beginning to look a little ominous. I was starving, but decided to say I wasn't hungry when it came to supper, which as it happened was cutting off my nose to spite my face, as he went shortly after that to collect his wallet from the car. He paid for the next drinks, and then drove me home, talking on the way about another date.

'OK,' I said, rather lukewarmly. 'If you like.'

'Shall I pick you up next week? What day would suit? Dinner? Or at the weekend?'

'Oh, what about dinner on Thursday? That would be fine, I think.'

But I had another date to meet, who looked divinely handsome in his photograph, and I didn't care what happened. I was very confident by now – this was going to be easy. I had Michael up my sleeve, and so didn't really appreciate a letter from Richard (his address was a good one in London – that bit was appealing) as much as I would do now.

I decided to drop you a line following our telephone conversation on Saturday. I think you know by now that I enjoyed meeting you last Tuesday, finding you both an interesting and attractive person.

The situation we were in was for me and I think for you a difficult one, in that it was an unfamiliar and chancy way of meeting someone. Because of this I was more reserved with you than I would have liked to have been and talked less of myself and what I am really about than I might have. I wonder therefore if you will have gained as favourable a view of me as you would have otherwise. You would very soon, I believe have used the following adjectives to describe me: affectionate, ambitious, reliable, sensitive, trustworthy, sophisticated, humorous, responsive, flexible, dependable, imaginative, responsible, realistic and interesting.

If you are looking for someone who leads an interesting and rewarding life full of contrast and who could potentially fulfil what you seek, then you will want to meet me again.

I will of course understand (and would certainly have to!) if you have met someone who on first blush you prefer, or if you are disenchanted with all of this. But if this is the case, maybe this letter would encourage you to meet up with me again? I do look forward to hearing from you.

I was touched by his enchanting and articulate letter, but my reply was firm.

Dear Richard,

Many thanks for your letter. I too enjoyed meeting you and having a fun day out. However, I've been debating as to whether or not to tell you why I feel our relationship would never develop into anything more than just friends and that's not what I'm seeking.

Well here goes. Do I have the courage? Yes, because as a friend this may stand you in better stead for the future.

I was surprised when you didn't purchase the cake as I was taking you out to visit my personal friends. To add to this I was surprised to find you had left your wallet in the car and that I was expected to buy a round of drinks and, to cap it all, at the pub when the bar lady was trying to assist us to find a meal, you suggested bar food and not a restaurant.

Richard, I do hope you take this in the manner it was written, as a friend. I'm not used to being treated in this way, when out with a gentleman, especially on the first date.

On his neat blue paper with the navy embossed address, I got a reply, a rather nice one, which, as I say, I would certainly give more attention to now.

I did appreciate your letter and the fact that you expressed your true feelings – such truth is always best and as you say might stand me in better stead for the future.

Remembering some of the things that have happened to you [I had told him some of my past life in the pub, including the fact that Alfredo, my third husband, had stung me for several thousand dollars], I can see it's hardly surprising that you feel the way you do in respect of those happenstances you relate and would see them as a signal of some fundamental flaw. I can only say that lack of generosity or stinginess are not failings that ever have been mentioned as one of my possibly many failings.

Admittedly, if I had been more careful of my presentation of self and social etiquette, I might not have fallen into the bearpits I seem to have dug for myself.

I'm sure you remember how much I wanted to have dinner with you that night (otherwise I would not have asked!). If I mentioned bar food to the bar lady, it was only because of my frustration and embarrassment at not finding anywhere to take you. I certainly did not expect you to pay for drinks – leaving my wallet in my jacket was a mistake I only realized when I came to pay for them. I would never (and obviously in retrospect never should have) asked you to pay if I had realized that I was making such a *faux pas*.

I do admit that it did not occur to me to buy the cake to take to your friends and that it would have been a very nice gesture for me to have made. Moreover, it seems that as a matter of social etiquette I should definitely have seen that as my obligation?

Of course first impressions are very important and I seem to have made a hell of a mess of it. I'm not sure why I'm writing this letter, other than because I wanted to tell you the way I saw things and you might even decide you would like to meet up again.

Well, now, of course, I would. In fact it is one of my greatest mistakes that I allowed our next date, a Chinese meal, to be our last. I would really like to see him again. Perhaps I will?

The next date, Mr Wonderful, was all I wanted in a man. Goodness, how lucky I was to have two such good men for my first dates, but it was also bad luck because I handled them both so badly. But I have put it down to experience, and I am a good deal wiser now.

Malcolm and I decided to meet in a restaurant in Littlehampton. The weather on the night we were to go was appalling. Snow was pouring down and transport was badly disrupted. I had ordered a taxi from a firm I often used, for 8 p.m., but when it hadn't come by 8.15, I was desperately ringing round for another. Eventually, I got one, and arrived in a terrible fluster at the restaurant, three quarters of an hour late. I saw this chap charging through, covered in snow, and realized that he must be my date, who obviously must have been delayed as much as I had been. He had come down by train, and was carrying a rather obvious overnight bag, which he stashed quickly in the cloakroom.

We made for the bar, hair covered in melting snow, snow on our boots and red faces. He was all I had expected. He never lost the twinkle in his eye, and was happy, outgoing, fun. I really fell for him, and hoped the feeling was mutual. He seemed to like me, but I wasn't practised in spotting the signs yet (not that I am that good at it, even now). We ordered hot toddies to warm us up, and while they were coming, we both had the chance to surreptitiously eye each other up. He was dressed beautifully – soft, dark grey leather trousers, tucked into expensive boots that looked like they had just walked out of Loewe in Bond Street. A grey tapestry shirt was worn under a thick sweater draped with a dark red and grey scarf. He was a little short, about 5 feet 10 inches, or perhaps a little less, but wonderful looking. And that smile! I wore a sexy black and red crepe number, tight-fitting, very sheer. I was very overdressed in fact, because I'd had no idea how people would dress in this restaurant. The restaurant staff were closing the kitchen because there were no diners that evening, so we hurried to our table in the pretty beamed room, with white tablecloths on the tables and flowers and pretty paintings on the walls. But the service was appalling.

Anything we asked for on the menu was off. I had garlic prawns in the end I remember, and I am not sure what he had; probably the same, considering the paucity of choice.

He was a delight to be with. We both laughed about the place and the weather, the food and the service.

'What do you do in your spare time?' I wanted to know.

'I go away about three times a year. I enjoy skiing and I'm going to Verbier soon. Do you ski?'

'I'm a sort of snow bunny,' I said laughing and pointing to the by now white windows. 'That's why I'm happy in this lot!' He ordered some wine which turned out to be delicious.

'I enjoyed the champagne in the States. It isn't really champagne, I know, not coming from France, but the grapes are the same, aren't they?' I said, trying to sound knowledgeable, oblivious to his answer, just captivated by his bright face.

He loved clothes and fashion. 'Your dress is beautiful. Expensive too. I've seen some like it in the States and they're hard to find, aren't they?'

Flattered, I told him where I'd got it, and before long he was asking about my life and my past. I told him a lot, and we discussed the differences between the States and England. I was still pretty fresh from America so could think of quite a few. 'Crossing the road – I've almost been run over a hundred times for looking the wrong way! And the supermarkets – fifty different sorts of everything. My girlfriend Marian and I used to make every possible variation of ice-cream we could – toffee and liqueur and nutty ones, chocolate chip – that's my favourite, and I do miss that. I miss going to football games – it's a family social event there, not like the very rough games here. I could go on and on.'

And did, and so did he.

'My dad's got a car accessory firm, and I work with him. I've just renovated my house in town – it's all white and grey and very uncluttered.'

'Exactly the sort of place I adore. Just what I would have,' I told him, entirely truthfully. My mother's house is rather fluffy and full of furniture, and it really is not my taste at all.

By now I was shivering in my dress, and he wasn't warm either, so he went and got our two coats. We looked ridiculous, sitting in an empty restaurant, drinking and eating and laughing and talking, muffled up to the eyeballs.

'You're the most attractive date I've had – I can tell you,' he said. I was blooming under his compliments, and falling more and more for him every minute. When we left, we held hands and found a taxi to take us back to Mummie's. We had some more to drink, and kissed and cuddled a bit on the sofa. I didn't want to stop, but he was more circumspect and was the one who held back and suggested we went (separately) to bed. I regretfully agreed that he was right and picked up the stray cat we were looking after to put her in a box.

'She looks really ill,' he said, looking very concerned, and taking her very gently from me.

'She belongs to the neighbours. We're looking after her because it's snowing so hard and they just leave her outside whatever the weather.'

'Poor puss. Poor puss. How's you doing then?' he murmured, stroking her, and putting her down on a hairy old blanket we had found in a cupboard for her to sleep on. In fact, the next day we took her home to our neighbours. Later they dropped by to say they had had to have her put down. They weren't a bit bothered, nothing like as much as we were.

Off we went to bed, me to have wonderful dreams of the future in my room, he to sleep in the guest room cleared out manfully by Mummie and me before he came, as we thought he would probably have to stay.

The next morning I wanted to impress him with my cooking. I asked Mummie's advice and she said, 'Just get on with it. Make him what you want, don't ask him and then take it up to him.'

So I had high hopes of my scrambled eggs, grapefruit and toast, but I burnt the toast, and the scrambled egg lay in a pale yellow granular lump in the middle of the plate, oozing rather dubious water all around it. I would have ruined the grapefruit if it had been possible, I'm sure!

I took the tray upstairs and walked in with my hands too full to knock. He was out of bed, clad only in rather small black underpants, which made it easy for me to have a quick look at his physique before he hopped, embarrassed, back into bed. I presented him with my culinary creation, and sat on his bed, talking to him while he ate half of everything, which was pretty good of him in the circumstances. It was romantic and friendly chatting that morning and soon after he had finished eating he asked what I would like to do today.

'I thought it would be nice to go out to Chichester,' he said, smiling.

'Oh God,' I said, weakly, 'Chichester is about thirty miles away, it's snowing and we haven't got a car. Couldn't it be somewhere else? I also have a crashing headache after all that wine last night!'

Basically all I wanted was for him to go and for me to die, but instead I suggested Worthing, which I knew would cost only £3 by taxi. He agreed, but I knew I had disappointed him by not being game for the longer trip.

I dressed up jauntily for our trip, and off we went. We held hands as we walked around the shops, but I noticed that we only stopped at things *he* liked. If I liked anything and wanted to linger, I was moved on sharpish to the next window. We looked at kitchens, we looked at clothes, at shoes. I have a feeling he was checking me out financially, but then he must have known from my circumstances and my conversation how I stood.

We then went for a walk on the pier. The wind was blowing my hair about, I had 4-inch heels on and was stumbling a bit, but it was bracing, and he kept smiling, which cheered me along. 'Race you to the end of the pier,' he cried, holding my hand even more tightly. 'Come on!'

'You must be joking,' I cried against the wind, pulling my hair out of my eyes. 'In these heels! I'll break my neck!'

'You're not very adventurous, are you?' he said, looking at me oddly, and right there, I knew I'd lost him. And I minded desperately, but by now there was nothing I could do about it.

He pulled at some red streaks I'd had put in my hair: 'What are these, then?' I smiled weakly, with a heavy heart, and didn't answer wittily, as I knew he expected me to.

We caught the train back, and I got out at Littlehampton. He didn't, putting his head out of the window to kiss me, gently, without passion.

'Thank you for a nice day. I enjoyed meeting you, Colette. I'll call you, OK?'

I knew he wouldn't and tried to smile cheerfully as if I believed him, as the train pulled out of the station. I turned to walk out, before his head was out of sight, and tried not to mind too much.

He never telephoned again. I see his ad every so often:

FELLOW SYBARITE SOUGHT! Do you enjoy romantic weekends in Paris, Vivaldi, bouillabaisse washed down with Chablis, fast cars, Italian clothes, shared baths, long evenings in front of a log fire? If so, please write with photo. I'm a happy and successful company director, thirty, dark haired, very attractive and well travelled. Looking for an intelligent and adventurous companion for permanent relationship. Midlands Based.

Another one he put in (I know this because a girlfriend answered it and found it was him):

CHANCE OF A LIFETIME! Handsome businessman, thirty, 5 feet 10 inches, dark haired, well travelled, cultured, affluent, graduate. Interests: travel, arts, skiing, good food, wine. Seeks attractive and vivacious companion, with similar interests and background, for permanent relationship. Photo please. East Midlands based but frequenting London and environs.

He's still advertising, then, and so am I. Neither of us has found the right person, and both of us are still trying. A lesson in patience!

I moved on to advertise in two Bristol papers, two in Bournemouth, one in Poole, two in Sussex, in a Santa Barbara newspaper, in a singles magazine in California, and in a Florida newspaper. I spent hours on the telephone as a result. Plenty of replies, all sounding positive, hopeful, interested and interesting. Some I would discard at once, because I very quickly became adept at spotting the horrors, the liars and the creeps. Others were more plausible, but, as I have already explained, looked at themselves less than realistically. Whatever their drawbacks, I should say now, they have all been nice. Some dates have turned out badly, some letters have been from unsavoury characters, or plain nutters, but I have never been assaulted or abused verbally or otherwise. Everyone has been sincere, despite frequent misrepresentation. I have had some 600–700 letters over the years, some three-lines long, some seven pages, so I have had plenty of practice in evaluating people on paper. I haven't always been accurate though.

In England this sort of thing is still seen as a little infra dig, a little declassé, something that nice girls don't do. Well, I'm not exactly an English rose, but I would certainly do it again. In America, it is a very different matter. There, it is entirely accepted, often applauded as a sensible way to vet future partners without the fear of getting AIDS or mugged. Professional people there don't have the time to mess about, although they have the money. People can no longer afford one-night stands, and older men (my age limit is forty-five, although I have stretched a point occasionally, sometimes without knowing it) want a secure family base – a wife, a real woman.

This has unwittingly turned into a full-time occupation. You have to be totally committed to the search, and that involves taking time over the letters, remembering who is who, and something about each one to make them feel good when they telephone. I have different sorts of paper for different people – some is really special thick de luxe vellum, some is just plain old Conqueror. If they are all lovey-dovey, they get apricot.

I have three wardrobes, and have to judge my date carefully – would he like classic silk or raunchy denim? When I dress for myself, I wear a jogging suit in the daytime, or cords and flat shoes. My summer wardrobe has all sorts of legacies from a racier past, like white leather mini skirts I don't have the heart to throw away. Then there are the glamorous evening dresses, the stylish day dresses, the sexy satin pants and sequinned tops for discos and casinos and the like. It all depends on so many things, the voice, the accent, the interests, the venue.

My telephone bill, or rather Mummie's, as she is financing this whole thing, with a view to being rewarded by seeing Moya and me happy when Mr Right comes along, is colossal. You can hardly cut short conversations just because it's costing a lot, and you certainly can't give the excuse that you have to call a lot of other men that day! Getting photographs of myself taken and developed, in different places, in different poses, to appeal, I hope, to different men, is also time consuming and expensive. This is no small undertaking, so if you are considering following my example, bear in mind the effort, the expense and the frequent disappointments. It's not all glamorous dinners, fast cars and romantic assignations, although I've had my share of these too.

Mr Right still hasn't turned up, but I am still hopeful, and determined to go on trying. I don't see any alternative. Mummie's finances are dwindling, her small private income getting a good deal smaller. I don't think I can go on living with her, on her, with my daughter indefinitely, although she loves Moya more than anything in the world. I need a husband and I want more children, and there isn't all that much time left. I want Moya to accept a new father, and possibly brother and sisters, and I feel that she will start to find it more difficult after about five or so, so that's another pressure. I haven't had a career, because I would only leave it the minute I got married and had a baby, because I would want to look after my children and bring them up myself.

Home is much calmer now. Everyone can see how hard I've

tried and am trying and with *Wogan* and the book and the radio interviews and all the publicity from the newspapers Mummie is very proud of me, and really does believe that I am doing my determined best to find the right husband. I'm too far down the line to give up now, and would urge anyone who cares to follow my example to remember that it doesn't happen in one year, two years or even longer. It might, but there aren't that many wonderful men out there; those that are available usually find their partners in very different ways. But perhaps, on an off day, on a whim, they might answer an ad. It is a constant spiral of ups and downs. One day, I will be feeling on top of the world, and that's when my last date was fantastic, I am full of hope for another meeting, and all kinds of developments, (but these are few and far between). It's when there is a fat pile of letters on the mat. It's when a photograph catches my eye, and the person isn't an unemployed labourer. And on other days, a date has gone disastrously wrong, I have said and done something stupid to make the man not want to follow up the meeting, I have been too insipid on the telephone, frightened of putting people off with the real me. That's when anxiety starts, when the downward spiral begins. I feel worthless, full of self-doubt, wondering whether anything is ever going to happen, if I'm ever going to get out, ever going to have another family, be loved by a man. And the more you worry, the more you doubt, and the more you doubt, the less well you present yourself.

So the best thing to do is to accept there will be good days and bad days, and that it is in the lap of the gods. Try to convince yourself it really doesn't matter all that much, if it doesn't happen today or yesterday or even tomorrow. And if you believe it, and you want to succeed, you have to keep looking to win in the end.

4

Magazine Advertisements

FACT: To find Mr Right you have to meet a lot of wrongs first.
FACT: People who advertise in magazines, advertise in many different magazines. So an ad in *Tatler* doesn't guarantee an encounter with someone from the upper classes. An ad in *Time Out* doesn't mean that they will all be vegetarian, bi-sexual, CND or into organic gardening.
FACT: To find Mr Right, you have to try everything.

So I did. I got all the relevant magazines I could, and pored over every single ad in them. The results were interesting, occasionally inspiring, often hilariously off the mark. Trouble is, after months and months of trying to laugh off the failures, my sense of humour was beginning to fade. But I continued. What else did I have to do?

Here are some of the wrongs I came across.

In *Tatler*, there was Mr Art Nouveau:

> SUCCESSFUL MAN with time on his hands would like to meet a very attractive, fun-loving and affectionate lady who would welcome a settled relationship. I'm good-looking, well dressed, fit, slim, and in my forties with an appreciation of style, wit and integrity. Naturally I'm looking for a counterpart – an especially beautiful lady in her twenties or early thirties who is presently on her own but would rather be with a partner sharing an affluent and sometimes exciting life in London and the country with considerable opportunity to travel. Please provide a recent photograph and reasonably full letter if you would like me to contact you.

This sounded just too good to be true. I sent a letter, and never expected to get a reply. But I did, and he kept calling me – three times, I think it was. He sounded very nice, not very well spoken but that didn't matter. He told me that he had been in advertising, and had owned one of the largest PR consultancies in this country. He didn't have a 9 to 5 job any more, but lived very comfortably on some private property deals, and an involvement with a hotel in the Cotswolds. He was very eager to meet me, and by now my appetite was whetted and I longed to clap eyes on this chap.

On the day of the date, I wore my full-skirted cream dress with a fitted bodice emphasizing my waist. It was in the days when I had to walk to the station as I didn't have a car then and needed to save the couple of extra quid on taxi fare. All the workmen on the building site made the journey hell. I would look down at my feet and totter past on my high heels, conscious that I looked like someone on their way to meet a man, and hoping to make a good impression. It used to make me smile – when I was not dressed up, and walked past in training shoes and a track suit, pushing Moya in the pram, they never gave me a second glance.

I took a taxi from Victoria Station to Julie's Restaurant in Holland Park. It is the place Prince Charles chose to have his stag night, and it is lovely. The wine bar next door is very popular with the local trendies, and I have often spotted a minor celebrity or two among all the dark oak screens that came from the demolished chapel of St Paul's Boys School. It feels very Victorian and heavy and rather womblike and comfortable. The restaurant is the same sort of thing, only more of it. The walls are white, and the ceilings are low. There are plenty of plants, and thick tapestry cushions on benches and chairs, rather hushed and exactly the place for a romantic assignation.

He was sitting there when I arrived – about 5 feet 9 inches I saw when he stood to greet me (I can measure a man at twenty paces now), and with silver hair. He looked in his fifties, not forties, in a jeans shirt and grey trousers, with a grey leather jacket hung over the back of his chair. He was OK, but would have been better if he had been some fifteen years younger. Still, he didn't look like Frankenstein's monster, and it could have been worse. 'Would you like a drink? They have some rather good new champagne here, and also some new glasses to drink it out of. Shall we try?'

'Yes, please,' I said, always happy to be offered champagne. It was good, and the glasses were wonderful – baroque, large, with painted flowers and grapes on the outside. I drank deep, as they invited me to, with their wide open mouths offering the bubbles.

He was crazy about cars. He had one of only three in the country – I can't exactly remember what it was, but it sounded foreign and snazzy, perhaps a Lamborghini or a Ferrari, one of those that sounds like the surname of a glamorous Italian (and is, of course).

'I have two sons, one twenty-two, one twenty-four,' he said, and the description of the older one sounded great. But I kept my thoughts on the matter before me, and tried not to fantasize about cradle snatching.

He did half the talking, a rarity, and the lunch passed pleasantly. He was good company and his life sounded tempting. 'I have a four-hundred-year-old cottage in the country. Rather ramshackle, but I am going to do it up. It has 5 acres of land with it, which is one of the reasons I bought it – it's on an estuary and I have a boat which I like to use at weekends. I'm a Londoner born and bred, so the country is only a bolthole for me, entertainment really, somewhere to rest and enjoy myself; I could never live there permanently.'

I talked about the States, and my life there, which as usual kept the conversation going for quite a while. I explained why I was doing it, in answer to the usual question: 'Why does a girl like you use the personal columns to meet a man? Surely someone as pretty as you doesn't have any trouble meeting men.' 'Why did you use them then?' I countered; that's always more interesting to me and allows me to find out some more about them.

'A lady friend of mine used them once, when she was feeling like meeting a man, and she did. She's still with the same chap she met through them – nine months ago now. I thought I'd have a go, and it's been interesting. I had some fifty replies, and I've met a couple of them. They weren't at all attractive, not like you, and I'm not interested in the others.'

'You're lucky you didn't receive revealing pictures of some of the less attractive ones,' I told him. 'Some men I have been out with have said that some women, usually the less attractive ones, send photographs of themselves sprawled naked on beds and things.'

We laughed, and finished our meal, chattering away. I looked at him, through my haze of champagne, and couldn't really convince myself I liked him enough to make a thing of it. His nails were too manicured, his whole appearance too neat, not rugged enough. He had puppy white flesh and was not tall enough either. We walked to his flat amicably enough, me holding his arm for balance on the cobblestones. It was a small, dark, thin house, like so many in Notting Hill. It felt like what it was, a bachelor house, with thick wood panelling on the walls and dark furniture and curtains. In his small and dark kitchen downstairs, there were lots of cookery books and equipment, all of which looked well used. His loo, which I stopped in on my way to his drawing-room on the top floor, was olive green and rather stylish, and when I reached the top of the house, I found myself in a fairly large room, chock-full of wonderfully precious and tasteful antiques, pictures, figures in wood and glass and bronze, all sorts of bits and pieces that looked delicate and valuable. I thought of Moya in there, and couldn't quite imagine it. I fancied I heard the crash of glass, the sound of canvas being torn, the thud of statuettes falling on the dark wood floor or the rich oriental carpets. And I imagined his face glowering at her, looking even more like a cross little puppy, a pug perhaps, or a bulldog, and didn't like the thought.

Pulling myself back to the present, I found another glass of champagne at my elbow and realized that he had gone downstairs again. He returned with a tray full of coffee cups, and a cafetiere puffing forth scented steam from the dark coffee inside it. I needed that coffee by then, I can tell you. I sat down on the 10-foot sofa, he chose one of the large armchairs, and we continued talking rather desultorily but without strain.

'I have to go about 8 p.m.,' I told him. 'It's quite late now, isn't it? Yes, about 7 – so I can't be long. I've enjoyed today very much.'

He called a cab and put it on his account, which was nice, and I bowled along to the station and home.

He called the next day. I was in a bit of a quandary. He was most of the things he had claimed to be in his advertisement, except perhaps good-looking. He wanted someone to share his life, that was true, but by doing what he wanted to do, with him. And I couldn't see him and Moya getting on.

'Would you like to come to dinner this time?' he asked. 'Then I think it would be better if you spent the night in the spare room, so you won't be bothered about trains and taxis and such.' I agreed and he met me at Victoria. I suppose that's where things started to go wrong for me. I hadn't felt entirely convinced about him, but wasn't violently opposed to anything concrete. When I saw him come bouncing towards me my heart sank. He looked short and old, and I felt embarrassed to be with him, not the best beginning to an evening. He also wore the same clothes – I thought he could have at least put on something different.

We went to the Pomme d'Amour on Holland Park Avenue, a warmly-lit restaurant with pink tablecloths and rather good food. At the back there is a sort of conservatory with a glass roof, full of climbing plants and flowers. We sat and talked, but quite honestly I was more fascinated by the conversation of the four gay men on the nextdoor table.

Remarks I have grown to mistrust began to appear: 'I see you as a classy expensive toy,' he said once, which was not at all how I wanted to be thought of.

Oh God, I thought. What a mistake. What on earth made me come here? This man is not for me, and I have agreed to spend the night in his house. What am I doing?

When we had finished, we walked what seemed a long way back to his house – I did think he could have forked out for a taxi at that time of night, so that was another black mark against him. I was beginning to look for them, I must admit. I also had thought he had been a bit mean with the ordering in the restaurant – the wine was not as good as it might have been, for instance. We walked in to the now familiar room on the third floor, and he opened the now familiar bottle of champagne. I drank gratefully, hoping that I could make myself feel a bit more enthusiastic, but I know myself, and know when I can't even drink someone pretty.

I had wanted to watch a programme on the television, so we sat on the sofa, side by side, and he turned it on, coming back to sit a little more closely than I wanted him. He motioned me to lie back against him, and, not wanting an argument or a fuss, I did so, rather gingerly. A hand came round my shoulder, and started to edge its way down towards my boobs. I tried to ignore it, and look as though I was fascinated with the programme, but then he began to play with one. I edged away. He withdrew it, and then, when I relaxed, back it came again, like the taste of onions after a particularly robust salad. He began to toy with my nipple, which made me feel precisely nothing. I lie, it made me feel thoroughly pissed off, and rather sick. I sat bolt upright, and said crossly: 'Look. I've told you I don't like that. I think it's time I went to bed.' My room was – you guessed it – small and dark, with navy blue curtains and bedspread, and the ubiquitous dark wood walls. I walked past his room – a duplicate of mine, only bigger – to see him lying on his back on the bed, fully dressed, looking at the ceiling as if he were asking it where he had gone wrong. I could have told him, but he didn't ask me.

The next morning was sunny, and we sat on the terrace in the sunlight, drinking tea. It was such a pity – the atmosphere was tight and strained; I couldn't wait to get away and I'm sure he couldn't wait for me to go. Eventually he called a cab, again on his account, and I got into it, sinking into the seat with a long sigh of relief. I never heard from him again.

Then there was Mr Diplomat.

> *The Director United Nations Centre invites you to a* BIRTHDAY PARTY. . . . with special guests The Countess Mountbatten of Burma 11 a.m. Wednesday 8th August The Royal Society of Arts, 8 John Adam Street Adelphi London WC2

This thick card came through the post one day in answer to my advertisement in *Tatler* which read

> VERY ATTRACTIVE fun-loving, affectionate lady, thirty. Brunette 5 feet 8 inches tall with two-year-old daughter would like to meet gentleman whose [sic] looking to create a happy family lifestyle.

A letter came too, saying, in sprawling blue ink, that 'I was attracted to your advertisement and wondered if you might care to join us at the Birthday Party I'm organizing. It would perhaps provide us with an opportunity to at least exchange phone numbers. I'll understand if you can't make it, but I'd love to hear from you.'

I would have been up there like a shot, except that the invitation came on the morning of 8 August. Still, he called me soon after my non-appearance, and I was soon glad I hadn't gone. He was so serious, so questioning. It felt like an interrogation, with no sense of humour to make his searching questions seem at least a little polite.

'Why did you leave the States? What are you looking for in a man? What have you to offer? What are you doing in this country? Where is the father of your daughter?' It went on and on, and he had no small talk to make it easier to swallow. He called twice, and I made excuses not to see him, and then he got the message and never rang me again. His wife had run off, he told me, and he obviously minded. If I had been feeling a bit braver, I'd have voiced my guess that he probably bored her to death, but instead I just felt sorry for him.

And there was Mr False Start:

> Let's meet together for lunch one day to see if we like the look of one another to begin with!
> Richard

This was another little note in answer to the *Tatler* advertisement. The paper was thick and white, but when I telephoned the number at the top, I could detect much giggling in the background. We set a date, he cancelled, and I couldn't be bothered to make another. I'm sure he was encouraged by his room mate to write for a laugh.

And Mr Weighty.

> Hi,
> I was intrigued by your advert in the June issue of *Tatler*. I've never replied to a personal advert before, but something about yours caught my interest.
>
> I am thirty-three years old, single (previously married) and have a pretty hectic existence working as the Managing Director of an international group of companies. I have recently just split from a two-year relationship, with a girlfriend and find it desperately difficult to meet the right kind of girl, someone who has the same interests as myself and who loves laughter and fun.
>
> I don't have a photo of myself to send you yet, but I did want to drop you a line and introduce myself. I'm 6 feet 2 inches, blond and my balance to my work life is eating out, dancing, travel, playing sport (squash, swimming, skiing and working out) and enjoying the company of good friends.
>
> I am a cynical romantic and love femininity in a lady. I've had only two relationships since I was eighteen; my ex-wife (met her at eighteen, married at twenty-one, separated at thirty-one) and my ex-girlfriend. I believe that I am an extremely affectionate and caring person. For me a good relationship means friendship first and sharing everything together.
>
> Honesty and giving are what I most look for in a relationship. I also love kids. I have one also by my ex-wife – a boy. I have a home in Chelsea. However, I am currently living in an apartment in the Barbican because the builders are in, for three-four months. My phone number is. . . .
>
> Should you be interested in meeting, please give me a buzz. We can catch up on all the rest over a bottle of vino.

I thought he was the answer to my prayers, I really did. Loving kids. Loving femininity, friendship, sharing. Flat in the Barbican, builders in Chelsea – mmmmmm!

'This is it, Mummie,' I cried, clutching the letter and brandishing it under her nose. 'This is really it.' She had heard it all before, so was a bit sceptical. We weren't getting on particularly well at the time, because we were both worried that nothing was happening. I was beginning to feel emotionally bankrupt, she was very definitely feeling financially so.

I called him, and left a message on his answerphone. He rang me back very shortly, and we arranged to meet at the trusty Grand Hotel in Brighton.

He was gorgeous. He looked just like a blond, blue-eyed Oliver Reed. His only drawback was that he was fat. Very fat. Not just overweight by a few pounds, but by a good many stones. He was wearing a seersucker blue-checked pair of trousers, and a white jacket, smartly casual. I wondered if it was a good idea to spend the day with him, my heart falling to my kneecaps at the sight of his waistline, but soon I was entirely won over. He was such fun, so in love with life, that it was impossible not to enjoy oneself with him. I soon thought he was great. We soon got on to the nitty gritty, as you do.

'I left my wife for my secretary – the old story. Then I got my come-uppance. I found her sleeping with my best friend. She is bad news, I know she is. Suicidal. Into drugs. A complete spendthrift. Untrustworthy. She wasn't the lady for me at all.' But he clearly thought she was, whatever he tried to make himself believe. He was obsessed with her, and the break had been too soon for him to be able to start another relationship with me or anyone else.

But we enjoyed the day. He smoked and drank like a fish, I was happy to notice, so we both kept each other company. No mealy-mouthed grumbling about fags and booze; we just got on and had a super time. He ate a lot at lunch, I noticed, which explained his weight.

'I do work out, and do a lot of exercise, but it is cancelled out somewhat by all the food I eat, at business breakfasts, lunches, dinners. It's a losing battle . . .' and he twinkled wickedly at me over his laden fork, which moved inexorably towards his mouth, to be followed by another and another and another.

We had a lot in common. He had had an office in Newport Beach, California, where a friend of mine used to work, in the very same building. We discussed his house's new colour scheme: 'All beachy colours, I think. Sunny and warm and beige and blue, like sand and sea. What do you think?'

'Lovely.' I was genuinely enthusiastic and entered into the spirit of the thing.

We talked about our children. He clearly adored his little boy. 'I took him to the zoo last Sunday. He loved it, and so did I. I really enjoyed watching him giggle at the chimpanzees' tea party and gasp at the elephants. This weekend we're going to see shire horses.'

He was a welcome and refreshing change, all man, with a wicked twinkle in his bright blue eyes. I knew if I got involved with him, he would hurt me, so I told myself it was just as well he was in no way over his girlfriend yet.

We got into his brand new red Audi Quattro, and drove into Brighton, leaving it in the car park nearest to the Lanes. We walked round them, arm in arm, and I loved being with him. He was so flamboyant, and he looked rich, which he was. People looked at us as we walked past, and he grabbed my hand; it felt entirely normal, and I walked beside him naturally.

'I'd like the new Whitney Houston album, Colette. Is there a shop we can go to?'

'Yes. Just round here. I've heard it's good – I like her very much,' I said, not hinting at anything, but pleasantly surprised when he instantly offered to buy it for me.

'What would you prefer? Tape or record?'

'Why thank you very much. Tape please.'

It did cross my mind then that if we were both getting a copy of the album, then perhaps he didn't think our relationship was going anywhere, but I put the thought out of my mind. I was having too much fun, and knew what the outcome was going to be anyhow.

Before we went home to Mummie, who I really wanted to meet this man, he bought hand made Belgian chocolates – half a pound for me, half a pound for her. We called her from the telephone in his car to tell her that we were going out for a drink but would be back later.

'Good heavens, it's 7.00. I had no idea. What shall we do now?' he asked me.

'Well, we could either go home, or we could go to a pub in the country.'

'That sounds like a good idea, then I can drop you home after that.'

So we drove happily to the Royal Oak, and had a lovely time, before moving on to the Shepherd and Dog, another of my favourite haunts. We stayed there till closing time, with hardly a pause in the conversation. He wasn't going to fall in love with me, but I knew he liked me very much, and I relaxed and felt at ease and didn't watch what I said. I didn't feel I had to. It was a wonderfully liberating feeling.

We sat in front of the fire, and he was the perfect gentleman, buying me drinks, opening doors, letting me go into rooms before him. He was complimentary about me without being gooey or sounding false.

I told him all about me, holding nothing back. Everyone likes talking about themselves, and I could tell he thought it was interesting. He didn't condemn anything, or look disapproving, or try to give advice.

'Tell me what you really think,' he would say, as we sat knee to knee in the pub.

'I don't know what to think of you,' I told him. It was true. He was unshockable, a workaholic quite obviously, and quite obviously mad keen on this girl, but not above a nice, flirty, fun evening with me.

He came back to meet my mother, who liked him, and he made himself feel at home in our little house. He was nice to Richard, my retarded brother, and polite to Mummie, who loved the chocolates.

'God, what a girl you've got on your hands,' he said to her, nodding in my direction. She couldn't be a bit offended, as it was meant complimentarily, and she took it in that way.

He was great, but he *was* fat. It spread everywhere when he sat down. It wobbled a bit when he walked, and when he smiled, although it was infectious, it also tucked itself into folds of fat on his arms. I don't think I could have borne to sleep with him, or could have tolerated seeing him naked.

When he left, he kissed me on the cheek, and quite honestly I never expected to see him again.

Some weeks later, a post card came from the Four Seasons Hotel 'where white sand beaches are just minutes away' in Newport Beach.

> Time seems to have rushed by since we had that lovely day in Brighton. I've been extremely busy and here I am back in good old California. The sun is shining and it's in the eighties. Spent the last weekend by the pool and on the beach. Back to work today, however, just as they are expecting a heatwave! Please give my best regards to your mum, and your brother. Take care. I get back on the 1st August. Will be in touch.

He wasn't. I wasn't surprised, just a little regretful, because he would have been a good friend, and someone to go out with just for fun. But his head was too full of someone else for him to want anything like that.

Then I met Mr Repulsive:

Dear Very Attractive,

Well, we seem, superficially, to have a number of things going for us. I have a three-year-old daughter, Alexandra; seem to have some joie de vivre, coupled with occasional manic workaholism (perhaps because I'm American, these Yanks are too intense), articulate, successful, etc. etc. etc.

Whether the chemistry is there, the eyes twinkle, one knows or senses, or hopes, that it's right, is another question. You forgot to mention sense of humour – indispensable for those ugly moments when nothing works and the world is crashing down. And caring as much for others as for yourself – as Mr Ego, I've finally learned to think about others first (well maybe first sometimes).

Anyway, if it doesn't work out, our daughters can play together in St James's Park.

Call me – let's have a drink.

The address was very prestigious, his office number a Belgravia one, so I did.

'Can't stop now. I'm going to the States. Give me your number and I'll call you when I get back,' said this rather gruff American voice. I was a bit taken aback at his manner, but couldn't do much about it.

Three weeks later he still hadn't got back to me, so I rang him. 'Sorry I haven't called you back. Perhaps we could meet next week. I have been so busy I've not had a moment, but lunch on Thursday suits me. What about you?'

'Fine. Where shall I meet you?'

'Do you know Ciboure? It's a small restaurant just behind Eaton Square. Can you make it there at 12.30?'

'Yes. See you then.'

Mummie wasn't thrilled at the prospect of paying for another train ticket to London as so many of my dates were a waste of time, but I pointed out to her that there was no point in advertising if I didn't follow it up, and I couldn't expect everybody to come down to Brighton to meet me.

I walked into Ciboure, and saw a man sitting by himself, a man who just had to be him, and a man I wished with all my heart wasn't!

He had said he was 5 feet 8 inches, but he looked shorter. He had said his hair was thinning. I should have known – it was non-existent. He was bald, with a few dark hairs clustered shyly together on his scalp. I should have known, and if, after all my experience, you are wondering why on earth I didn't, it was a simple case of desperation. My pitiful list of men on the go was dwindling, and no one looked likely to give me any of the things I needed. I was lonely and worried, arguing with Mummie, on edge with Moya . . . in short, I thought anyone with money would do. How wrong I was.

He stood up at once, and caught my arm. 'Come outside, please. Look, I'm sorry, but I have a business meeting in three quarters of an hour. I have to be on time – it's important. Perhaps we could have a quick drink here.' Here was the Ebury Wine Bar and it was full, and the seats were uncomfortable and it was the last thing I wanted. I was all tarted up for a smart Belgravia lunch and I was getting a glass of house red and a slice of game pie. Hmmph.

I towered over him, and, unusually, he didn't seem bowled over by me. With my luck, all the horrors think I'm their dreams come true, but this one was different.

We sat down and ordered and he told me something about himself. He had a nanny for Alexandra, and asked about Moya. Alexandra was down for Roedean, and his ex-wife had been there before her. Her father had been rather eminent at Christie's or Sotheby's and they had a wonderful art collection. Perhaps Moya could get a good schooling out of this one, I thought, but even that didn't help him look any better. You can't be considering carnal knowledge of this troll, I said to myself. You haven't sunk that low yet.

'I've got to get back,' he said, with his mouth full. 'Perhaps we could go out with the children on Sunday? I'll pick you up.' He phoned to make sure of the directions, and to confirm. He was annoyingly curt and businesslike on the phone. You would have thought he was plotting his way to the North Pole. 'I turn right then do I? Right? Are you sure? OK. Your directions look adequate. Expect us at 11.00 on Sunday morning.' I was amazed that I had let myself agree to this date, but there was nothing I could do about it now.

He had told me he had a 'rather nice convertible'. It turned out to be a Saab, which didn't make my heart beat any faster, and his little daughter may have had a nanny, but the nanny must have been blind. She was in a cheap dirty tracksuit, with a runny nose. His suit was beige and filthy and I began to dread the day ahead.

Alexandra went upstairs to Moya's room and quite obviously thought it was Hamleys.

'Well, yes, well, I live in a very tiny flat, and there's no room for toys there, I'm afraid,' said her father.

Alexandra picked up everything with big round eyes, and could quite happily have stayed there all day. But no – her father had decided that we were all off to the zoo – Drusilla's in Alfriston.

The journey was another nightmare. He was in a terrible twitch about the directions.

'Have we gone far enough? Have we gone too far? You're in charge of the directions – where are we?'

'We are on the A27,' I said through gritted teeth. 'As I told you. Why don't you ask those bikers on the side of the road where Drusilla's is?'

But no, he wouldn't do that and, amid much puffing and grunting, turned his convertible round and we motored back in the direction we had come, peering at every sign.

'Stop here. I'll ask these people,' I said eventually, tired of crawling along.

Of course, it had only been another hundred yards or so from where we were, so he turned his car round again, to the chorus of sniffles and whines from the little girls in the back seat, who were understandably getting bored. We got there eventually – it was hardly difficult to find. The sign to Seaford was obvious, and it was just a little further along.

He parked, and then asked where we should eat. There was the restaurant and the cafe. His meanness meant that we had to go to the cafe, although the pretty little restaurant with its diamond-paned windows was not much more expensive and I think the girls would have preferred it. Moya asked for a Coke, but he came back with an orange squash. I told him what she would like to eat – chips and beans – and he got that wrong, returning with a plate of something quite different, and obviously much cheaper, that Moya wouldn't touch. She was warming up for a real grizzle by now – 'Mummie, I want a Coke, I want a Coke' – which she only does sometimes. He got out 10p for his daughter to have a ride on the mechanical donkey, but said he hadn't got change for Moya to have one too. Of course, that set her off wanting a ride, and being very vociferous about it. I eventually cashed a cheque, paid for her to have one, and he paid for his daughter to have a second. He bought Moya and me an ice-cream to share, which was also just plain mean, and when we got to the train, I honestly thought he would pay the 50p for him and his daughter to go on the ride, and leave Moya and me at the gate. But even he couldn't quite do that, and we all went on it – in silence.

The journey back was as bad as the one out. Lots more grizzling from the girls, lots of puffing and huffing from him, and I couldn't have been happier when we got home.

'Can I use your telephone please,' he asked and, when I showed it to him, he muttered into the receiver until I left him alone. Then when he left, he told me, 'I really enjoyed today. Can we do it again soon?'

'Oh yes, certainly. That would be nice.' Why on earth don't I stop doing this. For some cowardly reason, I can never tell the horrible ones to their face that I wouldn't be seen dead with them ever again, but he obviously read the look in my eyes correctly and never phoned again.

Mr Labourer obviously picked up his mistress's *Tatler*, and wrote to me on thick creamy paper with a grand address embossed in red on the top.

> Perhaps I can tell you about myself. I am thirty-seven, about 5 feet 10 inches and at present going through a divorce. I also have a five-year-old daughter. I farm and run an electronics business, and as you probably gather from the address I *live in*. My main interests are shooting, skiing and sailing; in fact most outside activities.

Well, I wasn't taken in by that. 'Living in' probably meant that he worked on the estate and had had a spare afternoon. I never replied.

Mr Poet was another sad case. His advertisement in *Time Out* read:

> *A DEEP WINTER LOVE AFFAIR*
> *Oh to share a bathtub in the winter*
> *would be nice*
> *Just someone special to eat anything but*
> *rice*
> *Yes for a woman of feeling; one loyal,*
> *honest and true;*
> *Wouldn't it be grand to find somebody*
> *like you*
> *If you're young and very beautiful,*
> *being twixt twenty and thirty-five*
> *Would have our children and set all our*
> *lives alive*
> *I am single and forty-two, with*

experience of life quite rare
A strong yet tender man to hold, to love and share and care.
If you seek a romance that will last the rest of time
Then take courage, have fidelity and follow up the rhyme.
Just send a photo with a letter to my lair
And thence to meet and start our deep winter love affair.

Well, one couldn't help but respond, could one? Mummie is better than I am about this sort of thing and made up a poem and sent it back to him. I got a letter which was pleasant but the photograph which came with it was less appealing. He had a brown face, and was wearing a rather nasty short-sleeved shirt. His hair was grizzled grey, starting somewhere at the back of his head, and he had a domed forehead that shone in the sunshine. His sideburns were the worst thing about him – thick and grey like a sheep, and all the way down the side of his face and creeping on to his cheeks. Not for me. But of course, now he had my telephone number, I couldn't get rid of him. He called three or four times and wouldn't go away, until I told him that I had met someone else. My usual lie, *in extremis*.

Then came Mr Ugly Duckling:

Another ad in *Time Out* began 'GENUINELY EXCITING MAN' and so I answered it:

> Tall dark attractive intelligent warm-hearted considerate easy going and solvent, with one house, car and boat, seeks a slim girlfriend, twenty–thirty-five, status and nationality not important, children welcome.

We arranged to meet in the Clarence Bar in Brighton. He said he knew the town well, and knew a little restaurant that he was sure I would like. I didn't know it, but was willing to have a go.

'Dress casually,' he ended the conversation by saying. 'I shall be.'

I wasn't all that keen on this, but compromised with a blue and white seersucker trouser suit, and thought I looked casual enough for me, and white high heels, to make me look sexy enough for anybody.

I was a bit wary about the date, something hadn't clicked on the telephone, but I was prepared to give it a go. I went in to the bar and looked around. No one, so I ordered a drink, and a delicious-looking blond man came up and asked if I would have another with him.

'I can't. I'm waiting for someone.'

He tried again ten minutes later, and I said yes, because I was getting tired of waiting like a lemon. I kept a watchful eye on the door, but there was no one there who looked likely. Then an older man came in, looked around rather desperately, caught my eye, saw my companion and went out of the room, to return a little later. It was obviously him, and I felt miserable at having to give up the dishy man next to me for the new arrival. But I had to.

'If it doesn't work out, come back and we'll have a drink later,' Mark told me, raising his eyes to heaven.

I introduced myself to the man.

'I wondered if it was you,' he said, aggrieved. 'But you were with another man, so I thought it couldn't be.'

Now we all have different ideas of ugly men, but this man would have fitted into anyone's category.

A thick bulbous nose, two poky little ice-blue eyes, one of which I'm sure was glass, as it was a lot bigger than the other. He had a large paunch, and was on the solid side of fat. Oh dear.

His clothes were good, though, thick black cords, nice shoes, a thick cashmere jersey – he told me it was cashmere within the first ten minutes. That's the sort of man he was. I was humiliated to be with him, especially with Mark looking on, but there was nothing I could do about it now.

We went off – in his mouldy old Renault 5, M reg – to the aptly named Bottoms restaurant, and explored the set menu, for £11 a head, not including wine, but with VAT and service. I prefer things to be a little less cut-and-dried, a little more romantic, a little more stylish on the first date, I must say. When we got to know each other better we could feel more relaxed about the cost of dinner, but having it underlined in such a way makes me feel very uncomfortable.

He splashed out on half a bottle of house champagne, and looked at me triumphantly as he did so, as if to say, 'Look, I'm no slouch when it comes to spending money.' He pretended to be known by the patron, saying all sorts of nauseating things like 'How's business, then, Tony?' and 'It's been ages since I was last here.'

The owner was a bright businessman who knew a good customer when he saw one, and kept him happy with nicely vague comments like, 'Don't make it so long next time.'

Mr Ugly Duckling dropped names all the time – about people and places. Elton John. His tan from California. The wonderful party he had been to at the Belfry Club the other night. I left him to it, nodding at the right moments, and enjoying the food, which I have to say was marvellous. I had salmon in a bag which was delicious, and followed it, throwing calories to the winds, with a scrumptious toffee ice-cream.

'I take my holidays in Antigua,' he announced to the restaurant at large. 'I teach waterskiing, in exchange for room and board.' Oh really, said my face. You little cheapskate jerk. And as for sex, something I did not like to consider in connection with this awful man, he wouldn't leave it alone.

'How many times would you like it in a week?' he wanted to know. And then he played a game with me.

'What's your favourite animal?'

'A horse.'

'Why?'

'Because it's fast, powerful and large.'

'Well, that says a lot about how you like your sex. Fast, strong and large – har har har.'

He was constantly trying to touch me up, and it was disgusting.

'My ex-wife was a model, you know. Very well known. You may have heard of her, but of course I can't tell you who she is as we are not together any more.'

I let him run me home after the dinner, and at the front door avoided his flabby lips as they tried to find mine.

'I really enjoyed that,' he said. 'Did you?'

'Oh yes.' But he had got the message.

'I'll wait to hear from you.'

He's still waiting. I never telephoned and nor did he.

Mr Flower Power was next:

> GENTLE MAN tall, fair and considered very attractive, not only by himself, wishes to find an equally gorgeous woman. I am thirty-nine years old (young) borderline workaholic, but now ready for other distractions and even a committed relationship, where love does not mean ownership. I am currently successful and secure. I am an experienced and keen yachtsman, tennis player, artist, father and generally ready for anything.

This sounded appealing, so I replied promptly. He phoned back equally fast, and sounded pleasant on the phone, with an accent that came from some sort of public school.

'What do you do for a living?' I asked him.

'I am a partner in an art and design company. I earn about £30,000 a year, but I have divorce payments and a son at school.' He sounded nice, quiet and as gentle as he had implied.

'Would you like to meet?' he wanted to know.

'Well, yes, but I'd like to know a little more about you first.' I told him about my trips to Henley and Ascot, because he sounded so frightfully frightfully, and I thought it would be the right thing to say. But it clearly wasn't.

'Er, I don't think my background is exactly going to suit you,' he ventured and then it all came out.

'When I was fifteen I was chucked out of school for drugs. I spent two years in Israel and then went on to India and lived in a commune. I was a confirmed heroin addict by then, and came back to live on a houseboat in Chelsea and try to get myself together. I met my wife, who straightened me out, and we had a child. I went to a treatment centre, and was all fine, until we split up, and then I had a few problems again. But I'm all right now, doing well at work.'

'I appreciate your honesty. Thank you for telling me all about yourself. I don't think we'll get on. I have a little daughter too and . . .'

He wished me luck, I wished him luck, and it was an amicable ending. I wish everybody was as straightforward. It saves so much time in the end, as it always comes out eventually. I hope he finds someone to suit him.

And then there was Mr Perfect.

> VERY ATTRACTIVE tall, dark, intelligent, successful (and lucky!) City of London director, thirties, seeks very beautiful lady, with attractive personality, in twenties-early thirties, who is looking for good-humoured, interesting company, and who would not rule out the possibility of a long-term relationship. Photo and phone number please.

He called me in answer to a letter I sent him. I was cooking a cake at the time, and arrived at the telephone a little out of breath, and wishing that the call hadn't come at that precise moment. But when I heard his voice, the cake could have gone up in flames for all I cared.

He told me he was thirty-six, 6 feet 3 inches, and a director of a company. He sounded very sweet, kind and sensitive.

'I'm too busy at work to meet women, that's the trouble. I rarely go out with the boys either – not really interested. I play a lot of squash and I love my children – I have two girls and a boy, aged thirteen, seven and four.'

He was the one who suggested coming to meet me in Brighton, thus saving me from a row with Mummie about another fare to London, and wanted to do it as soon as possible. He suggested a weekday, after work: 'I can just get home, have a shower and motor on down to you. Won't take very long.'

I told him about my learning elaborate cake making, and he laughed.

'My father and I went on a cooking course last year. I learnt a lot – fifty ways to slice a cherry! It isn't good for me, cooking well. I am about 7 pounds overweight, and could do with losing some of it.'

He was late (men often are) and I sat in a lounge chair, wearing my tapestry skirt and turquoise jersey, and sexy black patent boots, to the left of the bar at the Grand.

In walked a handsome man, trendily if conservatively dressed, with perfect manners.

'I am so sorry I am so late. The traffic was not good coming out of London and work took a little longer than I had imagined as well.'

'Oh, not to worry.'

'Well, I apologize. You look like you've finished your drink. Would you like another?'

He was lovely. I warmed to him, and he seemed to like me, although he told me he hadn't liked his ex-wife smoking, and frowned a bit when I lit up.

He told me a good deal about her – another man who was still hung up on a previous woman.

'She ran off with a doctor, which was pretty unethical, as he was mine as well! She was hopeless. Spent all the housekeeping and plenty more besides. I wish we hadn't split up for the sake of the children. They are a bit muddled about it still.' His children were clearly his life, which was fine by me, because Moya was mine.

'I had another date with a woman who answered my singles ad. She was pretty and nice, and I must say we ended up in bed together on the first night. I haven't seen her since though.' I thought firmly that he was not going to end up in bed with me, and felt that that was the only slightly jarring remark he had made.

He loved skiing, and we talked about that, because I had always wanted to try again. He went to Greece in the summer, alone. It all sounded perfect.

'I'll run you home,' he said eventually, at about 10 p.m., 'and then maybe we can make a proper date another time.'

'No, don't be silly. You have to drive all the way to London. I can get a cab.'

'No, I'll take you back. That's perfectly all right.'

His white Lotus was in the car park, and I was impressed. It was clearly a new toy, one he was still enjoying the novelty of. He was extremely attractive and very nice indeed. If there was a drawback it was that he had very little sex appeal, no animal passion about him. Perhaps he was too nice, because we stupid women are quite keen on bastards, aren't we? We never learn. To this day, after all this business, I still somehow respond to being treated mean to be kept keen. Groucho Marx said something about not wanting to join any club that would have him as a member. I wholeheartedly sympathize, and I am not alone.

He walked me to my door.

'I'll call you.'

He did, the next day.

'Thank you for a lovely evening. What are you doing next Thursday? Shall we meet?'

'Yes, that would be fine.'

'Good. I'll talk to you about it before the time.'

He didn't call me, and I was beginning to worry. Another date rang up and asked me out that night, and so I accepted. Literally as I put the phone down, it rang again.

'Hello, Colette. Are you on for Thursday night still?'

'I'm really sorry, but I am afraid I've made other arrangements as you didn't call. I thought you weren't going to be able to make it.' (I was sorry I had accepted the other date.)

'Never mind. We'll have to make it the next week. Are you free any night?'

We arranged another day, a day when he was coming down to check out Lancing College for his son and I was told to book a restaurant. I telephoned trusty Bailiffscourt in Climping, and they had a table for two, near the window, overlooking the garden. Couldn't be better.

The telephone rang.

'I'm sorry Colette, but I'm running late. I'm still coming, but perhaps you should change the restaurant booking or something.'

'OK. I'll get on to it.'

He arrived at last, at about 9.30, looking pretty devastating in his City suit.

Off we went, not to Bailiffscourt but to a Greek restaurant much nearer home, which had been recommended the previous week by someone at the sports club.

It was much less glamorous, but great fun. We had our own little wine tasting as we didn't know which one to have – we ordered three half bottles and decided on the one we liked best. It was a super evening. He talked about his son going to Lancing, which he had liked, and I chipped in with my opinions. He drove me home, and kissed me gently on the cheek at the door of Mummie's house.

He had mentioned frequent Covent Garden tickets which he got through his firm and I had agreed enthusiastically to go with him. He didn't call, though, and I was getting worried. I got a Christmas card, with a nicely worded apology for 'not being in contact. I hope to phone soon and explain.'

But he didn't and so I sent him a little note, which may in retrospect have been a bit uncool. Something along the lines of 'I'd love to hear from you if you are free to be with someone.'

I called him three or four weeks later, still having heard nothing.

'Oh hello, Colette. How nice to hear from you. I've literally just walked through the door from Los Angeles. How are you?'

We talked amicably, and he really did seem pleased to hear, but he didn't ring me again, even though he had said he would. The old agonies began – would he? wouldn't he? If not, why not? What had I done? What had I said? Perhaps he was really busy? Perhaps he was hanging off a cliff in the Alps, his fingers clawing at the precipice, only one thought in his head, to call Colette . . .

Nonsense. If someone doesn't call, it never means that they are hanging off a precipice. It means they don't want to. I knew that really, but I didn't want to listen to the little prosaic voice of experience that kept whispering the truth to me. I was learning to ski in leaps and bounds, literally, and so I rang him (another excuse, I know) to ask the best place to go. 'You should come up with the brochures and spend a night here,' he said, welcomingly. 'Then we can look through them, and see where would be best.'

'Oh yes, that would be very – helpful,' said I, trying not to sound like a desperate woman.

'I'll ring you next week and we can make a date,' he said, but of course he never did.

He had said he would ring me when he went down on trips to sort out his son at Lancing, but of course he didn't. I asked him to be an escort for my friend Mandy for a ball, and he agreed, even going so far as to say that he would be mine and would find someone to go with Mandy. He never called.

When I was asked to do the BBC radio programme, I was asked by the producer to find someone who would say what it was like to go on a date with me. I phoned Mr Perfect, who was still as polite as ever, but just as politely refused.

'I would just like to say, Colette, that it wasn't that I didn't like you – it was that someone else from the past came back into my life, although it's over now. It didn't work out. I also couldn't cope with your smoking, I'm afraid.'

Mummie was crazy about him – any mother would have been. He was tall, dark, handsome in a classic way, he oozed reliability and friendly charm. I should have been more exuberant, I think. He was such a gentleman, I wanted him to know that I was a lady, so I think I was too stilted, too stuffy. I should have been more myself and I think he would have been charmed by me more than he was. He was really Mr Perfect – he would have been the perfect lover, friend, husband. He had money, looks, charm, he was nice.

Ah well, the best one that got away. . . . No use pining – on to the next.

Mr Africa was from Nigeria, a French Lebanese. He saw my advertisement in *Singles* magazine which said:

> MR WONDERFUL, THAT'S YOU Gorgeous looking brunette, thirty, 5 feet 8 inches, 9 stone 4 pounds, privately educated, travelled, has joie de vivre; seeks confident, original, internationally minded man of the world to create a family life, along with my adorable year-old daughter.

I asked a girlfriend who came from Zimbabwe about Nigerian men, and she told me that there were a few very rich men there. He could certainly afford the phone bill. He called me about ten times from London and a few times from Nigeria, for half an hour at least, often a lot longer. He told me he was the chairman of a board of international companies, and it all sounded like big bucks.

His wife had died, leaving him with five kids, and he was looking for a replacement. He was charming and very well spoken, with a wonderful accent, concerned about me and Moya. For instance, he was shocked that Moya's father should never have seen her, but then that wasn't unusual. A lot of my dates said that.

'You should come over, Colette. I'll send you a ticket, or we could meet in London. I'm often over.'

But the drawback was that he was in his early fifties, which was just too old for me. I eventually wrote and told him this, as nicely as I could; there was no point in going on, because he was lonely and wanted to get married quickly. It was a shame, and I wished him luck.

Mr Poona Poona lived near Bristol and answered the same ad. We wrote to each other to establish contact. His writing was appallingly difficult to read, but I could make out this:

> I have been divorced for over three years, I live mostly on my very small stud farm and go to the London office one to two days a week. I also have an office here, where I operate as a food importer. Horses seem to dominate my life, I hunt, point to point and breed from a few mares. I'm also a mad keen skier (snow and water). I am a sun lover. I've had business interests in the West Indies and still have to go backwards and forwards (especially in the winter). All this may sound as though I'm rich. I have to tell you I'm *not*, certainly after my divorce settlement!
>
> I am also 5 feet 8 inches, stocky, ride at 11 stone 7 pounds! I am extrovert, typical Sagittarian, kind, generous, affectionate (and respond to the same), suffer fools badly, untidy and fairly laid back. California would suit me. I don't have children but think I've missed out. . . . Do try me here all week or leave a message with a girl groom. Hope to hear from you. PS I liked the photo.

I called him back and we talked on the telephone, as usual, before making an arrangement to meet in London, outside the Old King Lud pub at Ludgate Circus, just below St Pauls. I wore my stilts, my black patent boots, and my camel coat, and looked very nice all dressed up for lunch but felt a berk standing out in the rain waiting for a man who 'will be wearing a navy wool coat'. Well, in that part of town on a weekday lunchtime, who isn't? I looked from left to right, trying not to seem too much like someone waiting for someone they didn't know, and then along he came. He was stocky, and very bright and breezy. He had one of those jolly, suntanned faces, and his manner was very up, very positive. I quite liked him, although it did seem a bit contrived.

'Hello. Hello. How *are* you? I have been looking forward to your coming up. Jolly good. I've found us a nifty little place I know for lunch, nothing special, you know, but I like it. This way.'

We walked down narrow, winding cobbled alleyways, rather like something out of Dombey and Son, and my heels clattered and slithered off the stones. He strode out jauntily beside me, talking and gazing at me in what any blind person could have spotted as naked admiration. I'm not sure I felt the same for him, but smiled a lot. I was hungry, and could do with a drink. We got to a little archway, which had obviously once been the entrance to a cellar, underneath the railway line. It was better than it sounded. Inside, there was a mass of male faces, on top of bodies in dark suits and with glasses of claret in their hands. There was sawdust on the floor, a bar, with tables and chairs, and then a restaurant with flowers and bare brick walls. Sporting print pictures were on them, depicting some spindly jockey hurling himself off his horse in 1896. It felt rather nice, busy and full of people who enjoyed doing business.

The waitresses knew my companion, and he ordered 'champers, don't you think?'

He was overwhelmed with me. His eyes sparkled and he couldn't wait to ask me why on earth I was having to advertise. I turned the question back on him, and he explained that 'everyone I know is married, and I come to town for business for such a short time that I just don't get the chance to meet new women – certainly no women as delightful as you!'

I smiled, flattered, and looked at the menu. We ordered something like soup, followed by game pie and salad with deliciously buttery new potatoes in their skins. Champagne went with all this very well.

'Broking isn't what it used to be, you know. I earn I suppose some £50,000 a year, but what with the cost of living, and the divorce, and all that sort of thing, it doesn't go very far.' It became obvious that he was the most frightful snob I think I have ever encountered.

'My wife left me, you know. I was having an affair with the wife of the Queen's vet, and so she divorced me. She has cancer, and so it costs me £20,000 a year to keep her in a nursing home. As it happened, I was taken for the most godawful ride. The vet's wife – no names, no pack drill, if you get me – got a country cottage out of me, and goodness knows what else besides, and then chucked me. Bit bad that. And Her Maj knew all about the affair and was a bit distressed, I got to hear. So persona non grata there too, I'm afraid.'

I couldn't help it. 'Surely she has more important things to think about than an affair her vet's wife is having?'

He didn't answer, and moved smoothly on to his interests in Barbados.

'Got to go there in the next month or so – check things out, y'know.'

His social life occupied a good deal of his thinking, and I was treated to a litany of names; some I had heard of, most I hadn't, although I had to pretend to, because he would stop and look at me like Wodehouse's seal waiting for a fish.

'I have to go fairly soon, I'm afraid. I need to buy some boots from a shop called Sacha,' I told him, after we had put our napkins down following some rather good cheese.

'Oh, great. Can I come with you? We could go shopping together for them – I haven't shopped with a lady for so long.' The way he spoke, it sounded as though he was going to buy them for me, so I agreed, and we caught a taxi to Oxford Street. I tried on pair after pair, looking at him for approval, getting rather excited as they became more and more expensive, and he nodded and smiled and suggested yet another.

'Oh, what about these, Colette? They look great. Or these – could she try the dark brown ones with the tassels?'

I was prancing about, showing them to him, and eventually, after trying on practically every pair in the place, we chose some. £80 or so, I believe, and I took them to the desk with him. But just as we got to our turn, he said, 'I can see it's just begun to rain, so I'll go and find us a taxi so you don't get wet.' And left me to pay for them myself. I wouldn't have expected him to pay for them if he hadn't been so misleading to begin with. But once he had given me the wrong impression, I had got the bit between my teeth and was now genuinely taken aback. Luckily they were boots that I would have bought myself, but I was a bit cheesed off by this. Particularly as we went off to his 'little place in Lancaster Gate' to meet a friend who was coming to give him some advice about selling it.

'Look at the boots Colette and I bought,' he said, making it seem for all the world as if he had bought them for me, so I smiled embarrassedly and put them on, again, to show them off. They were super, thank goodness!

'Perhaps in a year, if you are a good girl, I'll buy you another pair,' he told me – all it needed was for him to give me a hefty smack on my bottom and the picture would have been complete, but he didn't dare.

He was also very worried that any of his friends would find out how we met, so he concocted a story, and rehearsed it several times before his friend came round. I found it all a bit annoying and irrelevant, but I have been in this game for long enough not to retain the tiniest shred of embarrassment about it. He called again, of course, and I agreed to meet him – perhaps I had misjudged him, perhaps he would be better the second time, he obviously had good contacts and I would at least meet some new people.

'Would you like to come down to Tinycote House with me, Colette. Some friends have an apartment there, and it is quite something, I can tell you.'

'All right.'

We drove down in his ordinary car, the make of which I can't remember, and he never stopped talking. By now, my experience of garrulous escorts had taught me a good expression, a half-smile, a nod of the head, and perhaps an occasional 'oh yes?' or 'did you really?' and that meant they were happy and didn't need anything else from me. I was left to go on with my own thoughts. He covered galas, exhibitions, hunt balls, dances, parties of all kinds. He told me about his friends and their properties, and was obviously trying to be young and with it and yuppy, but his clothes were polyester trousers and a checked short-sleeved shirt, so that failed too!

It was a beautiful old house, with vast grounds and much history about it. It was supposed to be one of the most haunted houses in England, and I could believe it. Wood panels, paintings, everything you would expect in an English country house. Their apartment was very smart too, but not very big. We had a champagne brunch, all very lah di dah, and Mr Poona Poona was thrilled to be there with me. It couldn't have been that wonderful because they were serving André's Californian champagne, available at Jack's discount store for $1.99.

'Gosh, I say, this bubbly is pretty damn fine, don't you think? As good as Bolly any day.'

'Oh yes, we're rather pleased to have found it. Bolly is so overrated these days, and Californian stuff is splendid.'

Lunch had Sainsbury's claret, which also got the 'oh gosh, how spiffing this is' treatment; it tasted fine, but the fuss was excessive. The food was delicious, and the hostess prided herself on 'doing it all myself – so much better than getting other people to do it.'

(When she really meant so much cheaper.) She and I and another guest did the washing up, too.

The guests were odd – a terrible woman in an orange flying suit with an extremely mobile zip which went up and down like a lift. She stuck her chest and her bottom out everywhere, and wriggled in the most irritating manner. A forty-year-old man with a decidedly common accent was there – 'worth £11 million on paper you know. Deal went through last week' – and I made friends with a theatrical lady with far too much make-up who called everybody a throaty darling, and smoked like a gasworks.

Everyone thought I was his girlfriend, and came up to me to tell me that they hadn't seen him look so happy in ages. 'You're obviously very good for him, Colette. Hope to see you around a lot more.'

We left at about 7 p.m. after tea, and I was so happy to get back to my unclassy home in Littlehampton, with my mother who didn't drink André's champagne and my daughter who wasn't worth £5 on paper.

On the way back he had gone on and on about a big dance in Devon and please would I come with him.

'I haven't got a dress, and it's such a long way. I really don't think so.'

'Oh, we can take care of everything. We'll sort out your dress, and you can stay either in the same hotel, different rooms of course, or a different hotel if you prefer. Do come, Colette. It would be absolutely splendid.'

I allowed myself to be persuaded, but it soon became less clear about the edges. Nothing more was said about paying for a dress, (I couldn't pay, and I remembered the boots episode!) and I would have to make my own way to Exeter, or wherever it was, which I could see costing a fair packet. He wasn't the man of my dreams, and I didn't think another evening of his distasteful brand of snobbery could compensate for paying a couple of hundred pounds for dress and journey. So when he phoned, I said a very firm no, and eventually, he stopped trying to persuade me, and I never heard from him again.

Mr Sahara was a sad case. He replied to my ad in *Singles* with a sweet note:

> Dear Gorgeous,
>
> It was a real pleasure to read your advert in *Singles* and I sincerely hope you are the person I am looking for. I am young,

thirty-nine years old, well built, well educated, independent, enjoying everything in life, but hardly because I am a very lonely person.

Excuse my short letter and if you think you like to answer my letter please do so, which will only make me happy, perhaps we could meet somewhere for a drink or a meal and decide what we think of each other.

Please answer my letter because I've got that feeling that we could be for each other.

A friend said that he lived in a good area of London, so I wrote to him, and that started the avalanche of telephone calls. He was lonely, he wanted to hear my voice, and would call me all the time.

He was Lebanese, with a five-year-old daughter. His wife had left him and he loved his little girl with a passion. He would have made an excellent father – Moya and I could have had anything we wanted, I'm quite sure.

But I couldn't have married him. For one thing, I did all the talking on the phone.

'Hello, Colette?'

'Oh, hello, Mr Sahara, how are you today?'

'Fine.'

'What have you been doing today then? Anything interesting?'

'No.'

I told him that I was going for a skiing lesson, but would be back at 9 p.m. He got entirely the wrong end of the stick and turned up at about 6.15, and wondered where I was. Mummie explained, and he said he would wait. So he sat like a block of wood until about 9, responding to none of my mother's attempts to make small talk, and then, when I still hadn't got back, started getting a bit nasty. He had turned up with trays of goodies, strawberries (in December), chocolates, sweets for Moya, flowers, wine, the lot.

I got back at about 9.30 and was faced with a stocky man of about 5 feet 9 inches, with thin black and grey hair, and sagging white flesh. Attractive he was not – another reason for not being over-keen – and his clothes, though good, had seen better days. He was too fat to do up his jacket, for instance, which wasn't an appetising sight.

His eyes nearly popped out of his head when he saw me, though. He thought he had ended up in heaven, and he couldn't stop staring at me.

Eventually, like winkling out something from a shell, I found out that he had come to England as a multi-millionaire but things had gone badly wrong and now he was working for a very rich Arab, who lived in Grosvenor Square and Marbella. He, Mr Sahara, didn't have a house himself, but seemed to be well looked after by Abdullah, his boss.

'I don't want a woman who is just after my money, and that has been the problem.'

Mummie and I joked together later – what else did he have to offer?

He called me when he got to London, that night, to thank me for a lovely evening.

'You have given me a reason to live. I am so excited. I am so happy.'

He hadn't been transformed into a sunny little chap by the sight of me, but his tone had changed.

Next day he rang at 7 a.m. to wish me a happy morning.

'I want you to meet Abdullah. He is very interested and excited to meet you.'

'OK,' I told him. 'Arrange something with him and come back to me.'

The phone rang at 11 – 'we could be so happy together, I know it. Let's not waste time, Colette. [In my country people] get married without ever seeing each other. We've met. I think we could be so happy together. Marry me. Abdullah has agreed to pay for the wedding. He wants me to be happy, and knows I will be happy with you. Let's arrange it as soon as possible.'

'Hold on, hold on. This is far too quick for me. We don't do things like this in this country. We don't know anything about each other.'

'Ask me anything. Anything! I'll tell you anything you want to know, and then we can spend the rest of our lives learning the rest.'

'Look, you don't like sports, for instance, and I do.'

'I'll do anything you say. I'll learn to ski, to play tennis. I'll like them.'

'You know you won't.'

'I will call you later, to hear when we shall get married.'

And he did, in an hour.

'Look, I have hardly had a moment to think. I have been getting Moya ready to go out. I don't want to marry you.'

He called again.

'Abdullah wants to meet my future wife.'

'No, sorry, this is not going to happen.'

'When two people are in love, anything is possible.'

'No doubt, but we aren't.'

This went on and on, and I was getting really fed up. He got it into his head that he was going to meet me at the Grand Hotel in Brighton.

'Abdullah and I will be there at 7 tonight, and then we can go on to dinner to celebrate.'

'No, I can't make it.'

'We'll be there, so we'll expect you.'

'No, I can't come.'

'I know you will. See you then.'

Then at 7, the telephone rang.

'We're here. Where are you? We are expecting you.'

'I said I was *not* coming.'

'Well, now we're both here, what shall we do?'

'Oh, goodness. Come over here. Then we can all have a drink and talk.'

A grey Corniche slid up to our front door, and two men got out of it. Mr Sahara, small and flabby, and someone who was obviously Abdullah – gorgeous, tall and rich.

He looked exactly what he was, a flash Arab, complete with ruby ring and identity bracelet, and gold Patek Philippe watch. And he was no fool either. He took in at a glance what the situation was and never mentioned marriage, although Mr Sahara stared at me without blinking for a long time.

They left after we had talked, about mutual friends like the Middle Eastern Royal Family my second husband was connected to. I mentioned them because I knew that Arabs don't like women who hang around them, and I wanted to shock him and put him off. It may have done, but Mr Sahara was still panting like a puppy, and kept telephoning me without a break: 'All I want is someone to love me. Can't you love me? Please Colette.'

'No. I've got to go now, I'm afraid. I have to get Moya her lunch. Goodbye, and please don't call me any more today.'

I shouldn't have said the last word. The phone was blissfully silent, but only until the next morning.

'Look, I don't want to go out with you. I don't want to. I've told you a hundred times, so please stop bugging me.' He kept calling. Mummie would answer the telephone and say anything that came into her head, and then she became more specific.

'Colette doesn't want to talk to you.'

Then for the next six months or so, he reduced his calls to one every two weeks, and then sent me a Valentine card. I felt sorry for him, so sent him one back, which was foolish. The calls redoubled and I agreed to meet him for lunch at Richoux, opposite Harrods.

I was broke, and when he asked me how much I'd need to live on a week, I really did consider becoming his mistress – for half a second. Then his flabby flesh came into focus and I knew I would never ever be able to let him touch me for all the money in the world. I left feeling desperately sorry, but without giving him any encouragement. He still calls me every so often, even now. But however down I feel, I could never ever become his kept woman. Possession of such a kind, although I have done it in my youth, is something I now couldn't bear, not without marriage, children, love, security, all the things I lacked for so long.

I also advertised in local papers. In the *Bristol Evening Post* my ad read:

> VERY attractive articulate lady, thirty-one, brunette, slim, 5 feet 8 inches, possessing joie de vivre with sweet daughter aged two seeks successful businessman interested in forming a happy family lifestyle.

A pale card arrived, with a woman's face painted on it in water-colour and inside, a note in black ink said:

> Dear vivacious lady, I saw the advert in the *Evening Post* yesterday and if the GPO were able to deliver the thousands of replies, hi there, nice to hear about you.
>
> I am thirty-five and live and work at my house in Clifton. I am always interested to meet ladies who are interesting and like enjoying themselves. If you fancy linking up, please give me a call. Looking forward to hearing from you.

We spent ten minutes on the telephone, and he seemed fascinated by me and by California. He too had placed an ad, and answered a couple, and was bouncy, effervescent, and I looked forward to meeting him. He told me he was going to meet a friend in Croydon the next Sunday, so could we make it Gatwick?

'Fine.'

He was punctilious about the train timings, the platforms, where he would meet me. He called to confirm and we agreed on the Hilton, in the lobby, just under the large plane that is hanging from the ceiling in the middle of the tall atrium.

I was one hour late, because I had not taken into account the inevitable engineering work on a Sunday. When I got to the automatic doors into the Hilton lobby, I saw a tall, balding guy in a bright turquoise jumper moving around anxiously. He sat down, met my eyes and didn't flicker, so I thought, thank goodness, it's not him.

But it was. I was able to see that the bright jumper was matched by turquoise and green trousers, and matching spectacle frames. He had a large stomach, and wasn't balding, but was bald. Kojak had better look to his laurels. He was clearly nervous, sweating profusely, and there was a drop at the end of his nose.

We introduced ourselves, and he talked from then on, a mile a minute, very positive, very assertive, very American. He wasn't, but the States and their way of doing business fascinated him.

He brought over some tea and cakes, and I put into action my new policy. No longer was I going to be the meek and polite little lady. I didn't offer to be mother, I helped myself to cake, without waiting for him.

He didn't even notice. He launched into a crossfire interrogation technique, and I gave as good as I got. I didn't hedge, but answered truthfully and straight from the shoulder. He was trying to seem very intelligent, and was using (sometimes wrongly) lots of long words. He was dynamic, but it would have been even better if he hadn't kept telling me he was. He interrupted all the time, and I sat back while he held forth about himself. He didn't mind my smoking, which by now was a major point in his favour, and I listened to his tale of working from home and making a success of it.

The next day he phoned, and told me how much he had enjoyed meeting me. 'Would you like to come up to London and meet me at the Hilton there – in Park Lane, not the Kensington one?'

'Fine,' I answered enthusiastically, avoiding Mummie's eye, which was beginning to get beady about all the train fares (not that I blamed her). And I had to admit, I had still not answered my own question – could I go to bed with a bald man, however nice? He was nice, if a bit brash, and I enjoyed seeing him again. I spotted the top of his head gleaming above the back of a chair in the Hilton. He had got tickets for a Canadian Ballet company and we went off to Covent Garden and I loved it. I wore my cream dress again, and he paid for everything – supper in the Hilton restaurant beforehand (it couldn't be afterwards because I had to catch the 11.20 train to Brighton, and the ballet ended late), tickets, ice-creams in the interval, drinks at the Crush Bar and taxis all over the place. I felt deliciously spoilt.

'Not every man could afford to treat a woman like this,' he told me, rather spoiling the gestures again.

He did take care of me. I felt as if I was his girl all right, and I trusted him. It was a good, warm feeling, but there was still the question of his hair, or his head, anyhow.

He took me to Victoria and gave me £20 towards my travelling expenses, without making a fuss. I was grateful – it would calm Mummie down and make her better disposed to trips in the future. He held my hand when we ran for the train and then, when we got to the carriage door, gave me a whacking great kiss on the lips, which took my breath away. I was very embarrassed under the interested gaze of all the passengers – it was the last train, so quite full. As the train pulled out, I stood at the window and waved, looking at him and wondering where we went from here. I liked him more – he had stopped sweating and gabbling and was generally calmer and more relaxing to be with.

He called again and again. I agonized about whether to meet him or not, and he kept asking me down for the weekend to Bristol.

'There's a party on Sunday night – you should look 90 per cent sexy and alluring. But that won't be difficult for someone like you – you have a wonderful figure, and great hair.'

I accepted in the end. I was worried about the sex issue but thought I could deal with that when it came up, as it were. And then Moya saved me. She got herself a fever and a sniffle and streaming eyes, and I couldn't leave her in that state. Expecting the usual selfish disappointment, I rang him in Bristol and explained. He took it very well.

'I quite understand. I hope she gets better soon. Of course you can't leave her. Come another time.'

'If she's better, I will. Let's talk a bit later on.'

Mummie wasn't wild about a fare to Bristol – about £60 – so when he called again, I suggested another day in London.

'Fine. I'll meet you at the station, off the 11.56 train on platform nine, and we can go and have a lovely day together.'

He was there, precise as ever, and we did have a good time. Exhibitions at the Barbican, lunch, tea at the Hilton, drinks, and then a movie. That was his undoing – and was almost mine, quite literally. It felt like I was sitting next to a beast with six arms. He wouldn't leave me alone, and when a nude scene came up in the film, I worried dreadfully that he would move on to other areas that would be even more embarrassing. He didn't but he wanted to, there was no doubt about that. I was completely turned off. He nibbled my ear, he kissed my neck, he tried to play with my boob, he pinched my nipple and rubbed my hair and squeezed my shoulders, breathing hard and moaning suggestively in my ear. Oh dear – it was grim, and I couldn't wait to get out and home. He did the usual big squeeze at the station, and I smiled bravely, before turning to sit down in the carriage. When he called the next time, I unequivocally and for once said 'No thanks' and he got the message. He knew he had gone wrong, and I could feel him accepting the inevitable.

I put the same advertisement in a Sussex paper and a letter arrived in answer to it from a rather smart-sounding address in Cuckfield.

Dear Very Attractive Lady Full of Joie de Vivre,

I was not looking for advert, or any ladies, in fact I was looking for an osteopath, but there you were. Possibly the answer to my prayer, hiding in the personal columns of the *Mid-Sussex Times*.

If you really are as good as you sound, I assume, like myself, you are having difficulty finding that special person to share your life with – well, you might have found him here. Tall, 6 feet 5 inches, dark, well a few grey hairs, and handsome, so they tell me, divorced, aged thirty-seven, two super girls and one black labrador.

Very good job, unfortunately long hours, great fun, loves countryside, animals, entertaining, generally pottering about, trying to relax, not easy these days, and the good life. Do I mention drinking and smoking, well I could be persuaded to stop the latter, well educated, articulate, and unfortunately a perfectionist. Star sign Leo, so watch out, the rest I will tell you when we meet. . . . What I really miss is that family circle, the very special partner to share life with. . . . If all goes well, we can exchange notes over a candlelit dinner. Here's to the future.

Sounded pretty good. Cuckfield is a very pretty little town, his interests tallied with mine and he seemed to be looking for the same things. I called him.

'Hello, are you as good as Brigitte Bardot, then, oh Very Attractive Lady? Would you like to come out with me – I know a pub in Rottingdean and you may like it. Wear old togs when you come – I shall be wearing them, because I dress smartly for work and need a bit of a break.'

I didn't appreciate his hectoring manner, and he annoyed me, so I cancelled the date a few days later.

He was very nice about it, and apologized for his previous conversation.

'I had just got home from work and was feeling a bit ratty still. Sorry. Where shall we meet?'

We arranged the good old Grand, and I had to wait three quarters of an hour for him. When he walked in, I was pleasantly surprised. He had a good physique, very tall, and was smartly casual. He did, however, look like a car sales manager, which he turned out to be – funny how you can always tell.

I instantly didn't like his attitude. The goading was back: 'Am I what you expected? What did you expect? What did you think you had a right to expect? Have you had better?'

He was obviously very insecure, very lonely, but at moments when one is feeling a bit uncertain it is hard to think about someone else's plight as well. I stuck up for myself as best I could, getting crosser and crosser. I tried to give him the benefit of the doubt, but he kept on in this vein, and when he suggested his Rottingdean pub, I said firmly, 'No thanks. There's no point, is there? We're not getting on, you are obviously not interested in being nice to me, and I am not interested in having to defend myself all the time.'

He apologized at once, and so sincerely that I agreed to go. When we got there, he ordered a large drink, and I went the other way and had Perrier.

He got into his stride again. 'Do you expect a man to keep you, then, my girl? And what are you going to offer him? Eh?'

He insulted the way I dressed, the way I looked, my face, my figure, my hair: 'What gives you the licence to advertise yourself as attractive?' I decided that I was going to get a cab and go home to Littlehampton and hang the expense. I picked up my bag and made to stand up.

'What's the matter? Where are you going?'

'I'm not staying here for you to enjoy yourself being foul to me. Has anyone ever told you you are bloody rude? I'm off. Who do you think you are? No wonder you haven't found anyone. You smoke like a chimney, drink like a fish and you are ill-mannered and horrible to boot. Goodbye.' I was angry, and not far from tears.

'Oh, please don't go. I didn't mean to insult you, I really didn't.

I am so unhappy. My job is going no place, I feel no better than any other employee. I don't have many friends. What has life done to me? I don't deserve this, do I? Please don't go.'

'I think you had better sober up and we had better go, don't you?'

He took me home and was very sweet to me in the car, but I had learnt my lesson and didn't trust him not to turn nasty at any moment.

'Can I see you again? Please. I'll try harder, I promise. Here's my card. You will call me, won't you?'

But we both knew I wouldn't and he drove off sadly into the night. I was sorry for him, but my needs were important, and I was trying to help Moya and myself get a better life. I just couldn't take on another of life's casualties. I've only recently patched myself up!

Mr Get Rich Quick was an odd fish. Great fun but hard to work out. He answered my ad, with a compliments slip, on the back of which was written: 'Please telephone me reference your ad.' I did. He was out at least half a dozen times, but I eventually got hold of him. He was rich, and had all the trappings of newly acquired wealth – flats in Brighton and London, a Rolls Royce, farms, factories, all sorts of enterprises.

He was in building and development, but also had a stake in a racecourse and other ventures. He was going to buy a large boat, too, which whetted my appetite rather.

We arranged to meet, at Hickstead, which we both knew. A Mitsubishi Landrover ('My second car. I didn't want to look too flash in the gold Roller') was in the car park of the Castle pub, and in it was a man who looked like a criminal. A criminal with a twinkle in his eye though, and I warmed to him at once.

We had a drink at the bar, and were going to have dinner but then he grabbed my arm. 'Tell you what. Why don't we go up to London and make a night of it. I can drop you back later on, and it would be a good laugh. I often do it, but haven't had the time for a while. Or the pleasant company. What do ya say?'

I'm afraid I said no, not feeling like being that adventurous and knowing that Mummie would worry.

He looked disappointed but we went on chatting, and had a nice evening over dinner.

He kept horses at Douglas Bunn's stables – he owns Hickstead Showjumping Arena – and hunted three times a week. 'But it's getting expensive. I horsebox them to the meets so that they aren't tired by the time they arrive.' He liked gambling too, so I told him I was a croupier at the Metropole and he was interested in that.

I enjoyed his company, but he was dreadful-looking. He said he was thirty-eight, but looked more like fifty. However, over a meal it didn't matter. Particularly as he said I was 'delectable' and 'delicious' with a gleam in his eye. He was in it for a laugh, and enjoyed life to the full. When he was being nice he was charming, in a rough diamond sort of a way, but I wouldn't have liked to cross him in business. From what he said, he was known to be tough when he had to be, and wasn't above a bit of dishonest skulduggery if he felt it necessary.

In the car park before he drove home, he made a phonecall from the Mitsubishi and then, after he had put down the receiver, he turned and kissed me hard. He was a good kisser and I half responded, but didn't want to get into something I couldn't get out of. He walked me to my car, and kissed me again.

'I'll call you next Wednesday, shall I? We can arrange another date, gorgeous.'

'Lovely. I'll wait for your call.'

But I waited and waited and nothing happened, so I called him.

'What happened? Did something come up?'

'Yes. I got a bit tied up, darling. I'll call you when I've sorted it out. See you.'

But he didn't. I regretted it, because there was something ruthless and fun about him, and although I would have been unwise to have married him, I wouldn't have minded a bit of a fling.

Never mind. He wasn't that special. There are plenty of other fish in the sea. Aren't there?

5

Oddballs

Of all the men I have written to, spoken to on the telephone, and occasionally met, there have naturally been some who have been rather peculiar – unreliable, unpleasant, uncommunicative. For anyone who may wish to follow my example, I would stress that, provided you take sensible precautions about where you meet, and find out as much as possible about the man you're meeting, then you can usually weed them out before things get tricky.

Mr Cagey was one of the most sinister men I met. He wrote me a letter, on not very impressive lined file paper, in tight capital letters, which gave nothing away. The address was in Alicante, and it began: 'Please excuse paper but I wanted to get this off. I saw you on the *Terry Wogan Show*, where I couldn't help noticing your intelligence and sense of humour (two qualities I highly value in a woman).' So far so good. 'Perhaps you might like to spend some time at my place to get to know each other.'

Alicante didn't impress me madly, but it was an offer that included Moya, which was a good thing: 'I cannot guarantee we would reach the stars, but at least your sun tan would improve and your daughter should have a delightful holiday.'

He offered to 'have the plane tickets at a suitable airport for you' – an offer that I could hardly take up, much as I thought it a generous one, without checking up a little on his background, and his looks. The only information he vouchsafed was in a post script. After 'yours in hope and trepidation', he went on to say, 'I mention I am 6 feet 2 inches as you seemed very interested in height on the programme.' I wrote and got a reply in the form of a postcard on 31 October, postmarked, not Alicante, but Inverness. Oh well – perhaps he was staying with friends.

'Delighted to get your cordial letter,' it said. 'Will get in touch.

In haste.' He certainly *wasn't* in haste to get in touch, for it was not until 9 November that another card came.

'Recovering here on my friend's estate, back to town mid-week. Two lovely donkeys here for your daughter.' Once again from Scotland.

I had, in my letter, included all the usual questions. What did he do, what did he look like, could I have a photograph, what were his interests? Hardly unreasonable in the circumstances, but no answers were forthcoming. I repeated them, as gently and tactfully as I could, on the telephone, when he finally got around to dialling my number. It was an odd conversation. He mentioned four women he had known, and slavered over the memory of an encounter with a girl in a library who had given him a cigarette by lighting it first, which had made her, he thought, look very sexy. 'The end was still wet when she passed it to me.' He repeated the invitation to Spain, which I responded to cautiously but fairly encouragingly. I made it clear that I wanted to know more about him before I would commit Moya and myself to travelling away from home to see him in a strange house in a strange country.

'Tell me something about yourself,' I said, as reasonably as I could.

'Questioning, questioning,' he answered, sounding annoyed. 'Women are always questioning. My last girlfriend used to question me so much that I allowed her five questions one day, four the next, then three, two, one, until finally she couldn't ask any more. That's the way I like it.'

'How old are you, at least?' I asked, faint but pursuing.

'How old do you think, Colette?' he answered, infuriatingly.

'How should I know?'

'Well I'm young enough for you, Colette.'

Another time he told me sharply: 'You will find that out in due course.' What due course, I wondered. This relationship didn't seem to be going anywhere fast. Another extraordinary habit of his was not to end telephone conversations in a conventional way. No 'Goodbye, speak to you soon', but as often as not an abrupt stop, perhaps a curt 'Someone's coming' and the receiver would click down.

'Shall we meet?' I suggested one day. 'What about lunch?'

That didn't produce anything either, except a strange letter contradicting his first one.

'A friend who has a diet shop here (Inverness again) saw you on the *Terry Wogan Show* and assured me that you were very pretty.' He asked for my daughter's name for the plane ticket, and I had to come to the conclusion that this one-sided exchange of information was not the sign of a healthy future.

When he telephoned again, I asked him 'What do you look like? Perhaps you could send me a photograph of yourself?' which produced another reminiscence of the pleasures of women: 'I love to touch women with long hair. British girls are OK but the Norwegians are wonderful. I had a Norwegian girlfriend and I had a *lot* of fun with her.'

Trying to get him back on to the subject of himself, after some minutes of this, I asked, 'What do you do?'

'Oh, it's Sunday, so I'm working hard.'

'Working on a Sunday? Why do you have to do that?'

'Well, I can be doing paperwork or accounting, can't I?'

I had decided to let this one die a natural death, and when he telephoned again (from a telephone box – hardly calculated to instil confidence in his solvency) Mummie answered, and three times told him that I was ill or out or both. Then I got a card, a lurid get-well card with bright yellow and white capitals announcing that 'BEING SICK HAS ONE THING IN COMMON WITH SEX.' Inside it said 'IT'S BEST IF YOU TAKE IT LYING DOWN'. Ugh. I didn't care to think of sex in relation to this man, particularly since he had eventually sent a photograph in which he looked like a mad professor, with long grey hair parted to one side. In the card, because by now he had begun to get the message, he asked if he could have the photo and 'personal details' back. I'm not sure I bothered to return the photograph, and he hadn't given me any 'personal details' to speak of. A few more cards to Mummie, an odd little Christmas gift tag wishing us all Happy New Year from Spain, and that was the end of that.

Mr Creepy was altogether a different kettle of fish. His advertisement was tempting, to say the least:

> BUSINESSMAN – tall presentable, fifties, graduate (PhD), confident, original, wealthy, without heir (I liked that bit), just divorced, living in attractive country house (Surrey) swimming pool. Liking warm home life, love, social life, nature, pets, sport, travelling, dancing, gardening, etc. Wishes to share beauties of life with a very attractive, sincere, warmhearted, decent lady, thirty-two–forty-five, with adequate social background, liking to create warm home atmosphere, with similar broad interests, international minded.

I'm not sure how adequate my social background is, or how decent I am, but it was worth a try. After a couple of phonecalls and a postcard, he began to talk about his ex-wife, which I thought a bad sign. He was, it turned out, a lonely old man, living in a large empty house, missing his wife who had left him, and who was trying to turn their twelve-year-old adopted daughter against him. He would telephone late at night, usually about 11.00.

He reminisced for hours on end, and it was obvious that all I had to do was to listen to his descriptions of their happy life together in their mansion on Lake Geneva.

'You are a lovely woman,' he would say, in the middle of his long monologues. 'A lovely, wonderful woman. Please come to my house and spend a weekend, so that we can get to know each other better.'

'I'm sorry, but it is a rule of mine that the first date is always in a public place. Could we not make it a restaurant and then see how we go?'

'No, please, Colette. Come to my beautiful house. It *is* beautiful, and has a lovely garden that is going to rack and ruin. Do come and save it, and me.'

'I'm very sorry,' I insisted, as nicely as I could. 'But I really can't. After we meet, I'm sure it will be fine.'

Then he lost his temper with me, and began shouting down the telephone. 'What do you take me for, you silly Englishwoman. I am a respectable Swiss gentleman, and would not do anything that would make any problem for you. All I ask is for you to come to my house, and you suggest that I am untrustworthy. Restaurant? Restaurant? Why restaurant? My house is much more original, much more interesting.'

Sorely tried, I said, half jokingly: 'If you are so keen on being original, why don't you push the boat out, and take me to Kathmandu for the weekend, or to Paris for dinner?'

'Paris for dinner? Are you mad? No one does such foolish, crazy things.'

I didn't argue. It didn't seem worth it, and he was too annoyed. I didn't hear from him again, and had all but forgotten the encounter when a postcard fell on the mat one day. It had a spaniel sitting rather improbably on a beach, in front of a sea that had a very orange sunset on it. Although it was from Romania, he had written, 'not here'. 'Enjoying to meet you soon,' it said, which after our last exchange was puzzling.

Two months later, he called me. He had apparently met thirty-two different women as a result of his advertisement, and had only found one to compare with me.

'None of them understood me as you do, Colette. So can we at last meet? Wherever you like.'

I had steeled myself for the usual fuss about the venue, so was silenced for a second. Recovering myself, I suggested a restaurant in London.

'Fine,' he said. 'What about the Swiss Centre in Leicester Square? That would be appropriate, don't you think?'

We arranged a date and a time, but when he put the telephone down, I thought about it, and dashed off a note to cancel. I did not feel like being part of a line up. One is on trial enough in this game, and I really didn't need to know that I was being compared to another woman to see how I measured up, besides I was no longer really interested – he was too weird.

Mr Horseless was not an important encounter, but it amused me, in retrospect. At the time, I was furious with him for having taken me in and wasted my time.

I used to ride a lot as a child, and kept horses which I would enter for shows and gymkhanas. I was a good rider, still am, and if Mr Right comes along, I would welcome the chance to take it up again. I intend to introduce Moya to the pleasures of horses, hoping that she will enjoy them as much as I do. So when I saw an advertisement in *Time Out* that began 'STALLION, Late thirties', I read it with interest.

> Thoroughbred English stock, 18½ hands, stabled in SE London, affectionate – though frisky and responsive, seeks canter/graze with filly, view to possible stableshare. Details/photoswap. (Everyone answered, neigh obligation). Apply Horse Box No.

I sat down with a piece of paper and nibbled a pencil for some time, and after plenty of scratchings out I came up with a reply in the same vein:

> ROCKET TAH BELLA
> Description: Thoroughbred mare, thirty-one, 17 hh, attractive markings, sleek lines, chestnut flowing mane, vet's certificate, immaculate custom tack. History: Reared and schooled UK. Stabled loose box at full livery. Two years roamed grasslands Jersey, CI. Nine years raced California. Presently two years retired W Sussex. Ride: Interesting. Martingale – occasionally

hard to handle. Pelham, headstrong. Moves gracefully, jumps 4 feet. Requires experienced rider. Temperament: Good, warm and affectionate. Does not bite or kick, enjoys showing, travels well in horse box, good h, s and b. Responds to Polos, inseparable from two-year-old filly. Contact owner for inspection.

I was very pleased with the effort, and felt confident that it would show the recipient that at least we had a knowledge of horses in common. Ha. He turned out to be a common little man whose knowledge of horses is roughly comparable to mine of nineteenth-century Brazilian sculpture.

Of course there are people who sound marvellous, look all right, have all the right credentials, say all the right things and then let you down at the last minute. As they say, life's like that. I have two, Mr Unreliable Nos 1 and 2, who stick in my mind because they raised my hopes pretty high before disappointing me.

I wrote to the first one of my reserved, businesslike letters:

In response to your advertisement in *Singles* magazine I enclose a photograph of myself. I am British, twenty-nine, 5 feet 8 inches, 9 stone 7 pounds and I have a daughter. I am considered attractive and of a pleasing personality. Since June 85 I have been living with my mother at the above address. Previously I had been residing in the USA for the past nine years. If you care to correspond with me, enclosing a photograph of yourself, then maybe we could arrange a date to meet with a view to a happy future for all concerned.

He replied two months later, saying that he had been in Syria, and 'my circumstances haven't changed. If you still think you'd like to meet me, I'll be very pleased. Your photograph is so wonderful.' His wasn't bad – shining hair, nice open face, far-apart dark eyes, the edges of a leather jacket showing over a smart cotton shirt – he'd do. A little bit of flattery goes a long way after a hard week's advertisement placing.

So I telephoned, and we talked at length, about his family in Lebanon, his father who owned prize Arab horses there, but mostly, I have to say, about business. His business – he owned five companies, and was involved in computers, not a subject that I know a great deal about though I have some interest in it.

After a few of these conversations, it was decided that we should meet. He agreed to come down to Brighton – in fact, he said, there was a business conference there in a couple of weeks.

'Would you like to stay in a hotel there?'

I made it clear, as always, that there was to be no funny business about double bedrooms and paying in kind, and he seemed to take it on board. I was suspcious, however, when he phoned again.

'Colette, sorry, but I'm afraid I can only find single rooms in the hotel.'

'Oh good,' I said.

'No, it is not good, Colette, because I need a double room. I need space.' So that was that. Silence.

A month later, another phonecall.

'I have a good idea. Come to Nottingham for a few days. There is a very good health farm here, and perhaps you would like to stay there – I would of course pay for it.'

I was thrilled, and accepted like a shot. He called again, to tell me sensible things like times of trains, stations, where he would meet me. There was just one snag, which I told him.

'I'm sorry, but the fare is £55, and I just don't have that sort of money. There will be taxis and tips as it is, so I'm afraid I really can't afford it.'

'That's a shame,' he said, and nothing more. So another scheme evaporated, and I was beginning to feel a bit of a fool in Littlehampton, because of course I had told all my friends about going to stay in an upmarket Brighton hotel and then about my prospective few days in a luxurious health farm. Another month went by, and then came another telephone conversation. This time he wanted me to meet him 'somewhere nice, somewhere you'd like'. I said I knew Jersey, and *that* would certainly be nice. He was fine about this, and said that it was easier for him to fly from Nottingham to Jersey than to get himself down to the South Coast, so I was again put on Red Alert. 'Will you find out the hotel you would like to stay at – in separate rooms of course – and let me know?'

I knew all the hotels in Jersey, and spoke to my friends there who recommended a reasonably priced one, an expensive one and a very expensive one. I telephoned him back, and he picked the last. 'I think we should stay there, then it will be the most comfortable.'

Definitely, I thought, and phoned to confirm the booking. I had spent rather a long time on the phone by now, and Mummie was beginning to look ominous. She hadn't said anything, because it really did seem as if this was going to come off, but looked less convinced when he rang again.

'Colette, look, I'm really sorry. Something has come up. The marketing manager is ill, and we have a large order to get out by the end of next week. So I'm afraid I can't make it this weekend. Would you mind changing the booking for the following one? That's if you are free. Then I can get on with booking the flights this end, and I'll let you know where and when to meet. Looking forward to it. Is that all right?'

'Yes, fine,' I said, through gritted teeth, avoiding my mother's narrowing eyes.

More hours on the telephone, more rearranging, more explanations to ever more sceptical friends, and of course, you guessed it, he never called again.

The other unreliable man was, oddly enough, unreliable in the same way. There were the same sorts of arrangements, once for a meeting in Geneva. He would send the tickets, meet the plane, etc., etc. Nothing. I of course hadn't learnt my lesson by then, so again I had told everyone, and got all excited, and again had to eat my words and swallow my pride. Six months later he rang, and I told him I was off for a few days to Monte Carlo.

'Could I perhaps come down and meet you there?' he asked, ever so nicely.

'Sure,' said this lamb on its way to the slaughter.

Of course, he never rang to confirm, far less bothered to show up.

One year later, the phone rang.

'Hello,' said this vaguely familiar voice. 'Are you still looking, Colette, because I am?'

'No, sorry,' I told him crisply. 'I am happily married, thank you.'

The last oddball I shall tell you about I call Mr Raunchy. He saw my advertisement in *Tatler*, and replied to it on bright yellow paper, writing diagonally, which, while it wasn't that easy to read, certainly made him a bit different.

He was from Texas, and told me that he worked a 4000 acre ranch. I was a bit careful before I got too excited about this because he could easily have been the manager or even a ranch hand.

'I guess you have style,' he said, 'and I like that. As for me, I am fifty years old, with blue eyes and silver hair, and I'm 220 pounds.'

My maximum age was usually forty-five, but he had caught my attention, and I was prepared to stretch a point if he was very, very rich, not to put too fine a point on it.

I sent a letter off, one I made as wacky as I thought appropriate, and sure enough, a strong Texan twang was on the other end of the telephone before you could say, 'prime steer'.

'Hiya, babe' or rather 'Hiiiyaaa, Baaaabe,' he drawled and proceeded to chat me up in a way that either meant he had seen too many westerns or that the man was exactly what he said he was, which was 'born in the Yewnited Staaaates of Americaa; I've lived there all mah life. Ah'm a cattle rancher and proud of it. Ah've got me an oil well in Louisiana, and employ some mighty fine boys. Hey, I loved your photograph. Ah love your long hair. Ah can feel mahself running mah fingers through it when we are alone together, honey. Ah would like to take you gambling in Vegas, and with mah winnin's, ah would buy you all the purty dresses you want. Ah like to see mah women look purty.'

The telephone conversations were usually along these lines: 'Ah love women. Ah have a purty fine daughter ah'd like you to meet. Come over and live with me, honey.' This was all 'mighty fine', as he would no doubt have put it, but he had omitted one rather vital factor. No mention was made of how I was to finance this romantic-sounding venture, so I laughed softly on my end of the line, and didn't commit myself to anything.

'It's not a mighty fine picture of you that you sent me. Are you fat or thin? Ah can't see. Ah don't like fat women, ah don't like 'em skinny. Ah like ladies with thick thighs, because ah like something to get my hands into.'

Then he began to get more personal still, which became rather disconcerting.

'What bra size are you, honey?' he asked me one day.

'Well,' I said, very primly. 'I'm a 34.'

'No, no, no. Ah wanna know whether you're a B or a C cup, Ah wanna know what ah'm gonna be able to hold . . .'

'I'm a B cup, actually,' I told him, trying to sound unshocked but also not encouraging.

He didn't seem over-impressed with that.

'Hmmmm. Oh well. And your waist size?'

Feeling rather like a tailor's dummy, or a medical specimen, I told him 'I'm 27 round the waist, although I would love to say I was 24!'

This had obviously whetted his apparently prodigious appetite enough for us to move on to the nitty gritty.

'What's your favourite colour?'

'Well,' I answered. 'Blue, I think.'

'No, honey, ah don't think you quite understand me. Choose from black or red.'

'Black.'

'Well, ah'll be sendin' you some very purty underwear. Ah love women's underwear, don't you?'

'Well, some I like, some I don't,' said Miss Prim. Moving the conversation right along to the more respectable parts of women's clothing, I ventured: 'I've seen some pretty things in *Vogue*. Whenever I have a spare penny I buy *Vogue* or *Tatler*.'

But he was a dogged chap. 'Ah *love* the women in there.'

He called every two weeks, hotly excited and full of flattering ardour.

He did turn out to be too hot to handle, however.

'Ah sure am missin' you, baby. Come over and keep me company.'

'I can't, because I have Moya to think of.'

'No problem. Bring her over too. Say honey, ah wanna love a woman like you.'

This was a theme he expanded on in another yellow, diagonal letter, and 'Ah wanna love a women three, four days at a time,' he said in his next call.

'Perhaps,' I tried to say calmly, 'Texas might be too hot to spend all that time indoors?'

'This is the United States of America,' he said, in case I'd forgotten. 'We have air conditioning, designed for just that sort of eventualiteè.'

'What about Moya,' I reminded him.

'Oh, we'll be able to get someone to look after her,' he said, rather too flippantly for my liking. It was obvious that he was interested only in taking me to Vegas, and keeping me in bed festooned in all sorts of fancy frills. I had a vision of a tart's boudoir, all red and black nylon lace with a liberal sprinkling of whalebone to whittle my 27-inch waist down to more acceptable proportions, and decided I couldn't see myself there. More telephone calls came, with a lot of emphasis on wanting me in his bed, instead of just having a photo to look at. I wondered privately what else he used the photograph for, and the whole thing, despite transatlantic phonecalls, branding irons, the seventy thoroughbred horses he raised, his 4000 acres and the rest of the package, began to feel very dodgy indeed, and I called it a day. His being in Texas did have some advantages.

There were plenty more of these men. Some, like Mr Wishful Thinking, aged seventy-five, knew they hadn't a chance but thought they'd try anyway. One father wrote to me on behalf of his son, who had just had his heart broken by a split from his girlfriend, which really touched me. Despite some that were tacky, I mostly ended up feeling sorry for them rather than angry or revolted. One thing these last couple of years has taught me is a bit of tolerance. We're all looking. Some of us have to look a lot longer than others, that's all.

6

Mon Cheri Amour

The silhouettes of the palm trees were dark against the clear white marble of Monte Carlo. A soft rustle occasionally stirred the leaves of the trees and the crescent moon and stars were very bright in the black velvet sky. I sat back in my chair and sipped my gin and tonic, feeling the cubes of ice against my teeth, cloaked in a wonderful warmth that pulsed out of the stones from a month of sun.

I had been having a bit of a lull in the past few weeks. None of my advertisements were producing anybody worth spending an evening with, let alone the rest of my life. From America I had a sudden and very pleasant windfall from the sale of my car over there, which cheered me up a good deal. Instead of buying something sensible, or putting it all away in a building society, I spent all the £800 on a package to the most sophisticated place I could think of – Monte Carlo. I was just in the mood for a few balmy breezes, so I booked my three nights in Monaco, staying at l'Hermitage. I had wanted to be at the Casino, but that was booked solid, so I took what seemed like the next best thing.

It was really exciting to leave Littlehampton and stop worrying about the answers to the ads and jumping every time the phone rang and waiting for the post each morning, just in case. There wasn't anything 'in case' about this. I was ready for the time of my life.

The weather was pleasant when we touched down at Nice at about 5.00 in the evening. There was a smell of sunshine in the air, and the flowers were tossed gently by the light, warmly scented breeze. A helicopter was to take all the passengers to Monte Carlo, another splendid touch, and I went to check in with a sense of anticipation. The hotel was vast and white, five-star, but not as spectacular as I had become used to in California. It was old, and had always been very grand. The bedroom itself was quite large, with a big bed and the usual bits and pieces. There was fresh fruit in a basket to welcome me, some biscuits and some cheese. I was impressed with the bathroom, red marble mostly, with two basins, and a nifty hairdryer on the wall.

I changed into my baggy pink and black and white trousers, and matching top, put on a pair of white high-heeled shoes and decided to check out the town, looking like a classy holidaymaker, but also looking for fun.

First I stopped at the nearest cafe, and sipped my *café au lait*, looking about me hopefully. I began to have a few doubts about the wisdom of my choice of resort because the beach and the promenade were both deserted and I hadn't planned to spend four days in a ghost town. I turned to look at the Casino and that was much better. People were having dinner, and looked as if they had dressed for the occasion. It was about 8.00 by now, and the candle flames were throwing a warm light on the white china, thick tablecloths and the flowers in the middle of the tables. I smiled to myself, deciding then and there that that's where I was going to be that night. A few locals smiled back and some passersby eyed me hopefully, but I wasn't having any of them.

I went back to my hotel and into the bar, which was empty, but had a nice view of the harbour and what I later learnt was Adnan Khashoggi's yacht. The bar had a stone terrace outside, edged with statues of various Greeks in various degrees of tasteful undress, rather like some of the people I had just been watching tucking into their tournedos Rossini, or crepes Suzette. I had spent a good deal of my plane journey mugging up on places to see and be seen, and tried to top up my knowledge, already pretty comprehensive, by asking the waiter if he knew any good discos or bars. He didn't know any more than I, it turned out, and recommended a place I had already decided on: the Bar Brasilia. He asked me to meet him there later for a drink. Why not? I thought. He was tall, dark and quite good-looking, and he might save me from a lonely evening. I arranged the time, and downing the last of my g&t, I put down the glass on the polished bar, smiled at him, and went upstairs to prepare myself for what was going to be a fun evening. I chose my most glamorous clothes, and looked smashing when I put them on, and did my hair in a scoop on the top of my head, and added long diamante earrings to hang from my ears. I wore a white sequinned top and satin trousers, and high white pumps, and with a final slick of pink lipstick, and a last spray of Givenchy III, I tripped off to find my rich, handsome and delicious company director, probably American. First stop the Casino. The public part was full of Americans all right, but they were all spending their time in front of fruit machines, and the place was ringing with the chink of coins, the clatter of payouts, and the occasional scream of success or frustration. The Americans were mostly fat, over fifty, wearing those Crimplene trousers that must be given to all middle America at birth and saved till the owners leave the States to go to Europe. Luckily my package included a passport to many private clubs, and I hurried into the part of the Casino denied to these portly players. This was a completely different story. It was, in a word, superb. Tall, slim women blinded me with jewellery, setting off their £1000 outfits and putting my white sequins in the shade. Their escorts had their eyes on the tables, occasionally raising them to see who had come in before lowering them again with no change of expression. It was packed with Arabs, who looked me over appreciatively, and their companions, who looked me over very unappreciatively indeed. I beat it, feeling out of place without a couple of grand to play about with, not caring whether I won or lost. I again looked in for a drink in the cafe, full of locals and the cheaper end of the tourist market, and then moved on to the Laos Casino, frequented mostly by couples in their thirties and naturally, fat old men. I wasn't doing very well so far this evening.

Well tanked up by now, with all the gins and tonics I had sunk at the hotel, the Casino and the cafe, I went on to the Brasilia, and dived into one of the largest cocktails I had ever seen, all innocent umbrellas and long straws, but absolutely lethal. The waiter I was waiting for was there, and I was relieved to see a friendly face. He introduced me to his friend, a short, fat, ugly man with a big smile which gave his brown face a lot of charm. He was Karl Lagerfeld's chauffeur, they said, and he had to leave almost at once to pick up his boss. Or that's what I managed to glean from what they mimed and said. I imagine we looked like a Punch and Judy show. They left saying they wouldn't be long, and would meet me later in a disco, drawing me a map of how to get there.

I settled back into my chair, crossing my legs, and leaned back, holding my long, cold glass. Sipping it, I looked around me, without much hope, but still, something might turn up. I almost poked my eye out with the swizzle stick. To my right, I saw the most beautiful man I had ever clapped eyes on, from the tips of his toes to the top of his brown swept-back hair. He had pushed a pair of sunglasses back on his head, and around his pale blue-shirted shoulders, he had slung a camel cashmere sweater. His trousers were white-pleated denim and his tan was golden Monte Carlo. When he smiled his teeth gleamed and I thought I was going to pass out. I kept staring at him hopefully, but he didn't look at me at all and, of course, that made him all the more desirable. As I gazed, an English voice asked me if the chair beside me was taken, and reluctantly I dragged my eyes away.

'No. No it's not,' I managed to say, and then regretted it as I took in the speaker. Small, pock-marked, with bubbling acne, a pot belly and small moustache, he introduced himself.

'Hello, my name's Andrew. I can see you are British, so I thought I'd come and join you, if you are alone. But I can't believe my luck . . .'

'Mmmmm.'

I could barely be bothered to speak, and above all I didn't want the apparition on the other side of the room to think I was with this man.

'Would you like a drink?'

'Yes, all right, one of these would be nice,' I told him, and looked away quickly from his grease-spattered shirt. I then got every pick-up line in the book.

'What's your name? It must be something very beautiful.'

'Colette,' I answered him shortly. 'I'm here on holiday for a few days.'

'Very glamorous. But I couldn't have imagined you would be anything else. Where did you get your clothes? Dior?' The party on the other side moved closer, but he still wasn't looking. Then he did and his bright blue eyes met mine, and my heart moved up uncomfortably and stopped me from breathing properly. He smiled and, stupid fool that I was, I blushed and looked away.

'Look darling. You aren't listening to a word I'm saying. What's catching your attention?'

I turned to look at him at last and thought, what the hell.

'It's that man over there. Do you see him? The good-looking one in the blue shirt? I want to meet him but I don't know how.'

'Oh, is that all? I can do that for you. Shall I go over? Easily done.'

'No, yes, no, oh you can't, can you?' I babbled like a brook, and almost, but not quite put my hand on his arm.

'Just you stay here. I'll see to this.'

And he got up and walked lumpily across to the object of my adoration. I just sat there like a bump on a log, feeling completely stupid and wishing I was anywhere else, and also dying to see what would happen. Their conversation seemed to be going on and on and on – I could hardly bear it.

And then, he was there beside me.

''Allo,' he said, quite shyly and I looked up at him, grinning foolishly.

'Colette, this is Michel,' said Andrew.

We shook hands and looked at each other.

'He doesn't speak any English at all.'

'Oh God,' I said, laughing like a lunatic. 'I'm on lesson six in my French for Beginners. I can just about order a cup of coffee, and not much else. What on earth can I talk to him about?'

'I'm sure you'll find something,' said Andrew and translated all this, in what I have to admit sounded fluent French.

There was a lot of '*elle ne parle pas*-ing' and shaking of heads and smiling – all the things Frenchmen are supposed to do. 'It's OK. He says he understands and it doesn't matter.'

We had another drink, bought by Andrew, whom neither of us were paying much attention to.

He hung around, though, translating when we got stuck, so I suppose he had his uses. I wished and wished for him to leave us, but he didn't. Eventually, even he got the message and took off, making me promise to meet him the following night.

'I think I shall *frappe la route* now,' he said. 'But listen, Colette. I think it would be a good thing if you met me tomorrow, and you owe me one so shall I see you here at eight?'

'Sure, I'll be here Andrew.'

'Fine, love. *Au revoir*, Michel. See you tomorrow, Colette.'

We were alone together at last, if you discount the hundreds of people out and about in Monte Carlo that night. For all we saw of them they could have turned into butterflies and flown away. We tried to talk.

'You like. *Ce musique?*' I asked him, nodding.

'*Oui, oui,*' he said, and then came a bit of fast French, of which I could make out '*hotel*' and '*arriver*'.

'*Oui, ce matin, Hermitage.*'

I was relieved to see him smile as he repeated it. Lesson six had its moments. The music was blaring away, so he took my arm under the elbow and said something about '*disco*' and '*aller*' and looked questioningly at me. I trusted him, that's all there was to it, and I would have followed him anywhere. We walked out together and on to the pavement, after he had said goodbye quickly to his friends. He practically pulled me up the hill, as I had no idea at all where we were going, and explanations took too long. I tottered along willingly, watching his hair blown gently by the breeze. He spent most of the time trying to get me across the roads without getting run over.

We reached a very classy-looking place, Tiffany's, and went in to find that, although he was clearly very well known and liked there – all manner of waving and smiling – it was full and we had to try next door, another equally glittering spot. He held both my arms above the elbows, in a grip I had never realized before could be so masculine and so intimate and looked down from his 6 feet 4 inches, speaking very earnestly to me although of course I couldn't work out much of what he was saying. We went in and, holding hands, crossed the dark dance floor to sit down at a small table. The music was loud, and there were plenty of beautiful people dancing, sitting, talking, drinking. The waiter, who spoke English, brought us our drinks and also a few paper napkins because I asked him to. I found a pen in my handbag and we tried to talk to each other using drawings and gestures. We did fairly well or as well as could be expected with my head spinning and my thoughts making no sense at all. It was very funny at times. For instance, he drew a firework, which looked like a rocket, so I thought he was breaking it to me that he spent a lot of time away from home orbiting the earth. The whole evening was so odd that it seemed entirely possible that I should be spending the evening with an astronaut. Feeling the way I was then, my feet hardly touching the ground, we would have had something in common. Later I found out that in fact his hobby was making fireworks.

He was very patient, and when we had clarified one thing we moved on to the next. No rush, no bother, as though we had all the time in the world.

I told him I had a sister in the States – 'Amerique' – and cradled an imaginary baby in my arms to show that I have a child, and he understood that she is a daughter and I love her very much. And he would catch my face in his hands and stare earnestly into my eyes and I would return his warm blue gaze. He was wonderful to look at, like a Greek god, and I tried to tell him so. '*Vous avez un tres joli visage*', I stammered, feeling rather pleased with the length of the sentence. Unexpectedly he burst into pearls of laughter and explained it was something only to be said to girls – '*les filles ont des jolies visages.*'

But it didn't really matter, nothing did. To prove it, he kissed my forehead and we laughed together. He was attentive and romantic, not a groper or a creep trying to take liberties. If he had been I would have been off like a rabbit.

When the music slowed, he asked if I would like to dance. Would I? We moved on to the floor. I was held firmly but not aggressively against his lean muscular body and we moved to the song. It was pure heaven and when he kissed me I just wanted time to stand still.

We left soon after, and walked back dreamily, holding hands, to my hotel. It was safe but if there had been a spot of doubt in my mind I would not have worried because I could see security cameras everywhere. It took us half an hour to get back to the hotel. I asked if he would like a drink, miming the lifting of a glass to my lips. We tried to find the bar, but it was very late by now, about 3.30, and it was predictably closed.

Now I had a dilemma. I didn't want him to think I was easy. A few drinks, a smooch on the dance floor, and that was it – bingo. But on the other hand I couldn't bear to lose him. I wanted, needed, to spend some more time with him, and there was certainly no way I could hold a telephone conversation. By gestures, he suggested a drink in my room, which of course was the obvious thing. All I could think of to blurt out was '*non le lit*'. He laughed and put his hand on the back of my neck, to playfully pull my head into his chest. I felt he got the point.

We entered the waiting red velvet-walled lift, with its flatteringly dim light, and the doors slid closed. Before we pressed the button for the fifth floor he kissed me so carefully and excitingly that I had to lean against the walls as it moved. Once there, there was another problem to delay us. My clever little key card wouldn't go into its slot and it was beginning to seem as if we were going to be consigned to the corridor until it slipped in gently and the door opened with a click. I walked over to the small fridge in the corner and pointed to all the bottles, miming drinking and mixing. Halfway through this dumbshow, he stood up and reached into the shelves. He had a Scotch and soda and I my usual gin and tonic, with ice and lemon. I took a long time over all this, partly because my hands were shaking, and also because now we were here, the air was thick with possibilities. There is something very obtrusive about a large, soft bed, clearly meant for two people, standing empty in the centre of what is obviously a bedroom.

He found my dictionary and my French for Beginners, and passed it over saying, slowly, in French, that I should read him some. I wound my halting tongue around some of the words, some of which looked vaguely familiar, but quite honestly it could have been in Serbo-Croat for all the sense they made now. And somehow I couldn't build up much enthusiasm for the family life of the Duponts when this gorgeous man was half sitting, half lying, on the aforementioned object of furniture.

He smiled at my efforts, sitting up against the headboard, with his long legs stretched out. He pulled himself together when he saw my hurt face and pulled my head over on to his stomach and kissed the top of it. Then he kissed my lips and smoothed my hair, and we leant together for a while. Still no rush, he seemed to say.

I tried to tell him how exhausted I felt but got into all sorts of trouble with 'sleep like a baby' and 'dog tired' so I stopped and just yawned and stretched. I told him as much as I could, and as much as I thought he needed to know about my past. '*Un, deux, trois mariages,*' and showed him my ring finger, conspicuously empty.

He said he was '*seul*', wrote down his age and birthdate and drew a lion.

Now, you will forgive me if I wasn't at my sparkling best at this stage and the sight of this wild animal on the page quite took my breath away. I looked at it, and blankly at him, and '*quoi?*' I asked fluently. He meant he was a Leo so I told him my birth sign was Gemini and hoped we were astrologically suited.

Then the whole thing became a blur of scribbles and drawings and getting another drink, talking, hugging, dithering, kissing. I showed him photos of Moya and he made all the right noises. He explained that he lived in Bruxellais just outside Monaco. His hands were very rough. I took them in my smooth ones and rubbed his palms. '*Quoi?*' He waved his arms around and mimed climbing a ladder. He was a painter and decorator. He used to operate computers (that was a big one, TV screens and buttons and popping sounds but I got it) but he left it to make '*plus d'argent*'. Not exactly my sophisticated, wealthy company director but I was past caring by then.

By now it was something like 7.30 a.m. and many of my clothes were not in the same positions as they had been when I started. I was beginning not to enjoy the prickling of the sequins on my by now bra-less chest, so I slipped into the bathroom and changed into a loose beach dress and came back in to show that nothing more was coming off. Time he left.

Suddenly this man who had been intelligent about my language trouble all evening seemed to lose all power of deduction.

'*Ici*', I cried. '*Maintenant, now, sleep, dormir, seule, au revoir.*'

Instead of bowing out gracefully, which I half wanted him to do, he jumped up and went to the bathroom where I could hear him having a shower. Feeling a little nervous, I got into bed, and when he came back he joined me stark naked and not a bit worried about it. I fell asleep in his arms. How's that for sang froid? It felt fine in fact, very easy and natural. And when we woke up several hours later it felt easy then too. These things always do, even when they probably shouldn't. Lust is a great lubricator. And lust it was. He kissed my neck, my spine, the backs of my legs. His hands were everywhere without a trace of embarrassment or hesitation, which made it much less tense than it could have been. He pushed the bedclothes away, lifted my dress around my ears before he pulled it off, and continued his kissing, right down to my toes. Then we had the most erotic, exciting, marvellously liberating sex. The heavy atmosphere of doubt and unresolved longing was lifted, or rather changed to delight in each other's bodies. It took hours and every bit of me was touched by what seemed every bit of him. And my head was spinning, reeling, and I was gasping for him to stop and for him to go on. When we both came, together, it was a masterpiece of orchestration and I lay there, all my blood just below the skin's surface feeling rubbed and raw and ready for more. He understood and so we began again in different positions, with pillows placed by him in exactly the right places to support my shoulders, my hips, the small of my back. He stroked me sometimes, sometimes he pushed into me, quickly, slowly, gently, insistently. It was the best lovemaking I had ever had. He wanted to begin again when he had finished but I couldn't cope with this so I escaped to the bathroom avoiding his hands which were snapping at my ankles.

I couldn't summon enough strength to take a shower – I was quite incapable of standing – so I ran a bubble-filled bath and soaked thankfully in it, feeling the warm water wash all over me, drawing out the tiredness, leaving me with a warm glow and heavy limbs. When I went back into the bedroom he reached out to welcome me to bed. I whimpered that I couldn't do it again. '*Pas encore, Michel, pas encore.*'

He laughed, before leaping out of the bed to have a shower. We spent the next couple of hours in town at his friend's Chinese restaurant where the food was delicious and the wine delightfully heady. Or it could just have been being together. He was careful, attentive, pleased and proud to be with me. We kissed under the trees, held hands as we walked, laughed and mimed and laughed some more. Back at the hotel, we made more love and then fell into a deep dreamless sleep. I woke before he did, and was able to look at him, lying beside me, brown and lean and strong. He had told me that he had begun weight training, but had given it up to join an aerobics class to meet girls. I was happy that he had met me. I washed and dressed in an ultra sexy number, a long, tight, white dress stopping 6 inches above my ankles and showing all the good bits of my body to advantage, while camouflaging anything that wasn't quite up to scratch. I left him in bed but made sure he woke up long enough to see what I looked like and know that I was going to see another man. It was only awful Andrew who had introduced us, but it would do no harm for Michel to have a little time thinking about me, not being with me. We arranged to meet at the Bar Brasilia at 11.00.

Andrew showed up 10 minutes late, which didn't make me any more pleased to see him. My heart sank as he walked in breezily and obviously thrilled to bits with the picture he made in his brown polyester trousers, just that crucial bit too short, held up with a bright brown plastic belt, all mock croc and bright brass buckle.

'Hi, gorgeous,' he cried when he saw me, his eyes widening when he took in my clothes which he obviously thought were all for him. 'You look fabulous. You shouldn't have bothered, but I sure am glad you did. I was going to take us to the Casino for a noggin. Now I shall feel like a million dollars as well as losing a million, har har har.'

'Ha ha ha,' I echoed weakly, and wished myself anywhere but walking along the prom with this prune. We reached the Casino and went to the bar. I could see the barman, for whose company I would have swapped Animal Andrew at any given moment, thinking what's this lovely lady doing with this turkey, and I tried as hard as I could to show him how much I agreed. I told him pointedly that I had to be at the Brasilia by about 11.15, to meet Michel.

'OK, lovely lady, we can go along together. You might need me after all.'

Over my dead body, I thought. But as it turned out Michel didn't show until after midnight, by which time I was frantic inside, thinking we had missed him. When he walked in my knees and blood pressure went through the usual acrobatics and Andrew was forgotten. I don't remember what happened to him; he somehow melted away. Michel and I were cocooned in each other, with eyes for no one else. We stayed with his friends for a while, and eventually went off to a disco, yet another disco, where we danced glued to each other, as we had been in the bed at l'Hermitage. His hands played up the back of my dress, on my bare skin and I could only wish I had more available at that moment. It didn't take long.

We walked to the hotel as if we were taking part in a rather glamorous three-legged race, arms round each other. Hardly speaking we went to bed.

We made love, oh I don't know how many times, cuddled, slept, woke up and made love again.

Later we went out and he asked me if I wanted to go bowling with him that evening. This wasn't exactly what I had in mind for Monaco, and it was the last night for me to be sensible and make the most of my investment. I was supposed to be here with a goal, and a painter and decorator wasn't it.

'This is *au revoir*,' I told him sadly, looking into those wonderful blue eyes. 'You are no good for me. *Ce soir me aller* Jimmys. I think you are formidable, fantastic, wonderful, *mais* . . .'

It was a horrible moment. I realized then that he did not think I was just a quick lay, easily had and just as easily forgotten. He was hurt which made me feel rotten.

We walked slowly down the hill together and when we reached the bottom, I took his photograph and gave him my address. Couldn't help it. Then one last long kiss, and we separated, with him looking back at me as we walked away and me just standing there wondering whether I was mad to let this man go, but feeling that I owed it to myself to make the most of Monte Carlo.

It felt strange to be alone again. I took a short cool swim in the pool that afternoon and tried to catch some rays, sipping long cool drinks. I had a crisp salad for lunch on the terrace and felt myself getting brown.

Then it was time for my last outing. The sun began to slip slowly into the sea which turned orange, then bright gold, and then bluish purple and soon dark with bright highlights. It felt now as if I'd been there for weeks, not days, and the hotel had become my home. I decided to go out with a bang, if you'll pardon the expression, and so pulled out my green silk suit for maximum impact. Loose top, pleated hip-skimming skirt, all softly swaying and delicious to the touch. Subtle make-up: eyes aglow, lips moist and rich pink, skin flawless, scent Givenchy, recognizable at ten paces by those in the know, and I was ready, colours pinned to the mast. First a drink in the Casino. Not fruitful. A couple of old fogies tried the usual and I froze them out. Then on to Jimmys which was miles away and, as usual, I couldn't find a cab when I needed one. The contrast between being cherished by Michel and this was almost unbearable, but I soldiered on, and got there. Another shock – drinks were something like £10 each so I was cradling mine as if it were liquid gold, when an American youth, all 5 feet 4 inches of him, pounced. He was twenty-four, staying with his parents and dressed like a preppie catalogue. Lacoste shirt, pale pink, complete with yawning crocodile, slacks, expensive deck shoes, and a light aftershave. Nicely cut blond hair, a wispy moustache and some sort of tan on a face that was, well, open. I had too many drinks with him for want of a better alternative, and regretted the loss of my divine Michel. How could I have been such a fool? There it was, there for the asking. My own stupidity had just sent it away. No one had told me to leave him. I had done it all by myself. Did I fancy him? Yes. Did he fancy me? Yes. Was he wonderful to be with? Yes. Was he a wonderful lover? Yes. Well what was I going to do about it? It was 4.00 a.m. I could hardly ring him at this hour.

A few moments later, I could hear his voice on the end of a telephone. He sounded calm, not a bit irritated.

'*Bonsoir,*' I said.

'*Trouve un taxi,*' he said.

'*Oui, oui, oui,*' I wailed. I could hardly wait. I caught a cab as if by magic and it whisked me there. The fates were being kind. Michel came bounding out, and kissed me like I'd never been kissed before. One of his specialities, you will recall. We went up to his apartment like mice, so as not to wake his sleeping flatmate, and he sat me down while he went to open a bottle of wine. I looked about me, at a flat that could only have been given the adjective 'bachelor', in my experience roughly translatable as 'filthy'. But I couldn't have cared if it were a tent on the roof.

At 11.00 the next morning the taxi came to take me to the hotel and then on to the airport. It was dreadful to leave and he held me tight on the balcony, both of us almost in tears. Before I left Monte Carlo, I stopped for a few drinks at a bar called Flashmans. I met only ex-pats and was missing Michel badly already, so it was not an unqualified success. It was still hot and I was walking sadly along the pavement when a motorbike revved throatily beside me. Its rider leapt off it and, not bothering to remove his helmet, flung his arms around my waist. Three policemen arrived from nowhere but I sent them away with a smile and thanks. Michel, for it was he, took off his helmet and demanded we stop for a coffee. I seemed to have spent most of my time in Monte Carlo sipping at something or another, but I did want to spend a little more time with him, so we went into a café.

'*Colette, je t'adore. Je voudrais bien aller en Angleterre.* You see me?'

'*Oui, oui, oui,*' I said. I was helplessly, hopelessly in love and there really was no point in trying to be cool about anything now.

There were ten minutes before the helicopter flight to the airport, and the bus, which we could see from where we were sitting, had still not arrived, although I knew my bags had been brought down very efficiently to the hotel lobby. It arrived at last and I climbed on, followed by Michel who hugged me, much to the fascination of the other passengers.

'Laisé pas, Laisé pas,' he murmured against my hair, but I had to and we both knew it. He got off slowly when the driver turned the engine on, and stood on the pavement watching us drive away. I watched him disappear, and prepared myself for the journey back to dreary old England, comforted by the fact that I would soon be seeing Moya and not that long after that, I hoped, Michel. The journey was cheered by the presence of a handsome grey-haired man whom I met while buying a packet of cigarettes before we boarded.

He came over to talk to me during the flight. I cursed Michel briefly because this man looked eminently suitable and I looked like Dan Dare. I had slightly bloodshot eyes and my chin was cut to ribbons by Michel's stubble and looked like a plate of mince, despite all the make-up I had plastered on to hide it. He turned out to be called Monsieur Colette, a coincidence I remarked on, and we passed a pleasant flight together. Before we parted he gave me his card and said to call him if I felt like it.

It turned out to be a rather fruitful day. On the airport bus I met Fred Bloggs who was to take me to Ascot later that year, but at the time Michel was all I could think about. His souvenir on my face took ages to clear up so I was a walking reminder to myself every time I looked in the mirror. After two days I wrote him a letter, and six weeks later, after a few more communications came a telegram.

'*Chère Colette. J'arrive vendredi à l'aéroport de Gatwick à dix heures and je t'attends à l'endroit convenu. A bientôt. Michel.*'

It took me so long to decipher that I had reached the end before giving a shriek of panic. He was due the next morning. The house was completely upside down. Granny in the guest room, Moya sleeping with me, Mummie downstairs, my brother Richard in another bedroom. We dashed about like fleas in a fit, and Granny, who always comes up trumps, helped me move all the furniture and Moya out and in to her room with her clothes and her teddies. Chaos, but between us we got another bed into my room for Michel and me to sleep on.

I drove to Gatwick in plenty of time the next day, wearing a new pair of trousers, a new jumper and new shoes. I had rushed out to buy them the day before, anxious to remake a good impression. I couldn't wait to see Michel but I was also a bit apprehensive too, wondering if it would be the same, wondering if we could communicate at all any more, a thousand doubts and worries. I stood nervously at the meeting point and suddenly there he was, all 6 feet 4 inches of brown and beautiful man in camel trousers and a brown leather jacket, the thick sort that looks and is expensive. He was carrying a medium-sized suitcase and smiling a big sexy smile. My heart skipped all over the place, although I saw that he had had a perm, which was a pity, because his heavy brown hair had suited him much better straight. I didn't say anything – I wasn't in the mood to complain. 'Allo, Colette,' he smiled at me. '*Comment ça va, chérie. Ah, Colette,*' and he pulled me towards him, kissing the top of my head, pulling my body into his. I went easily, like a plug into a socket, and leaned there thankfully for a moment. It was going to be fine. We went off somewhere for a drink and tried to talk to each other in the sunshine.

This was a slight hiccup. I felt a lot more self-conscious talking French to him in England than trying to do so in Monaco. There people often helped with an odd word and smiled while they did it, but here everyone seemed to stare as if we were barking mad. But we got back to the house where everyone was waiting to meet this paragon, this Adonis I had described and whose telegram had reduced me completely to jelly. Even Mummie who is notoriously hard to please had to admit that here was the most handsome specimen she had ever seen, although she reserved her opinion until we were alone. He was very charming to everyone using sign language and then because he was exhausted, he sat about in the garden. We went to bed very early and made love very quietly so as not to wake Moya sleeping next door. It was even more wonderful for me than it had been, because it was in my home where I felt safe, and the magic intensified. Moya came in the next morning and sat on the bed with us lying under the covers. It was important to me not to be secretive about all this with her, because it seemed as if it was going to be important for us all. She was playing with a box of tissues, taking them out and leaving them in piles on the sheet. Michel sat back and watched us both, and then quietly said he wished I was as patient with his French as I was with my little girl. I thought I was being very patient indeed with it, but you can't be perfect, I suppose.

The next day was bright and clear and sunny, as some south coast days are, with the air full of salt and freshness. We felt happier than ever and arranged to go to Brighton to meet some of my friends. We took the train, and then walked down from the station together, past the Glass Animal Man Shop, various ethnic emporia and down to the clocktower, from which we could see the sea catching the sunlight on the water. We wandered about the shops, looking in the windows, stopping for coffee, holding hands like two summer lovers, foolishly romantic. I longed to meet some of my friends in the street, because I knew they would all be madly envious of my companion, but this was not to be. I took him to The Lanes, a mass of little streets, built in the eighteenth century or thereabouts, with all manner of small and interesting shops. We laughed and pointed and talked, and every so often stopped to kiss reflected in some shop window, full of antiques or records or clothes. We moved inwards, to the heart of the whirl of streets, and soon we were in Brighton Square, with benches under trees and more shops. In one corner there was a terrace restaurant called Vasso's and we climbed the spiral staircase to it in the open air, ordering a lunch-time salad and a cold bottle of white wine. It arrived with the condensation dripping down the outside of the green glass, and the liquid inside evaporated from our glasses as quickly. Lazy with the wine, and enjoying the weather, we wandered about some more, even more slowly, and went eventually to a wine bar to meet my friends. They all wanted to practise their French and I sat back and bathed in the reflected glory of Michel's charm, which won them all over, as I knew it would. He answered them politely, and they loved him, and flirted back outrageously, but he held my hand throughout and didn't respond to them with any answering flicker. It was lovely.

We went on to Choys, a Chinese restaurant nearby, and then, because it was late and we had missed our last train, caught a taxi back to Littlehampton. Michel paid, as he had for everything that day, and I began to worry because he was by no means well off. In fact he had said that he had brought £200 spending money, and neither of us had much idea of how long his stay would be. By now, we had our own secret sign language which hadn't much need of words. Our physical communication seemed to me to be uncanny. We loved being together. He understood what I meant when I had hardly begun the laborious business of speaking slowly and in words of one syllable.

But stories cannot go on being perfect, can they? And this seemed far too good to be true.

The next day we spent together with Moya, in the garden, in the bright sunshine, lying on the grass. He liked drinking, so I would bring him beers and wine, and wait on him hand and foot, which I didn't yet mind.

I have a friend called Jill, who is fluent in French, and I thought he might like to give the gestures a rest and talk in his own language for a little. And it would give me a rest too. I telephoned her and asked her for supper that evening. We went round before for a drink, and for Michel to meet her. I had explained that I wanted the two of them to talk as much as they liked, and her brief was to find out the works for me, all the dirt – 'is he married, single, gay, divorced, been in prison, does he like being whipped by bearded women in red? I want the lot, Jill. Don't spare me, and please try and get as much out of him as you can.'

'OK, I'll do my best. What shall I do if he has lived a blameless life as a monk in some remote monastery, feeding the poor and looking after the sick?'

'Well, I might be disappointed. Can't you make something dashing and dangerous up?'

As it happened, they talked a lot, but when he went to the loo, she had to confess that her questions had not been very fruitful.

'He really is pretty blameless, Colette. I've done my best, but all I can find out is that he likes England, is mad about you, and had a girlfriend for six years in Monaco, who is well and truly past history. That's it.'

We all went back to my house and I went to cook dinner. I think it was that evening that my passion for cooking started. My efforts could hardly have been any worse. I had a tin of salmon and some pasta, and I rather vaguely thought that the two of them would go together quite well. I had not considered all the other herbs and seasoning that normally go into making such simple-sounding food delicious. I just put the salmon straight out of its tin into a saucepan, and plopped it on to the over-cooked spaghetti. It looked and smelt disgusting, bones and all spilling out over the pasta which had congealed into a soggy mess.

Jill came in to find out what was taking me so long and saw me helplessly staring at the plate.

'My God, Colette, I wouldn't give that to the cat!'

We both began to laugh and went on and on and on. Michel came into the kitchen to find two helpless females doubled up over the sink, and was at a loss to find out what on earth was going on. I couldn't explain it either, and although Jill could have done, she didn't have time to draw breath before she began to whoop all over again.

'It doesn't matter,' I kept saying. 'It's too hard to explain. Just look over there at the plate.'

He looked over there, where I was pointing, but obviously couldn't see what on earth was so killing about the pile of food and smiled even less when I found some rather mouldy Cheddar and some bread, and half a jar of Branston pickle and gave him that, vowing that I would never allow myself to get into this awful position again. I would bloody well learn to cook.

Later on, when Jill had left and I had calmed down a bit, we went to bed but didn't make love. The atmosphere was all wrong, although I tried to cuddle him.

He tried to explain that he didn't always want to make love, even though he liked touching me and holding me. I am completely the opposite. If I get touched it starts putting ideas into my head, I cannot just relax and sleep when I'm madly passionately in lust but, frustrated as I felt, I did.

Next day, I couldn't spend all alone with him again. I had a life to lead. I had arranged a tennis lesson at the club which I'd already paid for. We went up there and I dumped him, fairly unceremoniously, on my friend Pauline, which she didn't mind but which he hated. I rushed off and had the remaining forty minutes of my lesson. He had been underfoot while I was trying to dress and feed Moya and then when I was trying to do the same thing to myself. He didn't seem to realize that life in Littlehampton had been going on for a long time before he hit these shores and hanging about on the lawn didn't get anything done. As a recreation, it's lovely. As a way of life, its effectiveness leaves a lot to be desired. He wanted to keep me in a little box, far from other people, and I am not used to living like that, nor am I able to, temperamentally and practically.

That evening he had me to himself, and he liked that. It was quite hard work for me, because helping around the house was not a phrase he knew in either English or French. I waited on him, bringing him food, and as usual plenty to drink. We went to bed fairly pickled, and made love. I was tired and a little peevish, so it wasn't as marvellous as it could have been.

He was more than a little peevish next morning, and stayed in bed as I left him to go and play tennis. Later I took Moya for a measles injection, so that put paid to any lovey dovey malingering which he had in mind. When I got back with her, I suggested we walk to the beach or around Littlehampton, which may not be Paris or Rome, but it is a pretty little seaside town with plenty for two people to do who are supposed to be mad about each other.

He didn't want to. He wanted to moon around the bedroom, or lie in the garden with me bringing him nicely iced beers or gins and tonics, with the lemon cut just so and exactly two pieces of ice in the long cool glasses. Sod that, I thought.

I told him I would be busy for the rest of the day, feeling tired and irritated by his apathy. He didn't want to do anything except go to a disco. '*Je voudrais aller au disco, Colette. Tu t'en veux?*'

I called my friend Nicky for ideas, as I knew the only good one in Brighton is Kings, but that's private and I wasn't a member. She wasn't much help either, but her friend Mike could help.

'Look, we're having a few people round for drinks this evening. Why don't you and Michel come, and then we can ask Mike if we can go on to Kings. I'm sure it will be absolutely fine. See you later? About 7.00.'

'Yes, we'd love to. Thank you, Nicky.'

I went downstairs feeling as though I had managed to do something right. But Michel told me emphatically in French that '*non*' he was not interested in meeting more new people, and '*non*' he didn't want to go.

'Look, cheri. It's only good manners to go to Nicky's party, even if you hate it and her, and everyone there. You have to be nice to people if you want something from them, and if you want to go to a decent disco, that's what we have to do. Unless of course you want to shimmy down to the Top Rank Suite and have a battle with a broken bottle after six pints of best and a boogie to some endless record, with your feet sticking to the floor, and somebody else's elbows sticking in your ribs.'

I'm quite sure he didn't understand this, but he understood my rising tone, and grumpily conceded that perhaps it was a good idea to go.

With bad grace he changed into his party clothes, looking pretty devastating in them, I have to admit, all in white, although by this time I could cheerfully have strangled him with the sleeves of the sweater he had once again casually slung around his shoulders. I wore my white cotton V-backed dress, and we got into a taxi and went round to Nicky's.

Everyone was impressed when he hadn't opened his mouth, and less so when he did. Mike's girlfriend could speak French and tried to talk to Michel, who irritated her with his arrogance and conceit. He told her that the only reason we were there was to get Mike to take us to Kings, which was neither tactful nor polite. It was particularly embarrassing because, as Valerie was translating all this to me, rather crossly, Mike wandered over and asked what we were talking about. Michel made a real pain of himself at the party, looking constantly at his watch, until Mike came over and said that we were going. He came in a taxi with us, and Valerie drove their small two-seater sports car there. I apologized to Nicky, and went out hoping that, now Michel had got what he wanted, he would remember his manners and be nice to people. A vain hope. Of course he hated the place, and sulked all the time we were there. I was beginning to get a cold, and was growing tetchier and tetchier. When he wouldn't talk to me, I really had had enough of him and his Gallic charm. He demanded to leave, so we left, as I was too tired, ill and fed up to argue by now. We had to catch a taxi, because it was late, which didn't please him, because it was expensive. Gone was the openhandedness of a few days ago.

On Monday things improved inexplicably. We went up to London and had a lovely day sightseeing, although not without its slight problems. He wasn't mad about Covent Garden, and was cross with me for leaving the British Museum till last. How on earth was I to know he'd like that best?

We ended up having dinner in Covent Garden, and he grizzled about the resturant. With reason, I have to say – it was pretty but the food was dreadful. He kept on about a boat that had sunk and eventually I deduced that he meant the *Victory* in Portsmouth. He was mad about guns and battles. We booked to go see it, and for some reason the day we went he dropped into one of his blackest sulks, sitting in silence in the back of the coach, with me fuming beside him about having to go to see something I wasn't interested in with such a nightmarish companion. Halfway there, he did a complete *volte face*.

Suddenly he was wreathed in smiles, whispering sweet nothings, in my by now none too receptive ear. He all but nibbled it playfully, and held my hand, opening my stiff fingers, and kissing my palm. By the time we arrived, however, I couldn't be bothered to keep this up, and had decided to make the most of the sunshine before it slipped behind another cloud and I was drenched in the rain of his disapproval. We both decided to bury our differences and be nice to each other. We walked happily around the war museum – he a lot more happily than me, but I was trying – and then on to an ornithological museum and a little castle, where he spent many moments looking lovingly at bullets. I stifled yawns. Everything I wanted to see he didn't, and vice versa. A real conflict of interests which didn't bode well for our future together.

I began to get a desperate cold, nose running, head thumping, shivers, shakes, the lot, and here he came into his own. He was splendid and got me home and to bed, cuddling me, and getting me tissues. This was a role he understood. I did the waiting on him when he felt he needed it, and he enjoyed being the capable male looking after his little woman when he felt I needed it. I was not in a fit state to argue: I was just thankful for the Kleenex.

Next day – yes, this was getting interminable – he decided to go to Brighton to buy a bullet, because he collected them. That morning I tried to call the antique dealers, who all said the same thing. He could not buy a bullet without a licence. You can imagine how that went down with merry Michel, who by this time had manifested a marked reluctance to have his will crossed. So we went to Brighton and visited about three antique shops who all told him the same thing. Now the country was at fault: it was '*stupide, ridicule, affreux, horrible, pas convenable*' and really, he should have applied those epithets to himself, getting all steamed up in the shops of these men who were only obeying the law.

I wanted to pop into a shop and buy something to wear. Mummie had offered to treat me, and I wanted to make the most of her offer as soon as possible, before she forgot about it. I thought I'd better be quick, and indicated on my watch that we would meet in half an hour. I rushed around those shops like a whirlwind, hardly stopping to look at myself in the mirror. It was sad, because most men like to help you pick and are interested in what you look like, but not this one. He didn't buy things for himself either, because he maintained that the clothes in England were '*affreux*'. A favourite word, I noticed. We went bowling, he having said how good he was, and he turned out to be only a little better than I was, which was not good – again the bowling alleys in this country were '*affreux*'.

When we got home, in silence, I called up Jill for help. She had just passed her driving test, so came over and picked us up to take us to the Shepherd and Dog pub, where she was meeting a girlfriend. Michel livened up at her arrival, and spent all evening talking to her, which was rather a relief. Horses were mentioned, and of course he rode '*très bien*' so we arranged to go riding. I knew that I would be better than all of them, and that it would be my responsibility to make them have a good time, so I did my best. But keeping an eye on two bad riders, and trying to keep your own horse under control, is not the easiest of tasks so, of course, I didn't manage to do it very well, and Michel was furious with me for not helping him all the time.

It was Moya's bedtime when we returned, and I sent him off to

Jill's for a drink, while I took her to her room. He pottered off, and when I arrived a little later, they were in full swing chatting to each other about everything under the sun, it seemed. I said that I had to go back as Mummie had cooked dinner, and he turned his attention from Jill for long enough to indicate that he would be along in '*un moment*'.

Some moment, or maybe my French wasn't even up to that. The hours went past, and I grew angrier and angrier. Jill's parents arrived back at 10.30 p.m., still no sign of Michel.

Now all I wanted was for him to go, to get out of the house, and take his unpredictable French temperament back to Monaco. It's funny now, but then I was in such a rage that I stomped into the bedroom, scooped up all his stuff and dumped it on the bed in a spare room. I stamped around like a Shetland pony, tossing my head a lot, moving myself out into Mummie's room, her into mine, and turning the house into a set for a Feydeau farce.

At midnight we heard, from my room of high dudgeon, the rather sheepish but defiant scrape of a key in a lock, and Mummie went down to deal with it. If I had I would have hurled a saucepan into his silly permed head. She explained the new sleeping arrangements, and he rambled on and on in French to her, none of which she understood, or was in a mood to decipher. She got cross too, and the decibels increased on both sides – an *entente* very definitely not *cordiale*. All the while I was listening to this, with my head on the pillow, spinning with disappointment and the realization that this wonderful affair was not to be. I wished the whole episode had remained an idyll in the warm breezes of Monaco, and not turned into a mega-sulk in Sussex.

Mummie flounced off to my room, and he dived into the bottom of a whisky bottle downstairs. We could hear him clanking about, the clink of glasses, the sobs – yes by this time he was in full Gallic flow. He went to bed about 2.00, past our unrelenting bedroom doors, with all of us pretending to be asleep, lying very still, with our eyes wide open and doomed to remain so. I heard him telling Granny, who haplessly encountered him on a hopefully stealthy creep to the loo, that he might go back to '*la maison de Jill*' and ask her for a lift to the airport. Oh yes, I thought, you're bound to get one at this time of night. I almost wanted him to have a go, but remembered that it would be my problem to placate the family in the long run. Granny was calm and sensible, and possibly because she was old and frail and not a bit threatening, he listened to her and trooped meekly into his room.

By noon that day the situation had reversed. We were all

downstairs and he was in bed. His flight was due to leave that day, and we were beginning to get restless – was he going to stage another drama, refuse to leave, haunt us for weeks? I took him in a cup of coffee at 2.00 p.m. and caught a glimpse of a pair of bloodshot eyes peering like a badger's from under the very rumpled duvet. There was nothing to say.

He got up, packed, came into the kitchen and looked at me sadly. That look had lost most of its power – once it would have moved mountains in my heart, but now my heart was hardened, although his limpid blue eyes (now streaked with red) did make me pause a little. He dropped his eyes, and said softly, '*au revoir, Colette*', before bending down slowly to pick up his suitcase. He shrugged his leather jacket on to his shoulders, and walked out, wearing sunglasses to hide his red-rimmed eyes. Later that day, we found a note to my mother thanking her for her hospitality, and two months later I found a letter, so crossed out and rumpled as to be almost illegible. It had slipped behind the bed; he had obviously written it in the early hours of this terrible morning.

That was the end of that. I would have to be madly in love to marry someone whose only possessions of note were a motorbike and several paintbrushes, particularly if it meant moving to Monaco with Moya. We needed to speak the same language. My French would have improved, but I have my doubts about any other form of communication.

7

California

California is a wonderful state – of mind as well as of America. It is sunny, there are vast expanses of sea and sand and surf, people are laid back, cool, funky, hip – all the words that seem to have been invented for California. I had spent a lot of years there, during and after my marriages, and it is a place in which I feel happy, where I can enjoy myself.

I like *things*: fast cars, lovely clothes, jewellery, houses. So do Californians. I like the sunshine, getting brown and slim, being thought attractive. So do Californians. I like Californian men – they have the right idea, or the ideas that I think are right. They look right, think right, behave right. At least the ones I met and went out with did, and there was no shortage of those.

So when the grey rain was mizzling on the windowpanes of my mother's small house in Littlehampton, and the clouds were a thick flannel blanket over a murky, white-topped sea, it was hardly a surprise that my thoughts turned to the West Coast of America. I had had a glut of men to see, vet, go out with and I had had a fairly nice time, but no one had worked out. I was left with a silent telephone and the patter of the postman's feet as he passed our house each day, or if he stopped, the plish on the mat was of a circular or an electricity bill. I was pale, uninteresting (so I was beginning to think) and depressed, it must be said. This happens in this game. For anyone who is charmed by the thought of all those men waiting to be met, remember that sometimes, fairly often in fact, the effort is not worth the result. You can meet wonderful men, but they don't feel that you are the one for them. You can meet half decent men, and wonder if perhaps you should give up the search and compromise, and then it really does seem a waste of the past months, so you don't. Then you don't have anyone left, and you wonder some more whether you have wasted your last chance, and whether you should give up and become a missionary.

But the personal columns are addictive, and there's always the chance that the next advertisement will be the one, and everything will have been worth it.

So I had another go. I had decided by now that if I couldn't get looks and money, I would have to think of Moya first, and so go for just money. I placed an ad in a Florida paper, beginning 'Marriage Minded', and saying the usual, I hoped, tempting things. It tempted 153 people to reply to me. One was from California, on thick cream parchment, and fourteen others caught my eye too. I wrote to them, and their replies came back, only to be rejected in favour of the Yellow Parchment, Mr Chirpy. His first letter began: 'Beautiful British Female' and went on in bright and breezy vein, sounding very positive and hopeful.

> I believe that my lifestyle and character meet with your requirements. I was recently divorced (last year) and I live alone in a new home next to a large 4000-boat marina.
>
> The neighborhood is a young family type. Most of the children are two–five years of age [good, I thought, friends for Moya]. We have a beautiful park, pool and playgrounds abound within a walking distance [better and better]. The area is ideal for cycling [I keep two bikes]. Bike paths are zoned throughout the hills. Along the ocean – five minutes from my house – we have the most beautiful scenic route, with occasional vista views. The surf is spectacular and obviously the surfing is great. California climate – South Orange Country Coast – is the world's greatest. [He didn't have to tell me – my mouth was watering at the very thought.]
>
> I'm absolutely bored with the Dating Game. Solidarity is the keynote of the manner in which I like to live. Yet – travelling etc. become more enjoyable when one has a place to come home. Don't you agree? [Yes.]
>
> If you feel that we can establish a solid relationship – come. The two tickets to Los Angeles, Calif, will be waiting for you. The single life is actually monotonous and dreary to my way of thinking and living. I'm ready for a 'family again'.
>
> My height is 5 feet 6 inches [hmmm – not promising, but I did say to myself that this time looks weren't a prime consideration] and from the outdoor living of California that I participate in the fullest, well – you'll have to see for yourself. For some

reason I cannot understand, and frankly care less, the women in my life have been tall.

Well there you have it:

Single man

financially comfortable

Well built, but 5 feet 6 inches

Reasonable looking – oh what the heck – attractive

Black hair and moustache – tanned

Sails

Cycles

Runs

Laughs

Laughs

LOVES LIFE

has good friends who care!

Loves the horses, likes Las Vegas (a player, not a gambler)

If you are what you describe and I am what I describe – that's a combo!

Please write regarding your ideas.

Well, I did, charmed in particular by the offer of the two tickets to California. No one else had come up with anything comparable, and the rain was still running down the glass. His answer was swift. He explained how he happened to be in Florida – visiting his brother – and said many positive things that perked me up even more, and pushed the fact that he was 5 feet 6 inches to the back of my mind. He sent a photograph of his dining room, with its thick cream carpet, and reproduction oak furniture – rather attractive, although I had to say in my next letter that with a toddler his carpet wouldn't stay cream for long! His photograph of himself was neither breathtakingly handsome nor stomach-turningly revolting. Standing by the water, on a rock, wearing brown trousers and a grey jersey, his hair was all there, dark brown and well cut, and his moustache didn't look bad on his smiling face.

'To my delight,' he wrote, 'your letter was extremely refreshing. You are a beautiful woman – that's obvious [well, that was a sweet thing to say]. It seems that we are philosophically compatible, so much the better. It seems apparent to me, after you have been emotionally clobbered, either you are down or the realization of what you want is perfectly clear. I choose to believe that we are of the latter group – am I correct [more than you know, buddy, I thought]?'

He said that he was a developer/builder, which sounded a nice, lucrative sort of job, and told me about his friend's ranch as I had mentioned my love of horses. It was all sounding rather good.

> Really do appreciate a feminine woman. Soooo if you want to wear high heels, makes you feel good – wear them! I'm a traditionalist – man takes care of outside, woman takes care of inside. Don't let that mislead you. No – I'm not a sexist, my firm belief is woman being maternal can bring to the home the warmth and love that is necessary for a good environment. Besides, you have a daughter and your desire to be a full-time Mummie should be realized.

This was exactly the sort of thing I wanted to hear, so after we had spoken on the telephone, and exchanged some more letters, his becoming more and more positive and encouraging, I decided to accept his offer of tickets, just for me to begin with, and see what would happen. I was very firm, as I always am, that it would be on a strictly friendly basis.

'I don't jump into bed with perfect strangers,' I told him firmly, and he seemed to accept this with no trouble.

The tickets finally arrived. Mummie wasn't too happy about me going, but I was determined to have a try at this one. If it failed, I would have had an exciting trip and a bit of a holiday. I arranged a child minder for Moya. Mummie grizzled a bit about having her in the evenings – 'I'm too old to look after her, Colette. If I'd wanted more children I would have had them' – but eventually I got round her, and she stopped putting up problems. I packed, and was off to the airport, full of nervous anticipation and excitement.

On the plane were a pop group, Maze – ten black guys looking cool and rather friendly. I nerved myself to go and ask for their autographs, and they were quite happy to oblige. As I stood up, I saw a man sitting alone – he was young and looked interesting and, as these things do, a conversation started between us, on general matters. He turned out to be a reporter from *The Independent* newspaper, a pop journalist, which impressed me no end. He had a happy face, and we moved to sit next to each other, and the booze flowed freely to pass the time away till we reached Los Angeles. He told me about his girlfriend, a nurse, and I told him about Moya and my life in Littlehampton. Not much comparison, was it? He had been covering the Maze tour, and told me about all the other pop stars he had interviewed and tours he had covered. Fortified with champagne and gin and tonic, I told him jauntily that maybe I had a much better story for him. I told him about my search for Mr Right, and that I was on my way to a blind date in the States, and I have to say that he seemed very interested.

'I'll tell the woman's page editor of the paper. I'm sure she will be happy to get in touch and take it further. Sounds like a good story, Colette. Too good to miss. Don't be surprised if you hear more.'

Well, I thought, any publicity is good publicity and it might well lead to something good, that is if this California trip fell flat. In fact, the editor did call, and Dave the journalist did end up interviewing me, over a delicious lunch at Little Thakeham in Sussex, with three bottles of wine to loosen my tongue. It took four and a half hours; I talked until I was hoarse, and the result was a long article, with a photograph of me at home, which led to my writing this book, appearing on *Wogan*, having a radio programme made about me, being written about as the 'Queen of the Lonely Hearts' in the *Sunday Express*. So I have a lot to thank him for.

But back to our muttons, as the great French philosopher might have said. I was beginning to feel seriously nervous as the plane moved nearer and nearer to my destination. As an idea, on paper, it had sounded fun and full of happy possibilities. Now after several hours, talking to a very nice British man about my life, it seemed that to be flying to meet an as yet unknown American one was nothing short of complete lunacy. We arrived. I got through immigration perfectly happily, despite a few misgivings. Sophia Loren had been on the plane with us, it turned out, which was a bit of extra interest, and took my mind off what sort of person I had agreed to spend the next few days with, even go on a trip to South America with, even, I recalled, possibly spending some weeks in Australia with if things worked out.

Once past customs, I walked through the double doors of the TWA terminal at LA airport, and looked around for someone who looked like the man in the photograph. Nothing. People came and went. There was the usual squealing and hugging and waving and buzz of conversation. The announcements reverberated over the tannoy, and my heart reverberated in my chest. Where the hell was he? Oh, God, had I made the most utter fool of myself? Was this all a hoax? Had I . . .? I pulled myself together and sat down to wait for a while. It was 5 p.m., and hot. Everyone had by now disappeared and I looked lonely and forlorn, and felt furious and sorry for myself at the same time. I got him paged a few times, but with no result. I rang him at his home, but just got an answerphone message saying he would be back later and would I please leave my name and telephone number so he could get back to me as soon as he got in.

I became convinced that all the staff were giving me pitying looks and whispering among themselves about the British woman who had clearly been stood up. I'm sure they never gave me a moment's thought, but you know how one gets paranoid. And I think I could be forgiven for feeling ill-used. I now had no coins for the telephone, so I couldn't even call my friends Carol or Marian who lived nearby. The plane had already been delayed one hour, so in fact, Mr Chirpy was a good two hours late in picking me up. I was near to tears, but couldn't leave the hall to go to the loo and have a good cry, because he might have arrived and then where would I have been?

Suddenly, an india rubber ball of a man, 5 feet 6 inches tall all right, came bouncing along towards me, beaming and waving as if nothing was the matter. He was skinny too, but he did look kind.

'Hi Colette, honey. Forgive me for being so late. I had so many things to do. I was trying to get a passport, and it took such a long time at the office. Here let me take that,' and he picked up my suitcase, which was almost bigger than he was. He looked like Timothy Town Mouse going to visit his country cousin, not a glamorous beginning.

I tried to smile, because he was genuinely apologetic, and was heaving my luggage through the doors to his car very gamely. He did not stop talking.

'Did you have a good flight? How's the weather in the old country? Gosh, Colette, I am glad to see you, I really am. I know you're going to love it here, really love it. I can't wait to show you my house, my area, the ocean. You've been here before you said. Well I wonder if it's changed at all. No, let me open that for you.'

He unlocked the door of his car. I was a bit disappointed with it. True it was a Cadillac El Dorado, but it was three or four years old, which in California, if you're anybody, just isn't on. People who have made it change their cars for something more powerful and better every year or so.

We drove off, me sitting beside him, and looking out of the window so as not to laugh at the sight of this little shrimp behind the steering wheel. He looked like a picture of Mr Toad at the wheel of his Rolls Royce, just about able to see through the spokes out of the windscreen.

The talk flowed, and I could hardly get a word in, had I had the energy. 'Gee, Colette, I am really glad you're here. I've said that already haven't I, just shows how much I mean it. I think we can really make this relationship work, and I'll take care of you and your daughter – enjoy doing it. It will be wonderful to have her here too. It will be wonderful to be with a woman again. You will adore my daughter, I can tell you. She's a dream, and pretty and talented.'

His driving was appalling; he nipped in and out of the traffic alarmingly, driving very slowly as he turned to look at me while he talked, and then very fast, right up to the bumper of the car in front, with liberal use of the horn. I clutched the seat with sweaty palms as I was jolted about in his erratic progress.

He was not the best-looking or best-presented man I have ever been with. Quite frightful, in fact. He wore grim polyester trousers, and a short-sleeved tight shirt that rucked up around his waist into tight little ridges. His face was very tanned but a mass of taut wrinkles, and I swear I could see the scars behind his ears that meant he had had a face job.

'What I lack in stature, I make up for in love. I wanna love a woman, I don't wanna just talk about it. I want to hold a woman and look after her and shelter her, and we will be so happy together. Women are for loving and cherishing, and families flourish on that kind of thing. I have so much love to give, Colette, and it's all yours for the asking.

'I can't wait for you to see my house at Dana Point. You can decorate it any way you want, any way at all. Or if you don't like it, we can move any place you like.'

As well as an investor/developer he dabbled in selling insurance – 'an easy way to make money, believe me. I'm worth in excess of a million dollars. Of course, it's tied up in the businesses, but it's there.

'I want you to buy a car, something sensible, because there's no point in throwing money away like that. People throw so much money away in this part of the world. I don't believe in that. I believe in having a good time, don't get me wrong, but there are good times and good times.'

I was dying for a drink. The view was of beach and ocean and pavements with people looking brown and walking along dressed in all manner of stylish or wacky clothes, and I longed to relax like them. Not to listen to this monologue. I know it was because he was nervous and that he wanted me to like him, and was terrified that I wouldn't. He wasn't brimming over with self-confidence, so had to over-compensate, but I would have been a much better audience with a cold drink inside me. Instead, I had to hear his views on designer labels. Yes, you guessed it. He didn't see the point of wasting money on such things. 'I don't throw my money away on designer clothes. Can't see what's better about them, anyway. You only pay hundreds of dollars for the label. These guys aren't stupid. Nor am I. I go to the warehouse down town and get exactly what I want, good quality, for a fraction of the price. That's thinking, honey, that's smart.'

I closed my ears to the babbling, and almost closed my eyes, but even in extremis like this, I can't be that rude. And I felt sorry for him too.

He had moved smoothly on to describing his house. His bedroom had an en suite bathroom, and he hoped I would like the arrangement.

'Look, John, do you think I could possibly have a drink,' I managed to put in between two of his breaths. I had been watching various jolly-looking cafes and bars slip past the window and could bear my parched tongue and throat no longer. 'Sure honey. Why didn't you say? Here, this is where we can get something.'

This was a petrol station, and with wicked profligacy he bought me a Pepsi, which I was to drink as he drove. The surest way of knocking out my front teeth, but that was that.

I said something like four lines in that two and a half hour journey, and boy, did I want a cigarette by now. I had given up smoking three months earlier, but this was not doing my resolve any good. I was dying for a cigi to give me something to do while he rabbitted on.

His house was quite nice, what a California realtor would have described as a very pleasant first home, or a quite nice second purchase. It would have set him back about a quarter of a million dollars, which for someone who was supposed to be a successful developer cum businessman would have been peanuts.

'What do you drink, Colette?' he asked, as he let us in through the white double doors.

'I drink champagne and gin and tonic, John,' I told him, my heart lifting, or should I say my spirits?

'Fine, we've got gin here, and there's a really good deal at Ralph's on champagne,' he said, very pleased with himself. Blimey, I thought, how cheap. In California, champagne is pretty cheap at the best of times.

Out we went, and I bought a packet of cigarettes, in brazen defiance of his oft-repeated healthy lifestyle. Serve him right, I thought crossly. He paid for them, however, still trying to make a good impression, and said that because Ralph's had closed, we would get the champagne tomorrow.

'Fine,' I told him, through clenched teeth.

When we got back to the house, he continued talking. Then, when at 1 a.m. it was obvious that I was worn out and bedtime was inevitable, he began to hover in that dreadfully pregnant way of men who are hoping for a grope. I've been there too often to be caught by that one, and nimbly sidestepped his advances, which at this stage were pretty tentative. In between this, I watched him, from a safe distance, put away about twenty pills, some for his heart and some for his health. He told me he had had a heart operation a while ago, and then came another lecture about how giving up smoking and drinking and eating carrots and pulses had kept him young and fit.

'I've kept myself real fit, Colette. I can tell you – I can make love to a woman any time, any place, and we'll both have a wonderful time.'

Smiling, I said goodnight and backed out of the kitchen, leaving him looking a bit crestfallen, but obviously consoling himself with the fact that it was early days still.

I was shown my room, and then he proudly gave me a tour of the house. It was smart, very plain, with brown and cream carpets, not cheap. Nevertheless, despite the care he had taken to make it look nice, it felt cold and clinical, and not somewhere I would have enjoyed spending time. The dining-room was to the right of the front door, the drawing-room to the left. A large, plump sofa, covered in a pretty pink fabric and chairs covered in plain beige and a sort of sham Liberty print looked welcoming, on either side of a rather unexpected brick chimneybreast, sporting a ship in full sail on the mantelshelf. The kitchen was on a slightly lower level, behind the dining area, and a carpeted staircase led up to the three bedrooms. Mine was pale and quite small but perfectly comfortable. His was more elaborate, but not much. The bed-spread was quilted, the headboard a reproduction contraption combining mirrors and shelves and cupboards in a dark wood. There were a few books, and, rather suspicious, a yellow teddybear with red paws, wearing a T-shirt. I always mistrust adults who keep soft toys about them.

I slept like a log, and got up early the next day. We had arranged to go for a bike ride, down to Dana Point so we could look at the scenery and the ocean. In the kitchen, a very healthy breakfast was laid out on the table, all vegetable juice, wholemeal bread and the usual pile of pills. Nearby I could hear puffing and groaning, so went along the corridor a little to see what on earth was sounding like a bear digging. It was my genial host, doing his exercises on the floor of the den. Even if I had been disposed to like him, and consider spending my life in his company, it would not have made me any keener to witness, on this my second day, his wiry little frame thrashing around on the carpet, and waving dumbbells so small Moya could have picked them up in one hand.

Before we left the house, he washed up the breakfast things meticulously, putting each item exactly where it came from. The monologue had changed to the tape marked 'Health' – I should give up smoking, I should do what he did, did I take enough exercise?

I was smoking, quite honestly, to put up a screen between us. He kept trying to creep up behind and put his arms around my waist, and slip a kiss under my guard.

We went off on our cycle ride, and eventually, after riding past what were really wonderful views, we stopped for lunch at a tatty little cafe. He ordered a salad (of course) and half a carafe of wine, and wouldn't have strawberries for pudding because he had bought some that were in the fridge at home, and so it was a waste of money to have these at three times the price.

We went for a walk along the beach, and he tried to hold my hand and put his arm around me, under pretext of helping me over the rocks. When I didn't melt into his embrace, he began to question me about it:

'You don't seem very responsive and affectionate, Colette. I expected you to be much more relaxed. Do you feel frightened or nervous? You needn't be. Trust me. I'm really going to look after you and make you happy.'

'It's because I have only just met you, John. Really, nothing more. I am not very demonstrative until I know someone and feel happy with them. Then it's different, but I've only just arrived.'

His little body fair quivered with sincerity.

'But, Colette, we have the rest of our lives together, so why don't you just enjoy the beginning, and relax? Let's start enjoying ourselves now. I want to look after you, to make you happy. You can have anything you want, anything.' Anything, that is, as long as I bought it at K-Mart.

To prove his good intentions, he asked if I would come away with him on a holiday of a few days, perhaps a couple of weeks. 'Just friends, of course. I know that. I checked some travel agents and they have vacancies on trips to Hawaii and Mexico. What do you say? It'll be fun, just the two of us . . .'

He looked at me appealingly, like a puppy, the corners of his moustache twitching in his effort to please.

But as usual he had not managed to impress me. Cheap, that's what he was, through and through. I had been to Mexico many times, a really inexpensive place to get to from California, and Hawaii – and it certainly isn't all it's cracked up to be. He had mentioned South America, a long time ago it seemed, when I was still enthusiastic about coming to meet him. He mentioned a cruise to Jamaica, but I thought that if I had to share a cabin with this little man (and I was bound to have to share; he would never stretch to two) I would slit my throat or his.

Seeing my disappointment, or rather, my lack of enthusiasm, he went away and came back the next day with: 'I've got it, I've got it. You'll love this, simply love it, Colette. What do you think of Acapulco?' He was still insisting on Mexico.

Oh God. This was hardly what I had in mind, but I let it go at that. There would be plenty of time to change my mind and the booking. It wasn't for a little while yet, and it was hardly likely that I would be staying that long.

We were to play tennis the next day, but I didn't have a decent pair of shoes to do it in, so, rather grudgingly, he bought me a pair. I pointed hopefully at some swimsuits but this time it was his turn to look unhelpful and they stayed on the rack. I said something about this in the end.

'I think you are extremely ungenerous, John. You keep saying how much you want to look after and cherish me, but baulk at buying me a cheap pair of tennis shoes. I haven't got that many clothes – I live with my mother and my daughter in England and I don't have a job, so how do you expect me to be equipped for all the outdoor living in California? I must say I am surprised at you.' So later he stretched to the purchase of two pairs of shorts and two T-shirts from a cheap store in town, and I had to be content with that. To cap it all, he told me that he thought I should try and lose some weight. I almost exploded with suppressed exasperation. I had made no personal comments about him, and I could have had a field day. He had talked me into the ground, and I had not complained once. He had made passes at me every time I was within reach, and I hadn't yet pushed him away in the abrupt manner he deserved.

The next day the saga continued. 'What about driving around the States together? We can stop and see my friends – I have plenty, all over the place, and it would be such fun, wouldn't it?' You would have thought he had suggested a trip to the moon and back, he looked so pleased with himself, but I had to bring him back to earth.

'John, these suggestions are fine, but I really don't think we are getting on well enough to go on holiday together. Why don't we call it a day. It seems like it has been a bit of a mistake, and I'm sure you'd like to be free to look for someone else, someone you will enjoy being with for life.'

'You'll grow to love me, Colette. I promise you that. Let's not give up at this stage. We have all the time in the world. There's no rush. Maybe I have been a bit pushy, but I was so bowled over by how wonderful you look, and I thought that you wanted all the things I want. I thought I had at last found the woman who would live with me and I could be happy with. My second wife ran off and left me. She's now had a boob job and a face lift, and is with another guy, who I know doesn't love her as much as I could. Maybe we'd have lasted if she had all that done before she left. She thought it was a favour when we had sex, as though she was giving me some kind of wonderful present.'

This was a theme he was to develop. He talked on and on about sex, until I began to feel that it would be simpler just to take our clothes off and get on with it.

'I want to touch someone, I want to hold someone, Colette, I want to hold you . . .'

Finally, when he ran out of breath, and could see that I wasn't being any more amenable to his suggestions, he changed tack.

That evening he took me to a smart French restaurant for a treat, obviously having taken some notice of what I had said. It was a pretty place, the other diners were worth looking at and the food worth eating. The only drawback was my shrunken companion, but I was getting used to towering above him now, and had developed a good line in glassy-eyed loftiness.

The amorous advances continued, and when we got home, he asked me to sit on his knee.

'No, thank you, John.'

'Why not?'

'I don't want to. I want to go to bed. That was a lovely meal, and I'm really tired now.'

'I have insomnia, and I need someone to talk to. No one ever wants to listen.'

So he talked and I listened. We had been here before.

I called Marian and Carol the next day, very careful about what

I told them, because I was sure he was listening to my conversation. I arranged to meet Carol on Sunday, and thought I could keep my distance until then, with a bit of luck and a lot of perseverance.

Costa Rica was his next suggestion. I agreed because I had friends there, and I could always run to them if the worst came to the worst. I did, however, do the decent thing and voice some doubts about the wisdom of this trip together.

'Oh no. I'm convinced you'll learn to love me there. Maybe we should marry before we go. Or in England, or wherever. I think it's time for us to make some kind of commitment.'

Marriage, I thought. When I couldn't spend a week with this guy, he wants to get married!

'I don't think I'm ready for marriage yet, John. Let's give it a bit longer and see what happens.'

'No, you should get married now. You need a man for Moya, you know you do, and I am just the guy you're looking for. I'll care for her.'

He needed to renew his passport in Los Angeles, so we drove there the next morning. It took the two and a half hours it had taken before, and the monologue repeated itself like an endless loop on a tape. As if this wasn't endurance test enough, when we arrived at the passport office, the queue was so long that it took four hours to get to the front of it. He didn't waste those hours. He talked merrily to everyone in the queue, telling them where we were going, who we were, and asking them their life histories. I was so embarrassed, and livid when I saw his date of birth in his passport. He tried to hide it but it showed that he was sixty-two. He bounced about holding his tatty briefcase and flashing his cheap watch, and I wished the ground would open up and swallow me.

It didn't and I lived to get back to the house. I cooked dinner for us and then we settled down in the drawing room in front of the video to watch *Out of Africa*. He talked all the way through it, and moved down to sit on the carpet at my feet, trying to rest his head on my knee. When it was over, we went to the kitchen to make some coffee, and he pressed his little body close to mine as I filled the kettle at the sink.

'I wanna kiss you.'

'Please, John, don't. It's embarrassing.'

He tried to touch my lips with his, but ended up missing and landing on my chin. He was very persistent, and I began to feel very wary of him – he wouldn't take no for an answer, and while he wasn't the Colossus of Rhodes, he was certainly strong enough to give me a hard time if he'd wanted to. Luckily, he didn't.

'Hug me, hug me, make me feel like a man,' he asked, and so I squeezed him gingerly which seemed to do the trick. His wriggling and clutching subsided and he calmed down enough to drink his coffee and for us to go to our separate bedrooms without any further bother.

I had agreed to go to Costa Rica, and I thought, what the hell, I may as well go and have a holiday. This wasn't being one, and anyway I needed some nice clothes, which he could well afford to buy for me.

I broached the subject as he was driving off to see his daughter in a play, and said that I would like to be dropped off at the local mall.

'OK, let's go,' he said.

'But, John, I have no money on me,' I told him. I would have been embarrassed at any other time, and would probably have bought my own wardrobe, but my blood was up by now. He owed me.

'We'll drop off at my office. I have some money there that I can give you,' he told me graciously, and drove us off. He emerged from his office with a few notes clutched in his hand, and proudly presented me with them.

'There you are, honey. Have a good time. Spend what you want, but try to keep some, as it is the only cash I've got this weekend.'

It was, dear reader, $100. At the present rate of exchange, as I write, something like £70. And I was to keep some back. What did he think I was going to buy – a pair of knickers and some plastic sandals, with maybe a lipstick thrown in as a final extravagance.

'This isn't going to be anything like enough, John,' I told him, squirming at having to labour the point. 'You can't buy an average dress for less than $110. I'm sorry but this isn't going to get me very far.'

He had the grace to look a little embarrassed, and gave me another $100.

'There, that's all the money I have. And here's a credit card. You can use that, and then clear it with me at the end of the day.'

Stuff that for a game of soldiers, I thought, and resolved to spend what I liked and deal with the consequences later. He dropped me outside the mall, one of those well-equipped ones, full of wonderful shops, boutiques, department stores. My eyes glistened, and off I went, relishing the sense of spending on clothes that made me look and feel good. I loved everything. And so I bought a lot – $200 on a blue and white-striped seersucker trouser suit, $100 on an Italian white linen dress, another $140 on a dress with blue flowers all over it, and a flowing cream dress cost me (or rather, John) $100. I didn't stop there. I was going wild – it was like the old days. A khaki suit caught my eye, so that went in the bag – $100 – and a pale green beach outfit, a short, sexy skirt and top, was added for $70. Oh, it was great, and the clothes were wonderful. I couldn't help myself, I was out of control, clearing my conscience by actually believing I would go to Costa Rica. I went after that to a bar, had a long cold gin and tonic, and talked to the barmaid, who was in much the same situation as I was, with a young daughter and no husband.

John turned up, and produced a Puffalump for Moya, which brought a lump to my throat and I began to feel a little kinder towards him and the buzz from the shopping spree helped.

I thought I would tell him about the credit card and did so, watching him wince slightly but for once not say a thing. Then I owned up to spending the cash too, and lo and behold, to my surprise he pretended to be pleased I had found some pretty things.

He drove in what was, for him, silence, probably in shock at the price of the clothes.

'Now we'll have to economize a bit on our trip to Costa Rica, Colette. I know you will look quite wonderful, but I can't afford to spend this sort of money all the time.'

When we got home I performed a solo fashion show, which made him keener than ever. He wouldn't leave me alone. He had spent all that money on me, he obviously thought, and he was now going to get his money's worth.

I brought up the AIDS issue:

'Don't you think it's a good thing that I won't sleep with you so early on. It means that I have always been careful and so probably haven't got infected. How do I know you haven't got it?'

'I'll use something, only please will you come to bed with me?'

'No, I'm sorry. I can't and I won't. Please leave me alone.'

'Just lie beside me and cuddle me Colette. I need you beside me.'

I spent a long time dodging him, in what by now had become a familiar pattern and, the next day, Carol came to pick me up and that was the end of that.

He wasn't a bad man, or even a cruel or unpleasant one. He had been bashed by fate and this had made him bitter, determined that 'no one is going to walk over John Chirpy. I'm a well respected person in this community, and that's how it's going to stay.' He really did his best to make me love him, and I suppose he wasn't to know that he did exactly the wrong things, designed to make me run as fast as possible in the opposite direction. He could have turned nasty – his pride, after all, was taking a hard battering – but he didn't. He was an essentially very kind man, and I hope he has found someone to be with, someone who can tolerate his non-stop talking and enjoys health foods and cycling as much as he does. And has the same attitude to money – that would help a lot.

Another encounter in California was at the very beginning of my two-years search.

Six months after I returned to England, Marian telephoned me from the States. 'Hi, Colette. How soon can you pack?'

This was a standing joke between us, because when I was having my ghastly last few months with my third and nastiest husband, I was always packing my bags and rushing over to her house. It got to a stage when I kept my make-up in small bottles in the back of the car, and I could pack the rest of my belongings in seconds flat.

So I laughed.

'Pretty quickly. You know that. Why?'

'Look, I'm going to send you a ticket, and you've got to promise to use it.'

'Sounds wonderful. But why on earth?'

'There's this wonderful guy over here I want you to meet. He's gorgeous. Just your type. He just split up with his girlfriend of seven years and is lonely.'

Tony, her boyfriend, could be heard in the background, encouraging her, and teasing me. He was a Californian who was independently wealthy and so had retired at forty-five, with no reason to go on working. His style was rude and cocky, and everything he said would have a double meaning if he could possibly milk one out of the most innocuous phrase. His company was a bit tiring, but Marian thought he was marvellous, and they did have a nice time together. His sexual habits, I had understood from some things she had told me, were a little on the dodgy side. They were into swinging parties, that sort of thing, not at all my cup of tea.

'This guy's French, Colette. Tony and I think you'd love him, and we're sure he'll think you're marvellous.'

'I have Paul [a blind date] coming over for Christmas, so I can't come.'

'You can. You must. Why don't you come over now and you can leave on the 22nd December?'

I was tempted. Paul might not turn out to be the man of my dreams, and a trip to stay with a friend, all expenses paid, to meet someone who might be, was very appealing.

Tony got on the phone.

'Look, darling. You must come. You'll be good for my friend. And it will be a great Christmas present for three people: Marian, you and Philippe. What do you say?'

What could I say? I said yes.

'Great. The ticket's booked for the 18th, and it's at the airport for you to pick up. See you on the 18th.'

I was very excited about going on such an odd but possibly rewarding trip – if it worked it would be a dream come true; if it didn't and we hated each other, well I would be in California rather than Littlehampton, and I can put up with a lot more hassle there than here!

I packed hurriedly, persuaded Mummie, who was understandably a bit wary about all this, to look after Moya for the four days I would be gone, and I was set.

I went to Gatwick by train, as usual, but things began to look up almost immediately. I picked up my ticket and saw that it was business class, an unexpected treat. I enjoyed it to the full, particularly as my neighbour was a gorgeous, tall blond man called Harry, who flirted outrageously all through the trip. Normally, I get stuck next to some awful old bag who wants to show me photographs of her spotty grandchildren and tell me their life histories, or worse still, next to some ageing businessman who thinks because he has a big fat bank account it makes up for his big fat stomach and he can still try it on. As far as I was concerned, this was a perfectly acceptable alternative. We talked and talked and by the time we landed in Los Angeles, we were the best of friends.

A little trouble at immigration rather put paid to my chances of pursuing this relationship. Harry said he would wait for me outside, while I was marched off to a detention room and given the third degree – 'How long had I been out of the country? Why was I only back here for three or four days? What was the point of my visit?' And so on – not very pleasant, and knowing I shouldn't be using my green card as I was now a resident in England made my excuses less convincing. I was scared they would relieve me of my green card and make re-entry into the States almost impossible.

Eventually they let me go, most likely because they had other larger fish to fry and I wasn't as much fun as a drug smuggler, or whoever else these people feel is a blight on the face of the American continent.

It was one and half hours later, but, polite to the last, Harry was still there, and walked out with me. I couldn't see Tony but, when he hoved into view, in his bright red gleaming new Porsche, I waved and turned to Harry.

'Thank you for waiting. I really enjoyed the trip and I'm sorry it was such a short one!'

'So did I. I have never thought flying to Los Angeles from London was fun before. Perhaps we'll meet again in the air or on the ground.'

We smiled at each other, and I felt really regretful because, red Porsche or not, Tony was no comparison at all, and heaven alone knew what his friend Philippe would be like!

So, Harry went one way, into the sunset, and I went the other, into the Porsche.

Tony never, for one single moment, stopped talking. I say talking, but it was a string of obscenities, interspersed with hip chat about sex and drugs. The radio was blaring all the way along the seven-lane highway.

'English girls really need a good fuck, that's what's the matter with them. Guys out here could screw the ass off them, and brother, do they go home with big smiles on their faces. My friend Philippe, he can handle his prick, and mind you give him a good time while you're here. I can tell you you won't regret it – most of the girls around here are dying for him to stick in between their legs.'

There you have an example of the tone of the conversation, and by now, a couple of hours into it, I was getting quite scared. As far as I could remember, Marian hadn't liked quite such straight talking. I remembered her as an executive Meryl Streep lookalike with many boyfriends (though they all seemed to treat her badly), but fun and a good friend. I hoped she hadn't changed as much as it looked as though she might have!

We reached his condominium, in a rather built-up area of Santa Monica. It was very 'bachelorfied' – three bedrooms, a living room, den, kitchen and bathroom. Lots of dark wood, mirrors and tiles, Tiffany lampshades, leather chairs and the odd bendy animal, like the emu or similar on top of one of the speakers. The bedroom was the best room in the house – predictably, I suppose. It had a brass bed, a thick counterpane and mirrored doors. The pillowcases were lace – all very pretty, but rather scratchy on the cheeks, I would have thought. Beige hessian on the walls, and an ethnic artefact above the bed – all tassels and plaits and South American zig-zag lines.

He had a parrot in a cage, a beautiful bird, red and yellow and blue. He didn't treat it at all well, poking it with a newspaper. I was shocked and told him so. Apparently it had once nearly taken his finger off (I couldn't blame it) and so he got his own back by abusing it eloquently.

'Fuck you, parrot.' Or better 'up your cunt, parrot.'

Another part of his repertoire with the animal kingdom was to play with the large wobbly furry balls of his bulldog as it lay on the sofa with a resigned expression on its squashed face. He could see by my face that I was horrified by all this, and so it was inevitable that I should become a butt of his humour. He decided quite quickly that he didn't like me. 'Your friend's too conservative, Marian. She needs a good fuck to get her loosened up, but I don't suppose she would know how to go about getting one. Still we've set her up, and all I can say is I wish Philippe lots of luck.'

Marian *had* changed – now she dressed sexily, in clinging low-cut things, with lots of make-up and jewellery. The Jewish American princess look they call it, and it did suit her more than her previous tasteful conservative dressing. She had had a nose job, so her nose was now a ski-slope, small and neat, like her figure which was petite and rather good. She had a good job in sales, and this had enabled her to have a large Mercedes car for herself. She was very hung up on sex, and her conversation (with a few fewer swear words) was along the same lines as Tony's – who they'd been to bed with, how many times they had done it, how they had done it, with what, who they'd like to do it with.

She stuck up for me in Tony's more extravagant moments. Like when he began teasing me, half-seriously, about being too prim to enjoy 'a little messing about, the three of us, you know'.

'Oh leave her alone, Tony, she's not like that.'

'I can see that. It would be a lot more fun for her, and for us, if she'd let her hair down a bit. Perhaps we'll all end up in my bedroom before she gets back, you never know.'

Oh yes I do, I thought firmly. I wasn't like that, and I had been around for nearly thirty years without having the slightest inclination to roll around naked in a bed with more than one other person, of the opposite sex only, thank you.

They were also into popping pills a good deal of the time, so were as high as a pair of kites, which made for rather a boring time for low-flying little me. Later I heard that Tony had been told that there was a chance that he would die in a couple of years, so he was making the most of his remaining time on earth. I would have thought there are a lot more interesting ways of enjoying life than imbibing chemicals, but I understood it from his point of view.

Later that evening Philippe telephoned to invite us to dinner at his restaurant.

'This you will like, Colette,' said Marian. 'It's the in place at the moment. Packed out with all the hippest people, the prettiest waiters and waitresses, and the food's really great. He's quite a guy, our Philippe, and quite a catch.'

'Yes, Tony told me.'

We drove down the beach to the restaurant, a huge airy bar-cum-cafe which was all Marian had said it would be. The atmosphere was fun, the music good, the tables fairly far apart and every one full to overflowing, with more people coming to take the place of those who had finished their drinks or their meal. Philippe wasn't in evidence – as the owner, he had to do a lot of socializing, welcoming and sitting at tables with favoured customers – and we sat down at a table near a window.

The conversation turned again to sex.

'Hey, Marian. Has Colette got good tits?'

'I don't know, Tony. Why should I?'

'Let's find out. Come here, girlie, and let's have a look. Or perhaps you'd like to leave it all till later, when we all get back?'

Oh God, I thought. How much more of this do I have to take? Luckily Tony spotted a friend and got up, without ceremony, to speak to him at another table.

Marian and I talked quietly for a while in his absence, the only chance I'd so far had to find out anything about her life. 'I met Tony at a singles party. There aren't that many guys around LA, Colette, and he treats me very well. He buys me things, pays my bills, and we have a good time.'

I thought he was a debauched old man, but nodded and looked encouraging.

'Hey girls, look who I've got hold of.'

Tony's voice came over my right shoulder, and I turned to see him standing behind me, beaming all over his bearded face.

'This is Philippe, Colette. Philippe, this is your Christmas present. Whaddya think?'

He was tall, pleasingly attractive, if a bit fat, and quiet, the opposite of Tony, who nevertheless seemed to be a close friend.

'Hallo, Colette. I'm so pleased you could come over for a few days. Marian has told me all about you, and I'm very happy to meet you.'

His slightly stilted English, in a French accent, did a lot to enhance his charm, and his manners were a refreshing change. 'It is nice to meet a European lady in this country, and such a pretty one.'

He kept having to disappear to attend to business, but I began to feel a lot better about the whole thing. He was no Adonis, and could have done with losing a stone or two, but his hair was brown and shiny, he wore nice clothes, his eyes were blue and his smile was kind. He also kept the champagne flowing, which sweetened the pill of being constantly referred to by Tony as his friend's Christmas present. I felt a bit like a parcel from Selfridges, and didn't enjoy the feeling, but I laughed along with it, not caring to alienate Tony still further.

I was dreading the night back at Tony's condo, but as it turned out, we were all pretty exhausted by the time we got back there. We said goodnight to Philippe, Tony with much nudging, me rather coolly, and drove off, weaving a little.

The next morning I did some telephoning. I spoke to Paul, my prospective visitor from Santa Barbara, who was by no means happy that I was in America. He had to delay his flight to England, and clearly felt that this was not on. Tough, I thought, as I put down the receiver, and then decided to phone Mr Happy, a delightful correspondent from an old advert, who seemed thrilled to hear from me. But we weren't able to fix a meeting in my very short stay. This all made me feel a little more independent, less tied to Tony and Marian and with some kind of a life elsewhere.

Marian and I then went out for a while, to look at the shops and have a cup of coffee by the sea, and when we returned, Tony said that Philippe had called me, suggesting dinner. He phoned again almost as Tony had stopped speaking, and I agreed to go out with him to Le Bistingo, a very smart and popular French restaurant. All I really wanted to do was sleep, because jet lag was still with me, but this was not practical in my short stay. And if I didn't go out with Philippe, Marian and Tony had already lined me up with the man who Marian had been in bed with when she had met Tony; he had made up a threesome.

The restaurant was beautiful, and I had dressed up. I wore a long black dress, about three inches above the ankle, with silver splashes all over it. It was figure-hugging, and very flattering, with slits from hem to just above the knee. The food was wonderful, the lighting subtle, the other diners had that indefinable aura of wealth and success. The walls of the room were white, and there were palm trees hazily reflected in the white marble floor. Philippe was very pleasant company, appreciative, polite, interesting, interested. I adored his accent, the clothes he wore and his car (a Mercedes 500). He was a practised man about town; everybody knew him and wanted to greet him.

We talked and talked. I told him about my life, a little about my past, something about Moya and my hopes. He countered by telling me about his – he had started his business with nothing, and had worked doggedly and cleverly to reach the top. I admired him and said so. I also told him about the pressure that Marian and Tony were putting me under to 'be nice to him' and he took it very well.

'Tony is kind and good really. Marian too. It's all just surface stuff. Don't worry, they'll be fine.

'It's such a pity you live so far away,' he said suddenly, changing tack. 'You are so wonderful. I could really fall in love with you. I haven't met anyone like you for so long. When are you going back? Can't you stay for longer, like for years? Bring your daughter.'

Imagine all this in a dark brown French voice, with throaty 'rs' and a charming slur, add a good helping of delicious food, plenty of champagne, warmth, pretty people, soft lighting and music, and you will get the picture. It was lovely – I hadn't been spoken to like this for a long time, and I revelled in it. But I kept cool, making him work, giving him the impression I wasn't really interested.

We left the restaurant, the drink mixing with very little sleep to make a heady cocktail. He asked me how much he should tip the man who brought his car round.

'Shall I give him $10 or $20?'

'I should think $1 would be fine, Philippe.'

'On second thoughts, it must be such a pleasure driving it, I'll give him nothing at all.'

Flash Harry jerk, I thought – how unnecessary, and felt less well-disposed towards him. We were to meet Marian and Tony at his house, and on the way, lulled by the warm night and his fast driving, I decided that he was all right really. He put his hand on my knee as he drove, and, cocooned in the leather intimacy of the car, with the blackness outside dotted with lights and cars and people flicking past the windows, I suddenly felt heedless and adolescent. I kissed his hand, bringing it up to my lips. Then I leant over and kissed his neck, and then, passionately, each fingertip, letting my lips linger. It felt good – I rediscovered the feeling of wanting to be kissed back, and of enjoying the sensations of sexual attraction. We pulled over and kissed some more, taking our time about it. Eventually, Philippe tore himself away with an effort and restarted the car. It purred into life, and we arrived soon afterwards at his house, where Tony and Marian had been waiting for a while.

'Hey, Marian,' said my tormentor, 'they look as though something good's been going on. Looks like my Christmas present is about to remove its wrapping. Are you two gonna fuck tonight?'

'The hell we're not,' I snapped, and followed Philippe out of the room to the kitchen, where we moved together and kissed and cuddled each other, smiling and touching. He was getting pretty excited about it all by now, and I was beginning to calm down, but I realized that I had given a strong come-on, and would now have to deal with it. Prick teasing used to be fun, but I now have more of a conscience about it. Men are human too. Tony and Marian, grinning from ear to ear, picked up their coats.

'See you guys. We're off.'

'Hang on, I'm coming too,' I cried, trying to find my bag.

'Oh no you're not, Colette. You're staying right here.'

'But I want to go home, to go to bed – alone. I'm exhausted.'

'Sorry, darling. We're not taking you. Bye.'

By this time, Philippe was annoyed, and I saw his frown.

'Who the hell does she think she is? I don't want her to stay. If you want to go, Colette, you can go.'

'Perhaps she's gay,' cried Tony, and began to laugh. 'Perhaps she can only get it on with women. Ten at a time. Eh, Colette. Is that it? Or are you frigid, like all English girls.'

I felt like bursting into tears. OK, I had been leading Philippe on, and perhaps I should have kept my passionate kisses for a time when I had more energy, but it was late, I had said I didn't want to stay, and surely they could leave me alone – at least until the morning.

Philippe saw my face, and collected himself.

'Look, guys. She's tired. Stop badgering her. We can talk about it in the morning. She's not going for a couple of days. Let's give her a rest. OK, Colette? I'll take you home.'

Which is what he did, and I was extremely grateful to him. I tottered up to my bedroom and kicked my clothes on to the floor, leaving them where they fell. I flopped into bed but was restless, too wound up to sleep. At the crack of dawn, whatever drugs Tony was taking that day worked a treat and had him up, playing music as loudly as he could, and taking the dog for a walk. I crept downstairs for a cup of strong coffee to beat my system into life, and met him coming back with the ballsy bulldog.

'Oh, if it isn't our Miss Prim. Philippe doesn't want to see you again, Colette. Isn't that what you want? So you can relax. I thought you were going to keep your half of the bargain and go fuck him.'

'Bargain?' I squealed. 'Bargain? I'm not a commodity, like a sack of rice, or a bunch of flowers for someone's birthday. Look Tony, I just like him, I like him a lot, but don't push me so much. Give me time to think, to sleep at least, so that my head's working properly.'

'We haven't got any time, Colette.'

'I know that, but . . .'

'You told Marian that you hadn't been laid in months. I thought it would be doing you a favour too. Look if you ever want to see Philippe again you'd better call him. And when you meet, don't lead him on, just fucking do it.'

'What on earth shall I do?' I said, panicking. I wasn't sure I wanted to get back into being the present again, but I did want to see Philippe.

'Send him some flowers.'

I called a flower shop, and arranged for a large bunch of yellow roses to be delivered to his apartment, with a short apologetic note. It worked. Philippe called again, and again we arranged to go out.

To take my mind off all this sexually charged business, Marian and I went out shopping, to buy a present for Tony for getting me a ticket. I didn't have all that much money, but Marian's access to his bank account seemed unhindered, so between us we bought him a Thai god from an art gallery for about $1000. I quite liked it, Marian said that he would love it, so I put in what I could and that was that. He was thrilled when he saw it, so she was right.

Philippe picked me up exactly on time. The first time he had taken me out, he had given me flowers, expensively packaged in a white box with a bow. This time I got chocolates, and a large bottle of scent – Opium by Yves Saint Laurent. Nothing but the best. The restaurant he had chosen this time was Nick Blair's on Sunset Boulevard. Another lovely place, with high white columns and gorgeous waiters trained in perfect, unobtrusive service. I wore my white sequinned top and beige satin trousers, and smelled expensively of my Givenchy III. We had lobster and champagne, and Philippe dressed and acted exactly as an escort in such a place should.

He was very amorous, very tender. He touched my hand a lot, and at one point, he leant across and said, very low and very sincerely:

'Colette, I think I have fallen in love with you.'

We talked sense and nonsense, I tried out my French on him, and made him laugh. His attention made me glow, and I responded to him warmly. He told me he had a yacht in Cabo San Lucas, and that he was buying his son (he had been married before) a computer for Christmas.

'It would be wonderful to bring up a daughter, Colette – our daughter.'

I avoided going any further into this. I didn't want to think about my responsibilities, my future. I glowed with the money, attention, glamour around me. We enjoyed each other, striking up between us a sort of needling rapport. We teased each other, made each other think, put each other on the spot with questions.

I confessed that the scene at Tony and Marian's was not something I felt happy about. I explained that I wasn't into drugs and certainly wasn't into threesomes or any other kind of kinky sex. 'I'm a bit frightened there, Philippe,' I confessed, and he put his arm around me.

'I'll cradle you in my arms, I'll not let them hurt you or upset you. Trust me.'

We went on to a disco when we had finished eating, and it was good. By this time we were drunk as skunks. We had a ball, dancing and then retiring to our quiet corner to be together.

One thing I didn't like was that by now, the alcohol and the smooching made him act a bit possessively, pulling me towards him rather roughly, almost manhandling me at times. I knew there would have to be a confrontation about the dreaded bed. I didn't want to go to bed with him, I would think one minute, then I would change my mind and think he was quite attractive, then again I would tell myself that, although I didn't find him that attractive, perhaps he was better than no one. Moya would want for nothing, and nor would I, as long as we were together.

I was very confused. I still hadn't slept for more than an hour or so, so was almost hallucinating by this time. We had left the disco at about 3.00 a.m., and spent another hour or so in the car before I got out and let myself in to Tony's condo and went to bed separately.

The next morning there was the usual cross-examination.

'Well, did you? Did you fuck him? Did he give you a good time? You didn't! Christ, you stupid bitch, if you don't hurry up you are going to lose him, I swear.'

That day, to prove him wrong, and give me a bit of respite, Philippe called three times, just to say hello. He wasn't messing about, just in case I changed my mind. He may have been staging this elaborate seduction just for the chance of getting me into bed, but it seemed more than that. His professions of love were a bit over the top if that was all he wanted. I find men say a lot about the way you look if they're after a quick roll in the satin sheets, and avoid any mention of children or futures.

We all arranged to go out to a jolly restaurant called the Palm, with sawdust on the floor and rustic wooden tables. You are given a large bib, to save your clothes from the buttery sauces from the copious quantities of lobster you eat there. We ate pounds of the stuff, which was delicious, but the meal for me was spoiled by the now familiar chorus from Tony.

'Hey, Philippe, what's she like? Eh? Did you fuck, Colette? Was he all I've told you – not that I know first hand, but, my, the news has travelled. You didn't? Well when the fuck are you gonna?'

He didn't bother to keep his voice down so I was scarlet with embarrassment, wishing he would just shut up or, if that was impossible, keep his conversation at decibels low enough to prevent everyone else in the place from being party to it. But, oh no. He wouldn't give it a rest.

'If you don't fuck her, Philippe, I will. I can't see a good cunt go to waste . . .' and so on.

I wished Tony's witticisms had been a hallucination – but they were all too real. My voice began to leave me, to add insult to injury, so I spent a while croaking weakly before it practically vanished altogether.

'What's there that you haven't told us, eh, Philippe. Have you had Colette on the floor of your new Mercedes, giving you head? Does she give good head?'

My attention was briefly diverted by seeing a fairly well-known actor come into the restaurant. I went up to him and whispered that I would like his autograph. He gave it to me, asking for my telephone number at the same time, which was gratifying if insincere. He said he'd call me whenever he was in England next, and smiled his famous smile.

The others now wanted to move on to a piano bar, and as I was being driven, and being paid for, and had no voice to express an opinion I had no option but to go along with them. It was ghastly

– dark, dingy, smelling of booze and sweat, with lots of red plush on seats and walls, and a black guy singing throaty jazz very close into the microphone.

We had more drinks, and I felt ever more tired and fed up with the torrent of innuendo. I honestly don't know why he did it, because it was gross, boring and not even remotely funny. And he had had his joke if there was one, at least a hundred times by now. He obviously liked to get under my skin about Philippe not getting into my knickers and if I had been feeling a little better, I would have tried harder to stop him. But as it was, I let him ramble on and on and on.

The next tack was that we should all do some drugs. 'Oh, leave her alone, Tony,' said Philippe. 'Can't you see she doesn't want to?' Which was nice of him, but didn't go far to make up for the effect all the booze was having on him. His manners sank further to the bottom of the gin bottle with each glass he filled, and his hands began to run around my body like a demented hamster. Up my knickers, on to my breasts, under my top, squeezing, pressing, rubbing, pulling me towards him. He too had got into a groove, about me being his Christmas present, the best one he had ever had.

'Please stop,' I croaked, pulling his hand out from under my skirt for the millionth time. 'Please, I don't like it.' And then, finally, at the end of my tether, I snapped as loudly as I could 'What they should have sent you is a whore for Christmas!'

'They did!'

Before I quite realized it, the snap of anger in my head made me hit him hard across the face with an open hand. The crack it made silenced the whole bar, and everyone looked at me rather nervously. I had shocked myself, he could see that too, and I just fell against him to rest. I was emotional, drunk, tired and miserable, and thank goodness, it was so obvious that no one said anything.

'I'm so sorry. I couldn't help it,' I managed to say against his shirtfront.

'Nor could I, but I should have. It was a dreadful thing to say, and I didn't mean it.'

We had all rather sobered up, and Philippe was very kind to me. We drove back to Tony and Marian's very subdued, and even Tony didn't make one of his terrible cracks. They got out and said goodnight, and waited for me to follow.

'Goodnight, Colette,' said Philippe, kindly.

It was his tone that made me say, almost to my surprise, 'No, I'm staying with you. Provided you let me sleep.'

Without saying anything more, he drove back to his place, a

beautiful house in the centre of Santa Monica, another very male establishment, with a bar and a billiard table in the living room, and lots of South American carpets and pots about.

Rather unexpectedly, but very appropriately in the circumstances, he made me a cup of tea, which I drank thirstily and gratefully. He showed me the bedroom and the bathroom, and told me, 'I won't touch you, and you can say to Tony and Marian that I did, and get it out of the way, if you like.'

I was really touched, and thought how nice he was then. And he looked great in his nightshirt, into which he had changed almost as soon as he got in, leaving me in the kitchen.

I was overtired by now, so I said I would take a sleeping pill. Tony had given me a tablet, oval and pointed, and Philippe advised me against taking it, so I took one he offered me. I would have swallowed a tub of burning oil by now if he had told me to – I was too sick, past caring.

It worked slowly. We shared the same bed, and the rest of the night is wrapped in a woozy cloud of sleep and tablet and darkness. I vaguely remember making love, and recall a fat body pressing on top of mine, with a tiny, limp penis which he tried to stuff inside me. It half-worked, I think, and after a few whale-like heaves and wallows, he rolled off happy, and the world closed around me even further.

When I woke up I saw his body beside me and felt queasy. His flabby behind wobbled in time with his breathing, and I wondered how I could have done it. But the fact remained that I had, and so of course when he awoke, feeling me sit up, he tried to come on with the amorous French lover bit, all *je t'aimes* and *belles*. It really didn't cut any ice with me at that bleakly real time of day, and I said firmly that I would have to be going now, because I had to meet my friend Carol, which was true. I really liked him, and was very grateful for his kindness the night before, but I felt sad for the affair that could never be.

Off I went, and met Carol at Rive Gauche, a restaurant we both knew. It was lovely to see her again, and we talked and talked. I told her about the débâcle the night before, and explained that the sex had been awful, but perhaps it could get better. She nodded encouragement, having taken in the good points first, like the house and the car and the job and the manners and the finances and the niceness. I was almost convincing myself, but still wasn't sure what to do. Tony and Marian were off to Mexico and would have to leave me at the airport at six the next morning even though my flight wasn't until the evening.

'You can stay with me tonight.'

'No, I think I'll stay with Philippe. He's been so understanding, it would be churlish not to. We'll work something out about the sex business.'

'OK, but if you need to stay with me you only have to call.'

After lunch Carol helped me get my cases, and I said fond farewells to Marian and shook Tony's hand. I left with Carol to meet Philippe, and alone later that evening he took me to dinner at the Bistingo again. I was settling back into this lifestyle very painlessly and put out of mind the small house in Littlehampton and all the rest of it. Just for a little longer – although Moya is always a delight and I never ever want to forget about her, the constant worry about money and men and the future is wearing.

But for now, I was with a well-dressed, well-off man, not perfect but pretty good, murmuring all sorts of delightful things into my ear. 'I have fallen in love with you. I know I have – please don't go. I love you. Bring your daughter over here. We'll make a home for her. I'll treat her as my own, and love her, and give her everything. We'll make this relationship work, I know we will. Give it a try, Colette.'

He wanted me to go skiing in Aspen with him instead of going home, and the offer was tempting, but I couldn't take it up. Moya was waiting and so was Mummie, not to mention a rather peeved Paul.

He was very pressing, very plausible, but even though it was tempting, I knew that it would only be temporary. I could never enjoy being with a man who revolted me physically, and with his clothes off, Philippe reminded me of nothing so much as a large cuddly slug.

On the way home, we passed a cart of soft toys, being offered for sale. 'Do you want to buy one for Moya?' he asked.

'No, it's all right. I've already got her something.'

'Go on, buy her one. Which one would you like? Go on, pick one. I'll buy it for you.'

There were lions and tigers, of all sizes and colours, and I couldn't make up my mind.

'Let's get out and have a look – look what about this one?'

He was so keen to buy her something I eventually chose a huge white animal, and he was thrilled.

'Now she'll know who I am,' he said enthusiastically, which was nice of him.

That evening we decided to have an early night. It was a pleasant evening, spent watching the video, although it broke in the middle which made him furious.

We went to bed together – I was determined to give this relationship a chance – but it was dreadful. Plenty of huffing and puffing on top of me, and, just to get him off me so that I could breathe, I dishonestly faked an orgasm, which thrilled him, of course. He thought it terrific, and did that awful business of wanting to know if I did too. Well, what could I say? No, it was awful and I think you fat and ugly and no good in bed? Hardly, so I said nice vague things and sighed and smiled a bit, and then took another pill and drifted off. I was going home the next day and wanted to have some rest before the journey. He got up early, and went into the jacuzzi, where I joined him, wearing my underwear at his tactful suggestion. It was a lovely way to start the day, and his compliments made me feel even better: 'You look lovely without make-up – so few women do.' He dressed, putting on one of his silk shirts with a discreet monogram on the cuffs, and looked good. I wore white ski pants tucked into black suede cowboy boots, with a black and white top and chains – sexy, slightly tarty, rather good and put some make-up on; I may look all right without it, but I feel a whole lot better with a dash of lipstick and some mascara.

'I'd like to have lunch with you. May I? It will be my last chance before you go back to that other guy. I am really jealous of him. Who is he anyway? Don't meet him. Why can't you give the jerk the push and stay here with me? I'm going up to Santa Barbara to check him out.'

As it turned out, there was no time for lunch, so he took me to the airport and went on declaring his love for me.

'I'm glad you're going. I love you. Too much. You're bad for me to be around, Colette.'

'Well, I think you're a pigheaded arrogant bastard for not taking me to lunch,' I teased him. Lunch would have been a nice way to end my stay which now felt rather unfinished; I was sorry and rather surprised.

I was beginning a streaming cold, however, the follow-up to losing my voice, and my thoughts were moving from lobster and champagne, to a bowl of thin gruel and lots of hot Lemsip.

'Please come back to me,' he wailed. 'Call me collect any time. Come back to me.' It was all getting a bit monotonous. With Tony it had been sex and drugs, and with Philippe it was love and sex – both by the fiftieth repetition rather tedious. But I did say I would think it over, and if Paul was a washout, I would call him, and anyway we'd keep in touch.

I checked in, leaving him behind, waving as I passed through the departure gate. I sat down at a table with a cup of coffee, and a tall, good-looking guy came up almost immediately to ask if he could join me. You know how it sometimes is – lots of compliments and being treated nicely makes one look and feel better, and then you can conquer the world.

I was feeling sad to leave Philippe, but I wanted a breather, a while to think things over – it had been a hectic few days, bad and good, and it felt like too much too soon.

I talked to this chap for a long time – he was a teacher, so I wasn't interested, but he was nice to be with for a while at a busy airport waiting for my plane.

Suddenly over the tannoy I heard my name.

'Colette Sinclair, will you please go to the British Caledonian desk?'

So of course, puzzled, I went. The stewardess reached under the desk and came out with a long gold box. I took it, from under her interested gaze, and the card that went with it, without looking at either. Philippe again, of course, I was extremely embarrassed but inwardly thrilled. I looked around for him, my hopes were dashed, he wasn't there. When I sat down and recovered myself I opened box and card. The box held a single red rose, and the card said 'from a pigheaded arrogant bastard who's glad you're going because he's fallen in love with you.'

Mike the teacher beside me looked at me worriedly. 'Are you all right? I've never seen anyone receive flowers and look so white.'

So, of course, longing to get it off my chest, I poured it all out to him: should I stay? Who should I see – Philippe or Paul? Was I mad?

He was sympathetic, but not helpful. I wanted to speak to Philippe then and there, but when I called, I got his son. The message I left was straightforward and not as emotional as I felt – 'This is Colette. Just to say I'm leaving for England now, and I called to say thank you.'

After a long flight, on which I took a couple of pills and slept most of the way, I got back home with a streaming cold, a temperature, and feeling generally miserable. I unpacked as best I could, and sat around feeling sorry for myself.

Paul was coming the next day, which I really wasn't looking forward to and, when he did arrive, I wasn't that impressed. Phillipe called me later on Christmas night, to wish me Happy

Christmas and also to ask if I had decided about Paul. I told him my disappointment, but also that I was feeling like death and wouldn't be coming skiing.

'OK, Colette. Please call, please call. I'll call you from skiing to see how you are. Think of me. I'll think of you all the time.'

He did call, but by then, I really felt the moment had passed. It was all a bit too much, and the unsavoury elements had given it a bad flavour. It had not been what I'd expected – sleazier and more unfriendly. I worried about Marian, and certainly was not getting myself into a similar situation. And Paul had turned out to be an altogether more interesting proposition – clean-living, slimmer, more handsome, and not best friends with raving sex maniacs. I was cool and I never heard from Philippe again.

8

Marriage Bureaux

May 1987. I had turned thirty-one. I had written hundreds of letters, spoken to many many men, all unsuitable. I had had a mad passion in Monte Carlo, to be followed by a sad let-down in Littlehampton. I had been charmed by my first and second dates, and foolishly let one go and lost the other. I had been bored out of my mind, or treated to Ascot, Henley, the theatre, smart restaurants, airplane tickets across the world. What more could I ask for? Mr Right, of course.

I still believed that he existed – I have never lost sight of that – but I was getting a bit exhausted by now. The routine of going through magazines, vetting the advertisements carefully, disregarding their wilder claims, not getting too carried away by possibilities, writing back to the ones I chose, waiting for their replies (or not hearing from them at all), meeting them, and all the palaver that follows that – it had all got too much, and so I decided to let the professionals have a go.

I looked through the magazines and noted down the names of some marriage bureaux. I contacted about five, and also went into travel agents checking out singles holidays, without much luck. The prospect of eighteen–thirty beach parties in Majorca left me cold, and I wasn't ready to stroll around Florence imbibing art history for a vast sum of money.

'Hedi Fisher, marriage and friendship consultants' wrote me a letter. They wanted £75 for my enrolment fee, and when I didn't reply, not having £75 to splash out on an uncertain result, they kept sending me pieces of paper reminding me that I hadn't replied and asking me why I hadn't joined.

I replied eventually, explaining my doubts, and a nice letter came:

You sound a very attractive and interesting person. I should very much like to dispel your doubts about our agency – as in my experience, many high-flying, high-calibre people have met each other through our introduction service. Ours is an up-market agency which caters for the more educated, outgoing, successful type of person.

I would like to offer you now just one contact – and charge you only £20 for it.

We have a fairly new client who is an American citizen of Persian birth. He is forty-two, 6 feet tall, slim physique. He has lots of black hair and dark eyes.

He is an aerospace engineer, educated at Michigan University, and a very intelligent man, who speaks three languages fluently and is into sailing, skiing, tennis and other activities. He is widely travelled, generous, and is used to a high standard. He is divorced and lives in London.

Why not? I thought. It was not a fortune and he did sound rather a good prospect. I had filled in my forms from the agency as specifically as I could, and there was no excuse for them wasting my time with people who did not fit. I had described my personality as 'outgoing, fun-loving, affectionate, impulsive, stubborn, spoilt (a little), serious, refined, original, venturesome, confident, warm, intelligent, kind, enthusiastic, expensive.'

My interests I listed as 'badminton, tennis, riding, opera, theatre, dinner, travel (adore), table tennis, power boats (in USA), art, reading, concerts, parties, shopping, fashion, aerobics, cars, the business world.'

I said that my political leanings are conservative, and told them that I had been privately educated at a convent, getting eight O-levels.

On the other form, the one asking the type of person I would like to meet, I was very firm. I ticked the nationality boxes marked UK, Europe, USA, Australian, Middle Eastern, and crammed the lines for appearance. It is probably unrealistic to expect everything all in one, but more information left less room for mistakes. 'Must be over 5 feet 9 inches, must be fairly good-looking, more than just own hair and teeth, must dress either fashionably or with class, must have a reasonable physique, no skin and bones or beer bellies.' I continued, with an arrow, further down the page, because I couldn't fit in all I wanted to say about personality. 'This is so difficult. It's a question of clicking, but I suppose confident, original, strong, warm, kind, fun, different, travelled. I have found

European or Middle Eastern men to be attractive, intelligent, impulsive and in love with life, with a great respect and admiration for women.'

Special objections or remarks left no room for mistakes either, I thought. I knew what I *didn't* want. 'Not a Mr Next Door, Mr Average – i.e. works for a company from 9 to 5, makes £20,000, lives in a three-bedroom house, drives a regular car, goes on an annual holiday.' There. That gave them the picture, if a bit hard to live up to. I sent off my £20, and someone from the agency rang back.

'How tall is he?' I asked, with the caution of long experience.

'Over 5 feet 9 inches, as you said in your letter.'

'What's he like?'

'He's got oodles of sex appeal – I'm sure you'll find him attractive. Good luck.'

I couldn't wait to meet this paragon.

He telephoned promptly, with a strong American accent which appealed to me at once.

'Hi, Colette,' he said, in a warm, friendly voice which I liked. We went on to talk about how he heard of the agency:

'From a woman friend. I have only been in this country a short time, and she recommended Hedi Fisher as a reliable and up-market agency. Where shall we meet and when? I'm dying to meet you. Let's not waste time.'

His enthusiasm, flattering as it was, was also catching. We arranged, without further ado, to meet at the Grand Hotel in Brighton, that Thursday – in two days' time. It's one of my favourite hotels in Brighton, as it must be everybody's. It suffered terribly at the hands of the IRA who detonated the bomb that blew up at the Conservative party conference but it has recovered regally, and if anything, is more gracious than it ever was. It looks out over the sea, behind wrought-iron railings, and it is not hard to imagine Edwardian visitors driving up to the front doors and disembarking in a swish of expensive silk and satin.

When the day came, I wore my cream dress, anxious to look my best. I arrived first and sat nervously at a corner table, wondering, as I always did, who I was going to meet. Oodles of sex appeal, eh? I only hoped I could compete. If he was as good as Hedi Fisher had said, I thought he would have had his pick of all the girls the agency introduced to him. I tweaked a fold of my skirt, uncrossed my legs, crossed them again, and looked up as someone came in. It was him. I always know and there was no doubt that he had recognized me too.

I can describe him best as looking exactly like a balding eagle. His physique, if it could be called that, was skinny, and the idea of him without his clothes on made me feel very unenthusiastic indeed.

He sat down, full of enthusiasm, and bought us drinks. He was very generous with everything all that day, I noticed. In fact he was extremely nice to me, and I could only wish that I could see us in bed together without wincing. It's such a shame the physical side of a relationship is so important, but it is.

We talked about our interests. 'I'm mad about tennis,' he told me in his broad American accent. 'I play nearly every day. I always think I'm pretty good, until I play with people who are on the tennis circuit, and then I realize that I will never be world class! It's a bitter lesson, I can tell you!'

We went into the restaurant for lunch, a very good buffet, and he chose exactly the right wines to go with the food. He was well mannered and charming. I like it when men stand up as you do, to go to the loo or whatever. He did all that, and was excellent company.

'I've spent the last twenty-seven years in the States,' he told me. 'So England is an entirely new experience for me. It's great. I really like it, and meeting a girl like you has made it even better.'

For a change, I didn't have to do most of the talking. I did talk, about Moya and England and my life in the States. He talked of Moya with fond respect, which I liked to listen to.

'What is your work?' I asked him.

'I'm a financial consultant. My work's pretty confidential at the moment – I'm advising a German company about where it's going wrong and how to cure itself. No one really likes to hear the reasons why they aren't as good as they thought they were, rather like me and my tennis! But we're getting there, and it pays.'

He was obviously very keen on his job, perhaps too keen on it. He spent a lot of time at his desk or at his clients', so whoever ended up with him should expect not to see him for stretches at a time.

He may have been earning a reasonably salary, but quite honestly, his clothes didn't give that away. His cream silk suit had seen better days – it bagged and sagged, at the elbows and the knees. His shirt was a bit tired too, slightly frayed.

After lunch we decided to stroll around Brighton, as he had never been there before and it is a really pretty place, very English, and yet very used to tourists, since it began as the Prince Regent's playground in the eighteenth century. We didn't have time to go to the Royal Pavilion, the extravagant onion-domed palace designed by Nash for the Prince. We went around the Lanes instead, and he enjoyed this greatly. All Americans do. It is such a contrast to everything they are used to in a large town. For a start they are real, and fairly unchanged since they were built. They have obviously been painted and repaired, but no high-rise blocks or fancy anachronisms spoil their charm. He loved them, and we spent a happy hour or so wandering about. During lunch I had seen a little girl with one of those silver wigs on, the ones with a straight fringe and straight strands of what look like tinsel, and I said how much I'd love to buy one for Moya.

'If you would like one for her, I would be honoured to buy it. Look there they are, in the shop over there, beside the record shop.'

'So they are. That would be lovely. Thank you very much,' I said, smiling, and impressed that my throwaway remark two hours ago had made so much impression.

I wondered what to do next, and thought of taking him to see my friend Georgie and her parents at what can only be described as a manor house in the Sussex countryside. I had spent many months in my late teens with them there, and so I knew them well and respected their opinion. I also thought it would give him a treat to see an old English house. We bought a cake – he paid, unlike my first date who blotted his copybook by not putting his hand in his pocket – and off we went in his red BMW 320, which didn't thrill me that much. It was all right, but I would have expected something a bit better. I know it seems too finicky to fuss about a man's car, but men identify with their vehicles far more than women do, and I think they say a lot about them. It really didn't matter at all, because I had already decided that this man, for all his pleasantness and obvious desire to please, was not going to be for me.

He played nice music as we went, and I introduced him to Georgie's parents – she was away at the time – who liked him at once.

Mrs McDonald and I went into the kitchen to make tea and get the plates and forks for the cake.

'What do you think? He's from the Hedi Fisher agency,' I whispered.

'He's very nice indeed. Obviously very intelligent, but I don't really think he's your type is he, Colette?'

'No, I suppose not. The biggest problem is that he is so funny-looking. If only he were attractive, things would be different.'

We came out with the tea things, and some drinks too, and the four of us spent a lovely late afternoon in the garden, enjoying the amber sun, and the sound of bees buzzing among the roses. It was very peaceful, and I wished for a moment that I could have something like this and be happy with it. I would of course love it, but I knew it wouldn't be enough. I would always want more – excitement, variety, glamour of all kinds. Not that this wasn't glamorous in a way – the old stones glowed in the light, and it could have been a filmset for one of those BBC serials, or *The Go Between*.

Time passed, and we had to leave. Omar had been excellent company – no innuendos, no silly comments, just sensible and intelligent conversation, obviously enjoying his surroundings. We drove back, and as we reached my house, he stopped the car. 'Look, Colette. I would really very much like to see you again. I have really enjoyed today, and perhaps you would like to go to the theatre next week? I'll try and get tickets and let you know. Does that sound OK?'

He ended rather nervously, looking closely at my face, which he then tried to clasp in his hands and kiss.

'No, Omar,' I said quietly, and there was no fuss. He stopped straight away, and didn't try to be unpleasant about it.

'Yes, I'd like that,' I said, not having the heart to tell him the truth, that I liked him but had absolutely no intention of going through with it. 'Give me a ring, and we can talk about it.'

'Fine. It's been a lovely day, and I think you are lovely too. I look forward to talking to you soon.'

And he drove off, as I walked into the house, to tell a waiting Mummie that yes, it had been a nice day, but no, there wasn't going to be another.

He kept calling me, for the next couple of weeks, and then I spoke to the agency, asking them to do my dirty work for me. He stopped phoning, so I suppose they did.

A follow-up letter asked me what I had thought of him, and I called to say that I was sorry but he was not my type. They were very nice about it, and another letter arrived:

> We are very sorry to note that Mr Omar Alhazi has failed to attract you, even though you liked him in other respects. We would like to offer you a choice of three handpicked men – if you could send us £60, or four for £80, by post.
>
> Here are a few possible candidates for you:
>
> Dr A. A. surgeon/senior registrar, age thirty-nine

Mr P. P. American Corporate President, wealthy, age thirty-five

J. D. London architect, trendy, age thirty-three

Dr N. A. Irish doctor, medical researcher, age thirty-one

Mr X. Y. English, Investment Banking – very YUPPIE, very high income, age thirty

All these people are good-looking. Do let us have your decision soon.

Of course I telephoned, and was told that one was 5 feet 9 inches, which was too short for me, as she should have known. The senior registrar sounded all right: 'he's tall and dishy, blondish,' she said, and told me that the other man, the investment banker earned up to £90,000 a year. Money matters. I haven't had any for a long time, and now there's Moya too.

My appetite was whetted, and so I sent my money and waited. A form arrived.

'Thank you for your cheque for £40 to cover these two intros. (Your own choices!) Good luck!'

Under the investment banker she had written: 'He is a high flyer, with big mop of dark hair and brown eyes. (He is not keen on children, so please avoid the subject if you can.)'

This didn't seem the right beginning to what might turn out to be a long-term relationship. I have a daughter, I love her, and I have no intention of denying her existence to anybody. If they take me, they take her. That's one of the reasons I am doing this in the first place, so he didn't seem like the ideal choice, but they had cashed the cheque.

Under the senior registrar, it said he was '5 feet 11 inches, fairish, with grey/blue eyes. Educated at Edinburgh University, *likes* children. If you can, meet him first in London.'

I arranged to meet the second one first, not out of any real desire to put him above the other, but because John, the investment banker, called six or seven times before we managed to fix a date.

I wore a pretty flowered dress, neither too demure nor too sexy, and went off to our meeting place – the Old Ship Hotel in Brighton. I waited there for some time, feeling increasingly nervous and annoyed. Finally he arrived. He had fair to greying hair, rather thin on top, and swept over his scalp to try and hide the fact. Not a good sign! He dressed appallingly – his jacket was too tight, the sleeves too short, and his trousers were grey polyester and far too short too. They looked like Marks and Spencer's special economy range, and his clodhopping brown shoes finished a rather unattractive picture. We had a drink – I noticed throughout the evening that he wasn't all that generous with drinks – and as he'd asked me to find a restaurant, as I knew Brighton and he did not, I had really thought about it, and ended up booking a table at Stubbs. When I go out with my rare dates, I always try and make it a bit of an event. They have had to make the effort to come down to meet me, often from quite far away, we are both nervous, and making it as nice as possible usually helps us both get over our embarrassment. I hadn't been to Stubbs, although it sometimes seemed that over the past couple of years I had patronized most of the other places in Brighton. I had arranged to meet at the Old Ship because I was beginning to look like a hooker at the Grand.

Stubbs was lovely and I was thrilled that I had chosen such a good place. It was French, with dark oak panelling and green and red velvet trimmings – intimate, warm and classy. We were unfortunately the first people in there that evening, so it was still a bit tense by the time we ordered, although it did fill up quite quickly and the atmosphere lightened considerably. It isn't such a comfortable feeling on a blind date to have waiters overhearing every word as you fish about for information on your companion, and try to present yourself in the best possible light.

His menu choices didn't impress me very much – he chose the cheapest things, it seemed, and it served to emphasize my first impression of his stinginess. But I suppose he might just have preferred them.

We spoke at length about his job. I can say that he is the only one of my dates whose job turned out to be far, far better than I had been told: I shan't go into too much detail, because I do not want to identify him too precisely, but suffice it to say that he had worked all his life for success and now it was about to come to him. He was going to open a Harley Street clinic, and he was only forty – so he had a lot of potential for making a great success of himself as a doctor as well as a lot of money.

But even that didn't make me like him very much. He tried to be complimentary when I asked him about plastic surgery:

'Any doctor who took you on as a patient would be less than ethical, I can tell you. I would refuse you.'

'But I've always wanted almond-shaped eyes,' I told him. 'Couldn't I come to you and have those done?'

'No. Your eyes are pretty as they are.'

He was a fair and principled man, very honest, I think, and trying his best to make a success without compromising himself. I really did believe that he would refuse me, however much cash he could make out of me. But he wasn't very nice to me, despite this clumsy attempt at a compliment. He said that he had left emotional life out of his calculations for his future: 'I had a girlfriend I was very fond of, but I gave her up, because at that time, my career came first. Now it is a bit different, and I realize that I need someone to share my life with me.'

He proceeded to cross-examine me mercilessly.

'Why are you doing this? Why did you come back from the States? What do you want from a man? Don't you think it is unrealistic to think that you will find the right person this way? What do you want out of life?'

He was always bringing me down to brute reality, and I didn't want to come down at all. Life is dreary enough with the DHSS and money worries and the situation with Mummie – I don't need strangers trying to make me more depressed by smashing my dreams. I am happy in my dream world – I want someone to fly with me, not to come crashing down to earth together. My first years had plenty of reality in them – more than most people have in a lifetime, and that's been enough for me!

He realized that Moya is the love of my life, and played on that a lot. 'Don't you feel that you are not being kind to your little girl? Don't you think you should be more realistic? Doesn't she deserve a bit more consideration?'

By this time, the food had turned to ashes in my mouth, and I could have been sitting in a transport cafe for all the pleasure I was getting from my surroundings. All I wanted to do was to get the hell out of it and go home. My monosyllabic answers made him realize that he had not been saying the things that promoted his suit, and he apologized.

'I'm sorry, Colette. I didn't mean to badger you. Please forgive me. I think you are lovely, and I want to ask you something. I'd really like to take you to a dinner party in London, on a boat, that I've been asked to. Do please say yes – everyone always expects me to come with someone, and I cannot think of anyone I would prefer to take.'

But the truth was, I couldn't stand him, and although I nodded half-heartedly, he began to realize that there was going to be no future in our relationship. He drove me home soon after this, in a mouldy little Golf, and when he called a few times, I made my excuses and told Hedi Fisher to do the rest.

The investment banker, choice number two, seemed an altogether better bet.

We met in the cocktail bar of the Queens Hotel, a gaudy,

overdone place, all red and gold and tassels. It looked more like a French boudoir than a place to have a quiet drink, and I hoped that he would be on time, so that we could arrange to move on somewhere else as soon as possible.

I wore my khaki suit, because it was a bit trendy and he was thirty years old.

I waited an hour, feeling embarrassed, humiliated, you name it. Normally when you are waiting for a girlfriend you feel embarrassed if you are kept waiting, convinced that everyone thinks you have been stood up. When you really are waiting for a man, and a stranger at that, it feels a whole lot worse. He arrived in a terrible mess, all ruffled and bothered. His shirt was hanging out of the back of his trousers, he wore no tie, and was sweaty and puffed.

Instead of greeting me properly, or even looking pleased to see that I didn't look like Hilda Ogden, he said, loudly: 'Get yourself a drink. I've got to go and check in.'

He shouted at the waiter to come over, and disappeared to sign the register.

When he came back, he shouted for the poor man again, and ordered two large drinks. He took out a packet of cigarettes and lit one, without offering me one. He shoved a handful of peanuts from the bowl on the middle of the table into his mouth, spilling a good many down his front and on the carpet, but still forcing in as many as he could fit.

'God, Colette,' he said, with his mouth almost empty of this fistful, 'I've had such a hectic drive. It was terrible, and I'm sorry I'm late.'

'That's OK,' I said, smiling distantly, but trying to be polite. He was after all taking me out for the evening.

He swilled another drink and ordered another. I thought I drank quickly, but this man would have made a warthog blink.

'I've ordered dinner,' he shouted in the general direction of the bar. 'Where do we go?'

'It's this way, sir,' came the answer, as the waiter came over carrying an empty tray to pick up the glasses.

'Come on love, let's eat. I'm starving.'

He stood up and walked off, before I had the chance to put my half-finished drink down on the table. I stood up, leaving it, and followed him, as he swaggered off, carrying his gin and tonic, swishing about in his glass.

We were the only people in the restaurant, in which 200 people would have had plenty of elbow room. It was very pretty – white linen, salmon pink, lots of flowers, the usual expensive-looking place in a nice hotel.

He was generous, I'll give him that.

'Order what you like, love,' he said, and meant it. It wouldn't have mattered to him if I'd started with ice-cream and ended with onion soup.

'I'll have the duck,' he told the hovering waiter.

'Would sir like anything to start?' he asked unctuously.

'No. Can't be bothered with any of that rubbish. I'm not really interested in food.'

I ordered only a main course too, not wanting to be eating while he waited, but I might have saved my consideration, as he then called the waiter back.

'I've changed my mind. I'll have the soup of the day.'

'Very well, sir.'

He spent the time waiting for the soup in devouring every crumb in the bread bowl. He wolfed it all down, and I took one small roll primly and put a dash of butter on the side of the plate, becoming more toffee-nosed with every bit of bad behaviour from John.

He never complimented me, which was unusual. All he did was to tease me mercilessly. I thought I was being persecuted. He christened me Lady Colette: 'Would Lady Colette like another drink? Would Lady Colette like red wine or white wine,' after which pleasantry he would roar with laughter at his own wit. I hated him. He began to drop his aitches more and more, in an affectation of being common, and talked of 'me and me mates' until I could have wept with boredom.

His soup arrived and he hardly stopped to remove his shoes before he dived into the bowl. Then the main course appeared and his mouth opened automatically to ingest whatever he had ordered, duck I think. No nonsense about waiting for me, or anything like that. Four mouthfuls later, he pushed the plate roughly away from him, knocking over anything in its way, quite heedlessly.

'This is disgusting,' he cried, with his mouth full.

He poured himself another drink from the wine bottle, not waiting for the waiter to come and do it for him, although it was clearly that sort of place, and he was hardly overworked. 'What do you do?' I asked quietly, remembering my manners although he had clearly forgotten his. I was seething with fury, but would have died rather than show I was beaten by this slob.

'I'm a Eurobond dealer. My only ambition is to retire at thirty-five, but my company, a Jap one, is very strict about forty being the earliest. I'm under enormous pressure at work all day, so in the evening I like to relax and let my hair down.'

Hedi Fisher had got a lot wrong, and one of the mistakes was that he didn't mind children at all. That was the only thing in his favour that I could see, and I was quite certain he could stand me as little as I could stand him.

Eventually I took a deep breath. 'I wonder which one of us is going to have the courage to tell the other this date's over?'

'What? What do you mean?' He looked astonished.

'Oh, come on, it's quite obvious we don't get on at all. Why don't we just call it a day?'

'Why? I'm having a really nice time. Really I am. I don't know why you're saying this.'

'Oh come *on*. You have insulted me non-stop since you clapped eyes on me, and I don't like it.'

'I'm so sorry, Colette. I have obviously been too long with my mates. I don't mean to be rude to you. I had no idea.'

'I'm not staying here, for you to be rude to me all evening, John, I can tell you.' I was warming up now.

'Tell me what I've done wrong, please, please.'

'You know exactly what you've done wrong. You've been foul all the time we've been in this hotel. I'm not used to being treated like this, I can tell you. Look, I'm going. Sorry and all that, but that's how it is.'

I half stood to leave, but his face almost crumpled. 'Please don't go, Colette. I really think you're great. I haven't met anyone like you, and you make me really nervous. Please stay. I'll try and behave.'

'Well, stop being so rude to me all the time.'

And, believe it or not, he did. He filled my glass without me asking, he asked me about myself, my mother, my daughter. He stopped bullying the waiter, and when we got up to go, he took a flower out of the vase on the table and put it in my button-hole. What had begun as the world's worst evening, looked as though it would change to one to remember. It wasn't without its flaws even now, though. I wasn't wild about his looks, although they were better than average, and his youth and mop of dark hair weren't up my street either. But things were looking up. 'Where shall we go next? What would you like to do?' asked the saint sitting to my right at the table.

'Let's go downstairs to the disco,' I suggested, and off we went, with him clasping my hand tightly.

He was very protective of me in the disco, as though he thought that one of the many other single men would snap me up. There were very few women there, so if I had wanted to, I could have had a field day, but that sort of thing is hardly a hobby of mine.

We sat at the bar to begin with, and he ordered drink after drink, all large ones. There was no way I could match his capacity, and I was getting really sloshed on my one drink for his three.

'I'm really glad you stayed. You could be the right woman for me,' he murmured against my hair, pulling me very close to him. 'You could straighten me out.'

The music was loud and rather good.

'Do you want to dance?' he asked, and I said yes. I love dancing, and usually find that men are nothing like as good as I am. This was the exception that proved the rule. He was a wonderful dancer, absolutely brilliant. A one-man show. I could be as flamboyant as I liked without being self-conscious about it, because I knew that everyone would be watching him. He never looked at any of the other women in the place, but kept his eyes on me – the only one in that disco who did. We danced and danced and danced. When the music was slow, he was just as good. He didn't try to grope me, or to kiss me when he had pulled me close to him. After two hours and about as many gallons of alcohol, he began to get amorous, however.

'Come and sit on my knee,' he kept saying.

I made all the usual excuses – I was too heavy for him, I didn't want to because I wanted to go on dancing . . . After a little while, he just picked me up and put me on his lap.

'There. That didn't hurt so much, did it?

It was 2.00 and the disco was about to close.

'Look John, I've got to go home. I've got a full day tomorrow. Thank you very much for a wonderful evening.'

'Please don't go, I'll be so lonely in my little bed upstairs.'

'I'm not going to stay in it, I can tell you,' I said sharply.

'OK, OK, but can I see you tomorrow. I don't ever want you to go, Colette. Believe me. I think you are wonderful. Please stay.'

'Call me tomorrow. But now, I've really got to go.'

'OK, but I just want to smoke a joint before I let you go. Come upstairs and have one with me. I really want to.'

'I don't smoke dope,' I said firmly, although I was hardly shocked by it after my years in the States.

'Well, come up to my room. After I've had it, I'll take you home.'

'Don't be silly. You aren't in a fit state to take me home. Just let me get a cab.'

'Here's some money for a cab, then. But wait. Please wait.' We rang for a taxi, which took a good half hour to come; all this negotiating and hanging about had taken time too, so it was now about 2.45.

'I'm going to come back to Littlehampton with you. It means I'll have another half an hour with you in the dark.'

'Oh, for heaven's sake, John. All right, if you really want to.'

We got into the cab that had driven up and I gave it the address.

'I want to come and stay at your house. Can't I?' He was like a child, a spoilt child, angling to get his own way.

'No,' I told him shortly. 'You can't.'

In the taxi on the way he took out a joint from his coat pocket and lit up in the back. We rolled the windows down and he blew the smoke outside, but I'm sure the driver knew exactly what was going on. I would have much preferred him not to, but there was no stopping him, and after all, why should he listen to me?

When we arrived outside Mummie's house, he got out sharply and paid the cab, even though he had already given me the money to do so.

The cab drove away before I had a chance to do anything about it, and he looked triumphantly at me.

'There. You can't send me away now, Colette. Can I just come in for a cup of coffee and then I'll go and get a cab back to Brighton.'

Realizing that he had me beaten, I agreed and made him a cup of coffee, steeling myself for the inevitable cajolery. It came: 'Can I stay here tonight, Colette? Can I? Please don't send me back.'

'All I want to do is sleep, you nut.' I wanted to get rid of him then more than I wanted anything, but it was clearly going to be difficult.

'OK, you can stay. But you have to promise you won't touch me.' In my room I have a sofa bed as well as my bed, and I prepared this for him. He behaved very well, getting into it with his underpants still on. I fell gratefully into mine and snuggled the duvet around me, shutting my eyes as I reached out to put my bedside light out.

It was too good to be true.

'Colette. Are you awake? I can't sleep. Come over here and give me a cuddle. Then I'll sleep. Nothing more than that. Please.'

'Oh shut up. Just go to sleep.'

'Please.'

To cut a long story short, or you will end up as irritated as I was, I got out of bed, and went over to him. I slipped in beside him, wearing my passion killer nightie, and tried to go to sleep. He slid his arms round me, and I settled back into them. Predictably he tried to get on top of me, but I wasn't having any of that, and so off he got, I climbed into my bed and we slept. Moya bounced in, all bright and breezy, at about 7.00 the next morning, and I felt as though my head was about to leave my shoulders. I crawled out of the room and dressed her, as I did each morning, wishing my head belonged to someone else. John arose at about 10, and came downstairs looking disgustingly normal.

'Let's go to Brighton Beach, the topless one. It's going to be a lovely day and we can sunbathe.'

The only reason he wanted to go there, it was obvious, was because it was a nude beach, and I really did not want to arrange myself beside many other women on the pebbles like sardines drying in the sun, ogled by all the passersby.

'No, sorry,' I said. 'I don't want to do that. It's far too crowded.'

This didn't please him at all. He agreed to go off to Brighton to pick up his car – I had seen it the night before, something red, flash and sporty, all fenders and chrome. Returning at noon, he suggested West Wittering, near Chichester, because he wanted to look at property or land there. Fine, I thought, the day was hot and it would be nice walking together looking at possible places for him to live.

I also wanted to see him sober. If he kept up the niceness, maybe there would be some kind of future for us. It was refreshing to be with somebody younger.

But no. He was back to his old self. He was wearing a dirty pair of shorts and a white T-shirt, which didn't impress my mother much when she met him.

We drove off, and the night before might never have happened. He put on whichever tapes he liked in the car without consulting me. He got out of the car when we arrived, slamming his door and walking away, with no heed to where I was. He bought a paper and read it in a small restaurant where we stopped for lunch. He was surly, unsmiling, and ordered what he wanted without asking me anything at all. He was ghastly to me all afternoon, and made up for not going to Brighton Beach (he was clearly furious about my refusal – not a good omen) by ogling every woman's chest.

'Cor, she's got a nice set. I'd love to see her without that top. Look at that pair – wouldn't I like to get my hands on those.'

We drove home at about 6 p.m., and arrived at my door at 7.

'Goodbye,' I said coldly.

'Goodbye, Colette. I'll call you.'

Oh yes, I thought. Like hell you will. And I hope you won't. But believe it or not, he did. I was very surprised, and made an excuse not to meet him. He tried again a couple of times, but I wasn't going to expose myself to that sort of treatment again.

'I'd like to see you again, Colette. Are you free next week? I could come down.'

'No, sorry, John. I'm not. And I don't think I'd like to see you again. Let's call it a day.'

And I put the phone down before I got another torrent of pleading. I had given in the last time, and it had got me precisely nowhere.

No more Hedi Fisher, I decided, after these two dates – lots of promises but nothing at the end of it except two rather gruelling evenings, and a lot of hard work for me. Not that I think what I'm doing isn't hard work, but a bit of light relief would be nice too!

I told Hedi Fisher what I thought about John (Mr Slob, as I called him) and that, as far as I was concerned, should have been the end of it.

But a couple of weeks later the telephone rang.

'Hello,' I said, without much enthusiasm – it was that sort of a day.

'Hello – Colette. Hedi here. Look, I know you told me that you didn't want to go on with us, but I think we've found you a perfect match! I really do. He's gorgeous. Just flown into town from the States. He's from Houston, Texas, and worth plenty of dollars.'

'Look Hedi, it's really good of you to bother, but I'm not interested.'

'Please Colette, he really is the tops. He doesn't mind kids, is dashing and handsome, and – well, this man is for you. He's staying in a £400 a night suite . . .'

She didn't mention a fee, so I thought, as I have so often thought, what the hell?

He called a couple of times to make contact and arrange a date. His voice was brown and creamy and soothing and strong, and his self-assured manner really cheered me up – perhaps, after all this time, Hedi Fisher was going to turn up trumps.

'I'm staying six weeks in this country, Colette, and I'd really love to meet you. Hedi Fisher has told me that you are the best on their books, and I can't wait to meet you.'

The feeling was entirely mutual, and we arranged to meet at the Grand – again. I was beginning to feel decidedly shifty every time

I went there, and was relieved when there was an unfamiliar face behind the bar. But I'm sure they recognized me, and I often wonder if I was a bit of joke below stairs – 'oh look boys. Who's she got this time?'

This time as I entered the revolving doors of the hotel, I looked around and could only see a tall man with elegant glasses and greyish bold hair – Nordically handsome, with a square jaw, and high cheekbones. He was wearing a navy jacket, beige socks, a white shirt – very well-cut clothes, very classy altogether. I was still smarting from Mr Slob, remember, so I was noticing these things more than ever.

Cor, I said to myself as I breezed past. Wish I was meeting that one.

'Excuse me,' he said, looking straight at me. 'Are you Colette Sinclair?'

I was speechless. This delicious hunk of man, with a beautiful smile and a wonderful voice, was actually my date. Not a dirty-nailed shortie, or a yob, or a weedy little creep who made me do all the talking – no, for once, my spirits soared and I thought, blimey, it's going to be a question of when I go to bed with this guy rather than if! We had a drink at the bar, and then moved on to English's, a very traditional fish restaurant near the Lanes – old-fashioned, rather masculine, civilized.

He told me that he was a professional gambler.

'I'm here for a look around, before going down for a while to Vegas,' he told me, as we tucked into our avocado prawns and lobster.

'I was a croupier at the Hotel Metropole here some years ago. I was quite good I think – it got to the point where I could spin to a section of the wheel.'

'A useful woman to have on your side,' he smiled, and we were happily in accord.

The conversation flowed smoothly. We talked about the States versus the United Kingdom. I explained, as usual, why I came back, and what I wanted to do. He told me about his life as a gambler, and I asked if I could smoke.

'I don't really like it, Colette, but if you'd like to, I don't mind.'

Oh dear, I thought, and only smoked a couple of the Silk Cut I had already got out of my bag. I spent the rest of the day nipping into loos to have a quick illicit puff or two!

We left the restaurant at about 3 p.m., feeling very contented, and I took him round the Lanes, again hoping that one of my friends would pass and see me with this lovely man, but of course nobody appeared. If I had been with the hunchback of Notre Dame, knowing my luck, a whole posse of girlfriends would have met me, and I would have been trying to disappear under a paving stone as unobtrusively as possible.

We had coffee at Browns in Ship Street – a rather arty place where you can have spaghetti or a main meal or just cake and coffee or a drink. Palms and dark wood, and slow fans overhead in summer. It's been going for years, and I've been going there for most of that time, every so often, to meet people or sit and recover from shopping, or to meet and have lunch with a girlfriend.

He was greatly pleased with it. 'I like it here very much. In fact I like it much better than either the Grand Hotel or English's. I was getting a bit worried that those sorts of places were the only ones you went to. If that had been the case, I think you would be too much of a genteel Englishwoman for me.'

'Oh no, I like all sorts of places. Depends on mood and companion really. I'm glad you like it here.'

We parted company at the station, where I dropped him in my little Golf, and I drove home, paying hardly any attention to the road and other drivers, humming a happy tune, and smiling a lot.

'Looks like you had a nice day, Colette,' said sharp-eyed Mummie, as I walked in the front door. 'A good one?'

'Oh, he's divine. Handsome and polite and intelligent and rich . . . this may be the one, this may really be the one.'

The next day he telephoned, and asked politely if he could take me out again.

'Where would you like to go, Maurice?' I asked.

'Wherever you say. What would you prefer?'

'What about a day in the English countryside. I don't suppose you've had much chance to have a look around here. It's worth it – very green and pretty, and if it's a lovely day, I'm sure you'll love it.'

So that was that. I picked him up at the station in Brighton and we drove off homeward bound – I intended to show him some country pubs on the way. It was a little less of a perfect encounter than the day before, because he was rather different – a cold and a hangover made him rather snivelly, complaining that he had never been so cold in his life. True, the temperature was not in the 90s, but the sun was out, and it was a bright winter's day.

First we stopped at the Royal Oak, my favourite pub in the area. But that wasn't what he wanted. 'I'd really like to go back to your place and have a cup of hot coffee to warm up. Could we go now, do you think?'

Sure, we could, and we did, but I felt pretty cheesed off with my Sir Gawain turned into the Green Knight, shivering and no fun at all.

He drank his coffee, clutching it like the Holy Grail, to continue the Arthurian metaphor, and was very uncommunicative.

'Do you want the blower fire on?' I asked solicitously. 'I understand how cold you must feel. I was like this when I got back here from California.'

Five minutes later, he was lying on my bed in my room, saying he felt awful.

'Could I just have a little rest, and then we can get going?'

Trying to smile, and hold on to the last vestiges of my adoration of this angel, who was showing his feet of clay in a very embarrassing manner, I agreed, and waited till he felt better. By now it was almost noon, and I waited, hopping from foot to foot because we had booked the restaurant at the Baliffscourt Hotel for one.

We had arranged to take Moya with us. For some reason, he got everything just right with her. He wasn't all over her, he didn't shout at her when she was a bit naughty, he was firm and capable, and she was putty in his hands.

When he awoke, at about 1.15, I plugged him up with aspirins, pushed Moya into her prettiest coat and buckled her little red shoes, and we set off, at last. We arrived at 2.00, an hour late for the table. The hotel agreed we could have lunch, to my relief, and in we went to the large, comfortable, olde-worlde restaurant – old-fashioned without being twee. Bailiffscourt is a 'mediaeval manor', or rather a house built in the 1930s in the style of one, and it manages to achieve a sense of age and history. The restaurant ceiling was panelled in dark heavy wood, and the arched windows, set in stone, were diamond-paned, letting in a fractured light that settled gently on the cream walls and the large tapestried chairs at the tables. There was a sense of substance, of solidity, of good old England, and I thought he would love it.

He seemed to. He looked after Moya very well, generously asking the waiter to bring little bits from each part of the menu for her. She loved it, too, and her good behaviour helped the atmosphere, which was beginning to lighten. We had pudding in the living room, which was more of the same wooden magnificence and comfort. When Moya wanted to go to the potty he came with us to show us the way and, when she got fidgety, he came with me to take her out into the garden, where we walked about among the flower beds and down to the pool.

'This is lovely,' he said, and I felt at last that I had done something right. 'I would like to come here and stay one day soon.'

We walked over to feed some ponies apples and, when he threw them into the pond for a dog to fetch, Moya was giggling and screaming with glee. He was perfect with her, and I felt that to be a very strong point in his favour, and was almost beginning to forget the sniffles earlier.

I took him then on to the cottage of some friends of mine, Jane and Michael, which was still part of old England, and the atmosphere we had lunched in. Peacocks strut about on their grass, and they have dogs, cats, rabbits all over the place. They liked Maurice, and Moya liked her ride on Polly their pony, so all in all, I decided the afternoon had been a success.

Back in Littlehampton, I was forced to acknowledge that Moya had liked the day most. I was still feeling a little irritated, because his whining about feeling lousy had started again, when he didn't have anything else to take his mind off himself. I left him at the station, waving a thankful goodbye and wondering if we would meet again.

His occupation was a bit dodgy too.

'I run what you might call illegal poker games in Houston,' he said. 'People play with plastic chips, all above board, and then I go round later with some friends to collect the money they stand for. Sometimes there's a little resistance, but we usually sort it out.'

Sounded a little too much like Al Capone in Chicago for my liking. His '£400 a night suite' was costing him £96 a week, in fact, because it was off season and he had taken it for a while. In fact he asked me about more affordable hostels where he could stay and wanted to know about travelling cheap . . . not exactly what I had in mind.

It was just as well therefore that I didn't hear from him again. Although he said he was forty-four, he looked thirty-six, and very handsome, but his manner was more cold and aloof the second time I met him. He seemed a lot less taken with me than most of the men I meet – not to be big-headed, just factual. I wasn't offended, but it didn't help matters. He didn't have any sense of humour I could connect with, and I just don't think I got through to him at all.

So that was the end of Hedi Fisher's efforts – she certainly tried, and it wasn't her fault she wasn't able to pair me off with the right chap. It just goes to show that very few of the right chaps go to agencies, and so I decided to save my money and keep at it on my own.

But this wasn't the end of agencies in my life. As you know, I appeared on *Wogan*, and among my fellow guests was the woman who runs English Rose, Christina Rhodes. The agency finds suitable English girls for American men, and on the show, she told me and everyone watching that she would find me someone, and my membership would be complimentary.

I almost forgot about the whole thing, taken up as I was with subsequent dates and disappointments, until one day, one of my letters was from her, on nice parchment, reminding me of her existence, and giving me a list of men to choose from.

The first one was a television producer, 'gorgeous, intelligent, looking for a relationship perhaps leading to marriage'. Another was Jewish, and although I am not anti-semitic, I can foresee problems with orthodoxy, etc. Another was a physician/surgeon, but he lived in an apartment, which at the age of thirty-five, to me at any rate, meant that he wasn't doing all that well. You can't be too careful, but even after all these years, I can misread the signs.

Among the others, some disliked smoking, another was only 5 feet 8 inches and a Catholic. A vet seemed quite nice, and I had to laugh about the Jaguar specialist, who probably put 'mechanic' on his application form, and was suitably jazzed up. It was also amusing to note that many 'occasionally' smoked – I don't know *any* occasional smokers. All were slim, too – it would be cutting your own throat to admit to obesity, and a few extra pounds can be overlooked.

The selection didn't seem any different to the men I found for myself in magazines, but I suppose the hard work of weeding out the horrors was done for me. The television producer sounded the best, so I wrote to him. He lived in Vermont, so of course I looked it up on the map, and hoped that he would be a good bet. Another one was Muslim and a travel agent, and, as I like to travel, I thought at least I'd be able to do that. The vet was also a possibility – it would be nice to have a cat for Moya and I like people who are kind to animals.

So the possibilities, just before Christmas, seemed endless and exciting. Accustomed as I am to being disappointed, I still can whip up enthusiasm and hope, thank goodness.

I was disappointed – only the television producer answered. I had sent photostats of my photographs – one with me sitting on the floor in trousers, lots of necklaces and a heavy cardigan around my shoulders; another of me in a white dress smiling outside a novelty shop in the States; one of me with Moya and a friend's little girl on my knee (sitting on the floor again, I don't know why) and one of me looking carefree and summery leaning against a white wall overlooking the sea and some palm trees. Obviously most of the men didn't find these appealing, which was a sobering thought.

But the letter from the TV producer (my first choice) cheered me up and made me forget the others – more fool them!

'Dear Colette,' he began on grey paper edged with a thin white stripe. It was scented, too, a soft smell of talcum powder, sweet but not poofy. 'I have received your lovely letter . . . It was nice to hear from you and I am delighted to write back.'

He explained, rather embarrassedly, that 'it was most unusual for me to join the English Rose agency,' and lots of other excuses. I could sympathize – I felt like that too when I started and occasionally come over all flustered still. The interesting part of his letter was to come:

'I am 6 feet 3 inches and 185 pounds. Born April 1951. I like all the things you would imagine – theatre, music, sports, movies, etc. And if you haven't noticed yet, I have very bad handwriting.'

He did, too, half capitals, half small letters, almost completely illegible, but I got the gist. He worked for the BBC and CBS and went often to the UK. 'You mentioned that you lived in the US for nine years. I would like to hear [or it could have said wold luk to hoar] more. I live in Vermont, a wonderfully historic area just outside of Washington DC. I would like to hear too about the career you have postponed with the birth of your daughter. I will be coming to the UK in December and it is possible we could get together. I would love to get another letter from you.'

He asked all sorts of questions about the photographs I had sent, or rather the photocopy of the four pictures, and asked about Moya, always a good sign.

'In case you are wondering, I have no children. Mostly the result of all work and no play, but children are something I am looking forward to. Maybe that's a good sign for me.' There, what did I tell you?

His photographs looked splendid – he was tall and blond and bearded and looked 6 feet 3 inches and rather glamorous. I couldn't wait. But I had to, until December, and so I contacted English Rose again.

'Come down to our office,' said Christina Rhodes sweetly – her voice was saccharine sweet – so I drove down to Margate. It was like a rally drive that day. The wind was howling and the sea was thrown up over the wall on the sea front, and pebbles dashed against my windscreen as I screwed up my eyes and pushed on, hardly able to see.

I walked eventually into the Greek restaurant where we had arranged to meet. I was very late, and felt embarrassed, but the weather spoke for me. As we sat there, the rain hammered on the windows and, although I was too late for last orders at 2.00, I had a drink, and they managed a salad rather grudgingly from the kitchen. We were all cold and wet, me rather more than Christina and her assistant, Joanne.

After shivering through my lettuce, Christina suggested we go on to her office where I could have a cup of coffee in the warm, dry off, and look through her books at leisure.

She had a selection of men for me to look at. After glancing at about ten, I made four piles: totally yuk, rather nice, so-so ones I couldn't be bothered with, and those who had not responded to the letter she had sent out about me.

Let me reproduce it here. It is so fulsome that even I blush, and I came armed with one concocted by Mummie, which we both thought gave a truer picture of me.

Christina had written:

> I am writing to you with the personal details of one of our most outstanding clients, a young lady named Colette Sinclair. Colette is thirty-one years old, although she looks younger. She is 5 feet 8 inches tall, slim, with long golden brown hair and sparkling hazel eyes.
>
> Colette has been educated privately and has a charming, well-spoken, cultured English accent. She is fair skinned with a lovely English Rose complexion.
>
> Colette's interests include: fashion (she dresses beautifully and is immaculately groomed), travel, dinner parties, private clubs, the arts, theatre, cinema, concerts, museums, literature, drawing, sports (including badminton, tennis, squash, swimming, horse-riding, aerobics) and horse racing.

The next bit was the part Mummie had written, as Christina's first letter said nothing about children at all, and gave entirely the wrong impression:

> Colette loves children and has a sweet 2½-year-old daughter of her own. She enjoys both town life and the countryside, and

seeks a secure, happy homelife with a compatible gentleman who would also share some of her interests.

Then back to Christina's original:

He should be attractive and financially secure, with a good sense of humour, fun and adventure, kind, considerate, well mannered and enjoy a family life as well as socializing.

[She asked for photographs and told them to telephone, adding,]

Please accept my recommendation of Ms Sinclair as one of our most attractive and charming English Roses. I wish you success in contacting her, as I feel sure that she will be in great demand. She has a great deal to offer the right partner!

By this time, Christina had loosened up a bit. We had had quite a lot of wine at the restaurant, to make up for the wilting salad, and she began to laugh and had stopped sounding quite so sugary.

We had great fun, looking over each other's shoulders and making comments about the men.

'Yuk,' I would say.

'No, no, he's really nice,' she would protest.

'Well, you have him then,' I'd laugh and that would result in peals of laughter from all of us.

I asked about any funny happenings in the office, with all the applications Christina must get.

'Oh gosh, we get all sorts,' she told me, laughing. 'One chap asked us if we would like some nude photographs of him, and of course we said yes . . . They never arrived.'

Another one, she told me, sent photographs of himself, as asked. Some were entirely predictable, in a suit, on the beach, in his house. Some, however, were of him lying sprawled across his desk, stark naked with a sticker over where his penis should have been.

'Of course we couldn't resist. We set to, and scratched it off, but when we had cleared it, we found that it had already been scratched away!'

We got to one, and Joanne squealed, 'I want him, I want him.'

We all grabbed his letter, but when he said that he looked like Christopher Reeve, I was sceptical.

'Why has he only sent two long-distance photographs then?'

The rest of his letter said things about 'women should know

their own sexuality' – 'see, I knew he was sexy,' said Joanne triumphantly.

One chap had sparrows' legs; another, a vet, looked even less attractive. There were a couple of Mexican-looking men, who looked all right, but I wasn't mad about them. I pored through most of her files, and came to the conclusion that she had come up with the pick of the bunch.

I picked out one more, a rancher, but she said she hadn't included him because of his bad spelling. So I put him back, but doubtfully; my spelling isn't anything to write home about. I enjoyed the afternoon, and came home with some more to write to. I tried them all, and tried hard but they didn't work out. One was old and dull, an expert in real estate, with two stepchildren and an ex-wife who had become ex almost as soon as they got married. The conversation on the telephone was strained and I wasn't enthusiastic.

One man I wrote to in Costa Rica. He wrote back enthusiastically, saying he was successful and had a good job and sent photographs of himself sitting in his house. I got out my magnifying glass (I have really become a professional) and scrutinized his room. The books on his shelf included '*The Key to Success*' and I wondered why, if he was such a whizz, he needed such things so prominently placed.

Another sent a photograph of a large, low house, with a golf course outside it. He looked bronzed and rather handsome, and in the old days I would have leapt at him. I'd have been fantasizing about living in his house and enjoying golf and having a family among the rolling fields, but I know better now. He probably worked there in the summer and caddied for the rich people who could afford to go there. I dashed off a letter to him, and asked him about his finances and whether the house in the photo was his. I didn't get a reply.

At the same time, I was having an odd telephonic relationship with a man who had heard an interview with me on Australian radio. His letter was long and fulsome, his photograph rather a pleasant surprise.

'Throughout the interview, I could not help but imagine your physical appearance. As your personality and quality as a person shone through the ether, it was evident that I had to contact you. What is most interesting of all is that I am very much attracted to you.'

He would telephone me from Australia, and tell me some more how marvellous I was, what a sexy voice I had, how attractive he found me, and I was giving him very little encouragement by now. I had even been sent a poem, which made me smile and feel embarrassed. Hardly high art or great literature:

I don't yet know
What it is I feel,
But my heart never lies
So it must be real.

Out of nothing something grew
And here I am alongside you
I miss you at night
and all through the day
It's hard when you live
So far away.

It's only new
And yet to grow
The hours apart
Go much too slow.

I'm still not sure
What it is I see
But I know you mean
A lot to me.

There was no way I would have got together with him, but I think I helped him. He had a stutter when he began telephoning me, and my mother would get very irritated when she answered the telephone and it was him. But by the end of a number of conversations, the stutter had gone, and I felt that at least he would be able to deal with women a little better in future.

Our conversations were strange. He would ask me to describe myself.

'No way. I would be much too embarrassed. You already know, anyway. I'm 5 feet eight, slim, brunette.'

'You sound so pretty. Does it make any difference that I am shorter than you?'

'No, not really. How short are you – you said 5 feet 7 inches, didn't you?'

There was a pause: 'yes'.

My mother would be hopping up and down by the telephone,

waving her arms at me and mouthing 'tell him, tell him,' but I couldn't, I didn't have the heart.

He said he would send me photographs in his next letter, but this took a very long time to come. As I've said, when they did arrive, it was a pleasant surprise. Nice smile, white even teeth, well-cut dark hair, large brown eyes, smooth olive skin. Not bad at all.

'Have you met anyone else,' he would ask sometimes.

'Yes,' I would say, telling the truth. 'There's someone from America who looks hopeful. He's coming over in January – he's a film producer.'

Then he would become jealous and prying, asking questions about the way he looked, what exactly he produced, where he lived.

'Maybe I'll come over in December,' he said. 'Depends on my finances. I've just bought two houses, so I'm a bit tight at the moment.'

I didn't believe a word of all this, because once, in an unguarded moment, he had told me that he was living with his parents, but I didn't argue. I would get off the telephone, eventually, making some stupid transparent excuse, but he would always call back, to my disappointment.

'Hello, my sweetheart,' he would say. He always called me that – 'give me a kiss. I've been thinking about you so much.'

Sometimes I would be in a good mood, and then I would be kinder to him than at others, and give him a chance. Once I foolishly gave him too much of a one.

'Do you know what I really want to do?'

'No.'

'Make love to you.'

I could have kicked myself, and turned it aside with a laugh, but made sure that I wasn't so careless in future.

Eventually he stopped calling. I hope he found himself a girl. I wish him the best of luck, and hope that his long and fruitless conversations with me calmed him down and made it easier for him to have relationships with women in future.

The English Rose agency deserves ten out of ten for trying. Christina really did her best and sent me many men, most of whom were in my range, but some who weren't. These I felt sorry for, for there was no way I was going to write back to them, but I suppose she was hoping that something would catch my eye enough for me to compromise a bit. Many were well off, and would suit someone perhaps less choosy than me very well. I have been doing this for too long to settle for anyone who isn't Mr Damn Nearly Right. I have come down from Mr Absolutely Perfect, but a girl does have standards!

I hadn't heard from the television producer since I had answered his letter, and was beginning to feel that Vermont was going to remain a twinkle in my eye, when one day, after several English Rose conversations and letters which had led to nothing, I decided to call him, and find out if there was anything in it. Mummie was not very happy about me calling America, but I managed to get her to agree, as long as I was quick about it.

'Hello,' I said, shakily. I was embarrassed about making the call, and my voice gave me away. It got stronger quickly, though.

'I was calling to see if you had received my letter. I know the Christmas post is bad and I wondered if it had got lost.'

'How nice to hear from you. I was thrilled to get your letter, which has only just arrived. I was just going to call you, in fact. Look, would it be better if I called you back?'

'Yes,' I breathed gratefully. 'That would be great.'

Usually when people say that, they get round to it hours or even days later, so I was thrilled when the phone rang almost at once.

He did a lot of the talking, which even my mother noticed and remarked on.

His career was a good one; he had struck lucky just out of college, and was given a job as producer out of 200 people. He was working on a six-part series for the BBC, did lots of work for CBS, and was generally very busy. He told me he had had forty-five replies from English Rose, so of course, I told him I had had a lot too. Not *entirely* untrue!

'It's very pretty here in Vermont. I'm sorry, Colette, I'm afraid I can't meet you over Christmas like we said because my father's ill and I have to care for him. Another time – I'll come over in the New Year. Will I need to hire a car? We could spend some time together.'

I told him about all the country hotels in Sussex and around but he just laughed at that without saying anything, which puzzled me. But that was the only slightly wrong note – he asked about Moya, twice, and I really thought that this was just the ticket.

'Oh Mummie. It's going to work, it's really going to work . . . This might well be the one . . .'

But nothing came of it. If it had happened earlier on in my man hunt, I would have been devastated. As it was, I was very disappointed, hurt and puzzled, but got over it after about a week, using the effective remedy of looking ahead for the next possibility.

9

Married Men

Of course, the world is full of married men, men who do very well without agencies like Hedi Fisher or English Rose. Some women seem to be attracted only to married men. It seems to make the chase more exciting, the catching more dangerous, and the eventual tearing away from the wife a great challenge and success if it happens.

Look at all the women sitting in tears at railway stations, waving at trains pulling out with their lover on it, going back to wife and family, however. This is proof, if proof were needed, about what a very dangerous game it all is. Some wives know and don't mind, some even do it themselves, but on the whole men prefer to stay married if they can. They probably love their wives, in some way or another, and they feel secure enough to embark on all sorts of extramarital adventures, knowing they have the perfect excuse for lack of final commitment at home.

If marriages aren't working out, then I suppose it's a different matter, but how does one know what is the truth? Many men just say that they are about to divorce, women believe them and then they find out that the wife is pregnant and they have plans to move together to a much bigger house.

I played around a lot when I was younger and less experienced in the hard game of living. I don't mean that I am now equipped to give advice from a wealth of knowledge, but I do sympathize with the woman who said, 'You just need to look at how few men leave their wives for their lovers to realize the strength of marriage.' And now that I am looking for a *husband*, not just a lover or a boyfriend, I can put myself in the position of the wife, and I know I would hate to know my husband was having an affair, even if he stayed with me in the end. I am now truly sorry for the pain I caused to the wife of the man I was involved with.

Since I started looking for a husband in earnest, I have only encountered three married men I have had anything to do with. On my way back from Philippe in Los Angeles, I sat next to a tall, blond, handsome man. Well-spoken and polite, he offered me the window seat, and when I gratefully accepted, flirted with me for the nine-hour flight.

He told me he had married a woman with a two-year-old child, a daughter who was now eleven, and they had had another son. He had a happy enough life on the surface: 'She is a loving and devoted mother, but we sleep in separate rooms. Have done for the last six months. We haven't divorced because of the children, but that's all that is keeping us together.'

He flirted with the air hostess too, just to show me that he was well known among the flight attendants, and this did seem to be the case. We talked some more about our pasts. I told him a bit about my marriages, with the usual judicious editing.

'I hear once you have tasted Middle Eastern men,' he said, 'you don't enjoy going back to Europeans or Americans. Is that the case? Do you find them exotic?'

'Yes,' I told him, and then could have bitten off my tongue. Here I was sitting next to the exact opposite of a Middle Eastern man, and I was praising them.

Not that he minded. We chatted amiably, with twinkles in both our eyes, but with no thought of the future in my head.

We went through customs, shook hands cordially, and went away from each other, in different directions.

Six months later, I was amazed to hear from my mother that he had called when I was out at badminton.

I called him back – couldn't resist it of course. All keyed up as I was, I was surprised to find him not in.

'Sorry, can I help you?' said a male voice.

'Only to take a message please. Please tell Henry that Colette rang.'

'OK, will do, with pleasure.'

I purposely didn't leave my number – if he wanted to talk to me, he would have to look it up again.

He rang me later that night.

'I've thought about you a lot, Colette. I've just been to LA and the flight back wasn't anything like as pleasant as the one when I was sitting next to you. I'm coming down to Brighton in the next few days. I wondered if you would like to come and have lunch with me.'

I agreed, but he never called to confirm so I concluded that this situation was one best left alone.

The conversation had been slow and the veiled implication was that we were only to speak again if there was going to be something between us. It hadn't been just a friendly invitation, and I needed to know if he was still married. But he wasn't giving much away. Another trait of the married man who is watching his back.

A month later, he rang again.

'Sorry, Colette. But last time, I never did come down to Brighton so I felt there was no point in calling just for a chat. That's not really on the cards, is it? I'm going to Los Angeles again, next week. Is there anything I can do for you while I'm there?'

'No, it's all right,' I told him. 'I don't need anything. Have a nice trip. Enjoy the sunshine!'

'I will. Goodbye.'

But that still wasn't the end of it. He called again. I was out. He tried again, and got me. The conversation was stilted, as always, and I knew he was still married, although of course he didn't say so. He knew I knew, and we knew that this wasn't going anywhere. I recall a girlfriend who did marry the man she was having an affair with, and she never trusted him again, probably with good reason. Perhaps she was the love of his life, but perhaps he was just like that, and preferred extramarital activity to the sedate contentment of married life. As for me, chance would be a fine thing – give me a bit of sedate contentment any day of the week. I've had the hurly burly of the chaise-longue, I now ache for the deep contentment of the double bed, as Mrs Patrick Campbell so wisely said. But if Henry ever did split up with his wife, I wouldn't mind if he called me again, although I am well aware of his sparkling eyes, and unambiguous ambiguities, if you get me.

Another encounter was with Mr Ascot. On the way back from Monaco, with a chin sandpapered by Michel's stubble, and a spring in my step, I travelled on the coach from the hotel to the helicopter with a couple of men who were sitting a couple of seats away from me.

One was a joker, loud and jolly. His friend was better-looking, quieter, and softly spoken. He looked classy, about forty-two, 6 feet tall, with black hair. (I could get a job with a private detective agency or Scotland Yard, I've become so good at noticing things about men!)

The loud one was being just that, and I thought, oh God, what an obnoxious pair.

'Would you like a drink?' he asked me.

'No, thanks,' I answered coolly. Meaning not on your life,

which is how they took it, and I could see them thinking 'stuck-up bitch'.

'Do you have a peppermint?' he asked, not deterred for long.

'No, but I have some chewing gum. Will that do?'

'Oh, yes, it's only so that our wives don't catch the demon alcohol on our breath!'

'Where have you been?'

'Monte Carlo, visiting friends,' I said, and blushed when they both looked at my chin and smiled.

'I can see that by your face darling,' said the noisy one, and nudged his friend, who had the grace to look away.

I ignored them for a while, and then was asked, 'Why Monte Carlo?'

'Because I felt like some fun and a short holiday. No one is fun any more in Britain. No one is spontaneous.'

I told them a bit about what I was doing, and I could see they were fascinated, like most people are, whatever they think about it. 'No girlfriends would come with me to somewhere where I'd be likely to meet anyone, so I went by myself.'

'Brave talk, darling, but I bet you wouldn't go out with my friend if he asked you, would you?'

I was stuck now, and, not wanting to look a sissy, I said: 'Of course I would.' And turned to the good-looking one and smiled at him.

'Would you kindly escort me to Ascot tomorrow,' he asked, looking embarrassed but obviously pleased.

'Yes, I'd be delighted. Call me tonight, if you still feel like it.'

'Right, that's settled. We've got to go now, so we'll see you on to the train, and if the wives catch sight of us, we'll all have to pretend we don't know each other,' said the common one, which bothered me a bit, but I was too tired to argue, and decided that I would sort all this out later.

The quiet man did call that night, and said he would be round to pick me up at noon.

'That would be lovely. There's just one problem. I haven't got a hat. Does that matter too much?'

'Not at all,' he said. 'We'll stop off on the way and pick one up for you.'

As it happened, I didn't have to ask him to do that. It would have taken too much time, and I didn't know him that well. I put something together at home, late into the night, and although it did end up looking a bit flower-powery, it also looked very pretty

– strawberry leaves and net – with my white backless cotton dress.

He appeared in a large silver Range Rover, which fitted the bill very nicely, and off we went. He looked just right too, in a dark suit, expensive, with no embarrassing bits and pieces. There felt nothing bad about this jaunt – he told me he loved his wife, and showed me pictures of his son. No innuendoes or long looks occurred, and we had a perfectly smashing day together. He gave me £50 to play with, slipping it into my purse, with no fuss. We had lobster and champagne for lunch. He was great company, really normal, and charming. We both knew it wasn't going anywhere, so we could both relax and get on with enjoying ourselves.

He asked me for dinner. I agreed, and we went somewhere nearby, Chez Jean, I think it was called. The food was delicious, the restaurant comfortable and intimate and we talked away to each other without restraint. He told me that his wife worked on an airline, which meant long hours and lots of gay friends, which he didn't mind – 'better than lots of straight men wanting to take her out' – but it got a bit tedious. He was essentially conventional, public-school educated, and wanted a simple, comfortable, conventional marriage. Their social lives didn't go together. Hers was very camp, and his was down-to-earth, out with the lads sometimes, in with the family and friends at others.

We spent hours in the restaurant, and I began to think it was pushing it a bit when the clock struck midnight.

'Oh no. My wife won't worry. She keeps long hours too. I'm sure we will get to the stage when we will split up eventually, but I love my son, and I know I wouldn't get custody of him if we did.' What could I say? I made sympathetic noises, and soon we got up to leave.

On the way home he bought sweets for Moya at the petrol station, which was sweet of him. We said a nice goodbye, with no kissing or cuddling, and the day stays in my mind as no more, no less than it should have been – a lovely day out.

Mr Colette, you may remember, was another encounter on the plane back from Monaco. He gave me his card and told me to call him. The idea of the same name fascinated me. Not knowing whether he was married or not, I thought it might be amusing to be called Colette Colette.

He called me, as it turned out. He arranged a date, in his impeccable English: we agreed to meet in the hotel used by the Wimbledon players so, while I waited (he was late, something I find unforgivable) I saw Ivan Lendl, and knew that Martina was about, and there were several other familiar faces, including Cash, who hadn't won the title then.

This is a horrid little episode, and I am ashamed to say it was my stupidity that caused me to sit through it till the bitter end. I have now learnt my lesson, and don't intend to do it again, but at the time, I was rather caught up in the process, and didn't think of getting out of it. Not that anything awful happened; I just felt a fool.

He eventually appeared, after I had sat at the bar for an hour, and left a note in his message box at the desk. I should not have waited; if there's a next time, I shan't.

Mr Colette bought me a drink and one for himself, and then explained that the World Cup was on at 7 p.m., and he would like to watch it. It was now about 6, so he would have time for a bit of a chat now, but would I come up to the room and watch it with him, and we could then have dinner?

'I don't mind watching it in the bar,' I said, dutifully. 'But I'm not coming up to your room. I never do on a first date.' He was not pleased. I got the usual bit about how happily married he was, and he had three children, and all he wanted was to watch the match and wouldn't touch me. *All* my common sense had not deserted me, and I believed not a word. Why, if he was so happily married, had he called me in the first place? I didn't know he was married at all when we made the date, and was very surprised, although of course I should have checked, or at least been a bit more suspicious.

But nothing came of anything. I wasn't prepared to go to his room, he wasn't prepared to miss the match. I felt sure that what he really wanted was to watch the match and then, with me on his bed or on a chair, or even on his knee, have a bit of rough and tumble, for which he would pay by taking me out to a meal. No bloody fear. And when I saw him again, away from the glamour of airports and duty free shops and Monte Carlo, he looked a lot less attractive, so it was no blow to get up, say a polite goodbye and go home, wiser and crosser. I hope his team won.

10

The Love of My Life

Beautiful
British
Brunette thirty. Tall/slim with daughter aged one seeks confident, original, kind man with joie de vivre to create a family. Previous US resident nine years. Daughter US citizen. Presently residing UK. Write to Newspress Box AAA 1232 Santa Barbara

That was the ad that attracted Mr Conceited – Paul White, the third man I fell in love with. The second was Michel in Monte Carlo, and the 'half' I mentioned on *Wogan* was my second date – Mr Wonderful, for whom I was nothing like adventurous enough, alas.

I got fifteen replies from the advertisement but none of the others were anything like suitable. By the time Paul's letter arrived, I'd given up hope of anyone I'd like answering the advertisement, and anyway, I wasn't impressed with the paper he'd written on or his handwriting. What did catch my eye was the tone – very up, very positive, bouncy, ebullient.

Dear Beautiful,

I wanted to write earlier but I have been on the go lately. All of the possibilities sound wonderful. We must meet soon! I am thirty-two years young, have never married and I have established a very strong emotional and financial base for myself. I have my own business in Santa Barbara and own real estate (home, etc.) all of which I have acquired myself from hard work, etc. Now I am beginning to relax and enjoy my life. But in Santa Barbara it is not easy to meet the right person in which I can share my love and life with [dodgy grammar there, I thought]. As for children, anyone around me will tell you they are my real soft spot that makes my heart melt. I especially, being a man who grew up in a household of four boys, I am somewhat attached to daughters.

I am considered very handsome, 6 feet tall, very fit, intelligent, articulate, self-confident, sensitive, and very caring and loving . . . and much much more!

If you will wish to meet me, we will have so much to talk about and then look to our future lives . . . I am awaiting and look forward to hearing from you.

He didn't send photos, and he didn't whisk me off my feet by writing and calling, but when we did talk, he explained that my letter had been locked away in his brother's briefcase, which is why he took so long to answer me.

His background sounded fine – 'my father has an antiques business and I have a couple of dealerships – one with Yamaha and one with Boston Whaler' – and soon we were arranging for him to come over to England so that we could meet. It was lovely, fun and lighthearted, more like planning a holiday between friends, with no hint of sex, than beginning a relationship. There was no strain, and I began to look forward greatly to him coming, although he finally decided he would come in December before I expected to get photographs, so I had only his word to go on that he was 'very handsome'.

Eventually I got a card, a very English one with a picture by Edward Killingworth Johnson on it, very old-fashioned, full of flowers and trees and demure little girls.

Dear Colett, [I was a little put off that he hadn't bothered to get my name right.]

Your sunshine card has brightened all my days. I am sorry for the delay of these pictures, but most of the photos I have are of everyone else. So I collected these few recent pictures and am sending them especially for you! No! You didn't kill the cat! [I had said that curiosity was killing me, like it had killed the cat.] Honestly I am so excited about all of this, time seems to pass very quickly and I must make plans for England at Christmas. I think you will love the pictures . . . In the one photo I am holding my niece, and that's my dad beside kissing her. In the other I'm standing with my brother. Now you know what Paul looks like. But remember, great looks are only half of it . . . I have a heart full of love, sharing, sensitivity, and emotion! I'll call you in approx ten days or sooner.

Despite his enthusiastic sell, I didn't think he looked all that wonderful. He had a nice open face, but quite honestly I thought he looked a bit fat. His clothes looked good, though, and that is always impressive: loose denim jacket, and those rather sexy pleated khaki trousers in one picture; a smart red short-sleeved shirt in another, a big gold watch prominently displayed on an arm in a pale blue shirt casually turned back a few folds at the wrist. All rather smartly casual, showing that he took a lot of care with his appearance. He had a nice smile, although in some of the photographs it looked posed, a little stiff.

I wasn't interested in him as a prospect by now, but he did sound fun, alive, vibrant, and I needed a bit of a lift in the midwinter cold and depression. Whatever happened, at least he would provide that – some Christmas cheer.

I heard nothing for a while, and life went on as usual, with his visit a little thought in the back of my mind, but not much more. I had grown used to things not happening, but this one looked very likely. He phoned again in late November, saying that he had been away and was definitely coming over.

I believed him and threw myself into drawing up an itinerary to make his visit a success. He didn't want to commit himself, though, and whatever I suggested he would make approving noises about, but wouldn't fix a date or a definite arrangement. I suggested *The Phantom of the Opera* (not from entirely selfless motives, I admit) and said that, although the tickets were expensive, they would be increasingly so as Christmas drew nearer. No response. I suggested a New Year's Eve Scottish Night, in Brighton, but although he said, 'Mmmm,' and 'Yeah, that would be nice', nothing firmer was agreed. I was thinking along the lines of the Orient Express, and all sorts of jolly outings, but was hesitant about using my credit card, in case I didn't get reimbursed. Just as well I didn't, because although he said he'd send his American Express card number, it never arrived. 'Maybe he isn't going to come,' said Mummie, down to earth as ever. I still wasn't sure why I had accepted Marian's four day Christmas excursion to meet Philippe.

But she was wrong. He turned up, as arranged, in a hired maroon Mercedes, at nine on Christmas Eve. I was all over the place, trying to put together a large slide we had bought for Moya's Christmas present, and I could have done with an evening's grace, but it was not to be. In he breezed, as if the world was invented for him, and I thought, oh, my God. He was not my type – in Annie Hall glasses with red rims, he put me off *a lot.* He had said he was thirty-two – I thought he looked ten years older. He had said 6 feet – he looked shorter. I was decidedly disappointed, but I put a brave face on it, and resigned myself to having a pleasant, friendly time, and nothing more. I might even be able to persuade him to change his glasses! I didn't have any complaints about his hairy chest, which peeped out from his rather good Italian shirt, tucked into well-cut baggy trousers – they were all right too.

'Hi, Colette,' he said loudly, sticking out his hand. 'Mrs Sinclair,' he turned to my mother. 'I am so glad to be here, glad to know you.' He was like a large St Bernard puppy, exuberant, and oozing confidence.

Oh God, I thought. I'm stuck with this for ten days. How on earth am I going to be able to cope with it?

'I am so pleased to be here,' he went on. 'I think England is wonderful. And it is great to be staying for Christmas with such a warm family as you are.'

We went for a quick late drink at the Shepherd and Dog pub which of course he thought was 'wonderful' too. He didn't think my smoking cigarettes was wonderful, however, and I carried on regardless of his disapproval, hoping that it would put him off.

It was unfair of me – he couldn't have tried harder to be nice. He adored the 'warm festive atmosphere' in the pub, and did his best to be nice to everyone in it. He was brash and American, putting it on a bit more so that everyone would notice; he seemed to love everybody, and everybody seemed to love him.

'I love the pace of life here, in this country. It feels so slow and calm!'

I came in for my share of his enthusiasm too, of course. 'I love the way you dress Colette. It is really smart and tasteful. You are a very attractive woman.'

I had made an effort, I must say. I was wearing a very expensive black and turquoise sweater with a V-neck in beautifully soft wool, over a skirt that looked like tapestry, in a mixture of mauve, turquoise, black and gold. Black patent boots brought out the shine in the jumper.

Eventually, after I had overdosed on the enthusiasm, I began to see that he was a sensitive little boy underneath it all, needing a lot of mothering. He loved my mother, and was very respectful to her. Later she told me that she had noticed that, if there was any conflict of opinion between us, he would always stick up for her – it was as though he needed the stability of mother always knowing best.

He listened sympathetically when I told him about Moya's father, and about being dependent on my mother and the DHSS. He was appreciative of my mother's very plain English cooking, which he sampled after the pub.

'He was ogling you and eyeing you all evening,' said Mummie when he had gone back to his room in the Hotel Metropole in Brighton – he had even thought of that, instead of expecting to spend the night – and unfortunately I had to agree with her. But he just wasn't my type, and I was still thinking of Philippe.

On Christmas Day he came back in the late morning and I introduced him to Moya. 'Hi, Honey. My aren't you pretty.' He tried so hard to be friendly to Moya, who was not used to having men falling all over her in an effort to please me, but she was not impressed. He brought presents for us all. Moya had a jogging suit, with a bear in satin on the front of it, which cost $40 (I knew because the price tickets were left on all the gifts) from Bullocks Wilshire. Mummie got a bottle of scent (Je Reviens, by Worth, very French, old fashioned, charming) and I received the most lovely, elaborate necklace of black onyx, ivory and gold beads, in a suede box, inside a tiny green carrier bag. I was very impressed, particularly as I noticed the price on the bottom which he had forgotten to remove, like most men: $256! I had bought him a silly game with rings, which he quite liked, and a large book on England with beautiful pictures, which was perfect. He loved it, and I was glad I had chosen exactly the present he would have liked best.

I was very pleased with his efforts, but Moya had been up all night being sick, so I wasn't in the best of humours. His jollity began to grate pretty early on. We joined some people at my friend Mariella's restaurant, and everyone else thought he was super. He spent a lot of time playing with Mariella's little girl, and talked about his brother's child too. He seemed a good financial bet, and it was clear that he was interested in a stable family lifestyle, so that was a lot in his favour, but still I couldn't work up much enthusiasm.

'My mother works at an exclusive private club,' he told me, and I imagined a very elegant, refined old American lady. He bought everyone's drinks, and was most attentive to me, and by the end of a few gin and tonics, I was beginning to like him a bit better. The alcohol cushioned the puppyish gambolling and made me more tolerant, I suppose.

Mummie cooked Christmas lunch at about 4 p.m., and I mellowed further, after a few bottles of wine, and a couple of hours of sitting watching television, feeling replete and contented. It felt like being a family, warm and close, and when he left, he just held me very tightly around the waist, without trying anything else. It felt strong and supportive and very romantic.

The next day, we went out to feed the ducks in the village pond with Moya, who was less standoffish, although I kept wishing he wouldn't try so hard to make her like him. The feeling of being an old married couple continued, and was very seductive; I was definitely being converted, slowly, but surely.

'Let's drive into the country,' he said suddenly. 'Let's take Moya home and then let's just go out and be together.'

We went to the Royal Oak, and he drove beautifully. I sat, without smoking (a rule I had made for myself because by now I wanted to please him), and when we got there he predictably loved the place, going through his brassy American act again, much to everyone's appreciation. Even mine.

We talked about the future.

'You have a lot of class, Colette. I like that. Perhaps you could come out to the States and see how you liked it? I would love you to meet my family, and I know they'd adore you.'

We played Shove Halfpenny and he loved it, and then a man with a Great Dane, a local, the last person I would have thought would have given any time to this American loudmouth, told him in detail all about the different sorts of beers in the pub – an illustration of how people like talking about something they know about to an appreciative audience.

Outside, there were two girls on horses, and he wanted to take their photograph. They smiled and allowed him to, posing proudly and not a little flirtatiously.

'Wow, this is great,' he cried, clicking away. 'Is this a regular Sunday pastime in this part of the world?'

I smiled at him, and then because it began to rain, we ran back to his car, hand in hand. As we closed the doors, he turned towards me and kissed me very gently. I liked that. There was no insistent probing, nothing tried on.

It was an idyllic day. When the rain stopped, we walked in the woods, holding hands, and then looked over a bridge at a stream bouncing and bubbling over rocks below. I relished the greenness of England, and the valley around us, and the refreshing dampness of the air was soft on our faces. The trees rustled above our heads, and our feet swished through the thick, wet leaves. A robin flicked its tail at us from a branch and chirruped sweetly as we talked.

'The best way for you to live would be half in England, half in America, I think. Wouldn't it? I don't know if I can afford you, Colette. You are obviously used to the good things in life, but we could try. I would love to invest in another house here. Would you help me look?'

Would I? I couldn't think of anything nicer. I began to envisage all sorts of houses, large and manorial, small and luxurious, in the depths of the countryside, or in the centre of Brighton, in one of those elegant Regency houses.

I also began to think I would be going to California. We made plans together, and he was very enthusiastic about my visit: 'I'll show you around. It would be excellent.'

We talked about each other's pasts. I didn't tell him about all my marriages, judging that he might not approve of them.

'I was engaged three times, Colette,' he told me ruefully. 'I guess I just haven't struck lucky. The first time she broke it off, the second time I did. Then my third fiancée couldn't get pregnant, and I did want children – still do. I love my brother's children but that's not the same.'

We decided to go to London. I took him to Harrods, the mecca for any visiting American, and he amused himself by looking at all the men's fashions and accessories (not the women's, I'm sorry to say!).

Next to Covent Garden – it was just after Christmas so nothing much was open. We had a meal in Peppermint Park on Upper St Martin's Lane, which wasn't up to much, although he enjoyed flirting with the waitresses. I felt an ominous stab of jealousy at this; I began to feel that, as I liked him more, he began to like me less, and I didn't like the feeling at all.

I dashed him round to St Paul's in the dark – the sun set at about 3.30 – and then to Westminster Abbey, but he wasn't keen on anything old or cultural. Strictly modern and materialistic, our Paul!

Dinner was not to be – every restaurant was closed, so we drove home and ate there, with Mummie and my brother. She was getting a little tired of cooking for us, and had hoped for a night off!

He had moved from the Metropole to the Grand, and now I suggested he move to Bailiffscourt, the mediaeval-looking manor house in the countryside at Climping. He readily agreed, and so we drove there together, so that he could check in and I could have dinner later with him.

It is a very romantic place – old stone and thick walls, old roses and thick grass in the summer, and even the winter monochrome suited the Sussex grey walls, guaranteed to appeal to an American.

We went through the stone archway and straight to reception, where he checked in for his last three nights. My heart sank as I realized how short a time we had left, and then and there I resolved to seduce him if I could, that night. I could stand the strain no longer. We had kissed, and held hands, and walked together for hours, and he had squeezed me tightly round the waist, but this was only whetting my appetite for more. I was very keen on him by now, and, as these things work, as his enthusiasm diminished slightly, mine grew.

'This place is incredible,' he said. 'Wonderful. How clever you are to know about it.'

We walked through the corridors, our shoes clicking on the flagstones, until we reached his room. The dark wooden door swung open to show a large room, its main feature a four-poster bed overhung with a splendid tapestry. The ceiling was high and vaulted, bissected by dark oak beams. A log fire crackled in the autumn afternoon and hissed in the grate, filling the room with the scent of applewood and pinecones and a little woodsmoke.

'Wow, just incredible,' he repeated, and reached out to squeeze my hand.

'Look, a real four-poster.'

He bounced on the bed, chuckling like a child, and falling back happily on the pillows.

His brown eyes caught mine wickedly. 'Come here.'

I walked over slowly, my heart beating fast. His legs were spread apart and I fitted neatly between them; he hugged me tightly and I sighed, holding him close.

'Phew. Let me go. I can't breathe,' I gasped. He smiled.

'I'm famished. You must be too. Let's go exploring. Then we can see if we can find something to eat.'

We discovered the walk-in wardrobe behind one oak door and the huge bathroom, with its brass taps and raised tub, behind another.

We ordered room service, and a bottle of champagne.

Unfortunately the kitchen had closed, so we made do with ham sandwiches, which tasted delicious, washed down with the bubbles. Another bottle was inevitable, and the moment was precious, warm and full of expectation.

Paul didn't even seem to mind me sitting on the windowledge

and opening the tiny leaded glass diamond-shaped window to have a cigarette, summoning up the courage to make the move I had to make, or go out of my mind!

I stood up, and crossed the room to where he was standing at the foot of the bed, unpacking his case.

He looked up, and turned to me, opening his arms welcomingly, making it all so very easy. I stayed there, within them, feeling him rub my back gently with his strong hands. Our bodies pressed together, tingling with tension. My hands were wound in his hair, pulling his head down to mine. He moved willingly, running his lips up and down the sinews of my neck, kissing me lightly and quickly.

It was almost too much to bear. We undressed each other slowly, appreciatively, button by button, stopping to kiss, to press, to hold each other. His tanned body was beautiful, strong, hard, hairy and very masculine – I could hardly believe my luck. He found my breasts and caressed them with kisses, till they almost ached with wanting; I unbuckled his belt, unzipped his trousers, he slipped off my skirt, pulled the top over my head and, free of the inconvenience of our clothes, we fell back on the bed and gave ourselves up to pure animal lust of the most gasping, panting, desperate, delicious kind. It was wonderful, and my head spins now as I write of it.

When we had both climaxed, and felt drained and heavy, we looked at each other and smiled. He drew me closer to him, and put a small kiss on my lips.

'Thank you, Colette.'

I slid off him slowly and easily, without a word, and he fell back naturally on to the covers.

'There's a robe on the back of the door,' he called, as I disappeared into the bathroom to be alone, and to soak in warm scented bubbles, enjoying the sensation of release from the mounting tension of the past few days, feeling wanted and full and very special.

Like a kid he picked up the phone and called his mother in California. 'She's wonderful, she has a sweet little girl,' I heard as he held me close. He insisted I talk to her. 'When are you coming over?' 'I don't know,' looking to Paul for an answer. Eventually I said my goodbyes, full of hope for the future.

We lay naked in bed together, drinking more champagne and watching the sun set, in pink and gold and amber through the tiny leaded windowpanes. The trees went purple in the way they do in cold winter air, and the shadows lengthened to make dark ink blots on lawns and flowerbeds, mostly empty, but with a sprinkling of hellebores and winter flowering jasmine. We made love of course. The atmosphere was too romantic to avoid it, and this time it was just as passionate, but dirtier if anything. He kept whispering savagely into my ear: 'Talk dirty to me. Say how you love my great big cock, and how you want me.'

I didn't like it but I did my best. It felt rather strange, very artificial, particularly after the very natural coupling we had previously enjoyed. He wasn't as good as he thought he was, in fact; when he had finished, I could have gone on. He said he needed a rest, so I was left feeling only half satisfied, a state of mind that breeds insecurity and often resentment. The next morning we made love again, less desperately, more familiarly, warmly, still enthusiastically but less as though we were in training for the Olympics.

I took him to Oxford, or rather he drove me and I showed him around. Or, would have done, if he had been remotely interested. He couldn't have cared less, and when we got lost in the city's notoriously confusing one-way system, he frowned blackly at the steering wheel and wouldn't address more than an irritated grunt or two at me.

I was longing for a cigarette, and foolishly said so.

'In California you would never get a date, honey. No one smokes there – it's a really dangerous habit.'

He wanted to walk round Brighton by himself the next day, almost his last, which didn't show undying devotion, I thought. A distant alarm bell began to ring in my head. This wasn't how a man madly in love, or even a little, behaved just before leaving a woman. We talked when he got back, and, like many of our conversations it was intelligent, interesting, on the ball. He liked my ideas about business – 'You can do anything you like with the dealership if you come out to California,' he said. If, not when. And as if I would be an employee, not a wife. He would often compliment me on my hair or my clothes, always something specific, not about the whole of me. His manner had changed, indicating, I should think, that his feelings had too. I was getting the feeling that this was not to be a success, but by now I was hooked.

That evening we went to Dukes, and I had planned to try and find out where I stood. Out in the cold, it seemed. He was not even friendly, off hand, flirting with other women.

Eventually I could bear it no longer. Well-primed with alcohol, my blood was up, and I needed to know. 'What's happened? Why have you changed? Surely you must know how I feel about you?' I asked desperately.

'I do, but I've been thinking hard. I don't think you would be happy with me in America.'

After that, we sat morosely looking into our glasses, and he took me home. I felt abandoned, miserable, and I knew he wouldn't call before he left, even though we were supposed to be going to this stupid Scottish Night at the Grand.

I was exercising sweatily to my aerobics tape in my dressing gown – red faced, panting, always the glamourpuss, especially when I need to be – when the doorbell rang. Mummie answered it, and I shot upstairs, looking over the banisters to see him standing in the living room, all spruced up.

I threw on my dressing gown, hardly having time to slick a gloss of lipstick on my lips, and ran downstairs, trying to look chirpy.

'Look, Paul. I'm sorry about last night. I laid a heavy trip on you . . .'

'That's all right. Are you better now?'

'Yes, oh yes!'

Like hell, but it was our last day together, possibly for ever. He said nothing about that night, and I was too shy to ask him, so we both sat squirming in the troubled atmosphere, until he finished his coffee and politely took his leave.

It was dreadful. I suffered that afternoon an agony of indecision. Should I call him? Should I just assume we were finished? Was it accepted that we would go anyway? My stomach squeezed together, like a monkeywrench, and I could hardly breathe at times. I looked at the telephone balefully, willing it to ring and put an end to my misery, but it sat smugly silent, implying that it was up to me.

I dialled. He answered.

'Hello?'

'Hello. It's me, Colette. I'm really sorry to bother you, but I was wondering – are we going to this dinner tonight or not? I mean, you didn't confirm, and . . .'

'I thought you didn't want to see me any more, Colette. I'm so sorry. I seem to have misunderstood things completely. I didn't know what to say. I will be delighted to take you, if I can get us in. I'll try the restaurant, and call you right back.'

He did so. 'I had cancelled our booking and it was snapped up. There aren't any more places, I'm afraid. But there's a midnight buffet in the cocktail bar. How does that sound?'

'Fine. Will you, er, when shall I be ready?'
'I'll be right there.'
And he was. Thirty minutes later his Mercedes purred up, and I was made up and dressed to kill. I had borrowed an elaborate dress from my friend Nicky, and knew I looked terrific. It was long, heavy black jersey splashed with silver, the material folded and pleated cunningly to flatter the figure. He was thrilled. 'You look amazing. A pleasure to be seen with. It's going to be a lovely evening.'
I did hope so. I was still nervous, but the compliments helped. We drank champagne all night, and I could see that everyone thought I looked wonderful. Unfortunately he thought some other girls in the room looked pretty good too, and was itching to dance with them. To save my face, I said coolly that he should do so, and so he did, returning regularly to check on my champagne level. I sat there feeling humiliated and resentful, and sipping from my glass trying to show that I couldn't have cared less.
At five minutes to midnight, he came back, picked me up, and spun me round in his arms.
'It's going to be our year, Colette. I know it. I think you're just beautiful.'
Mollified, I smiled and kissed him back, but it still didn't feel right. We went up to his room shortly afterwards – it was much smaller than his previous one, and we had to sleep in his poky little bed. Lovemaking was nothing like as good as it had been, and I put in all the effort to try and salvage some enjoyment, as the bedsprings creaked, and our elbows were cracked on the wall and the bedside table.
I wore his jogging suit back to my house the next day, and he stayed for breakfast briefly before going back to his hotel and then, I thought, to his own country.
But he decided to stay a couple more days. I was getting used to his unpredictable changes of plan, and I was happy to have him for longer.
We went to Hampton Court but I should have remembered his indifference to history. He liked the gardens but whizzed me round the building, me following in his wake like a little dinghy after the mother ship. He was cool, often ignoring me altogether, and I was nonplussed again. In retrospect, I should have just got out of the car earlier, or refused to go out with him, but one never does the right thing when in the grip of unreasonable attraction.
He wanted to have dinner at a Greek restaurant opposite the

Kensington Hilton that his father had recommended, so we went there before going to the theatre in the West End.

We finally made it to *The Phantom of the Opera*. Because he had left it so long, we had to buy vastly inflated tickets from a tout outside the theatre, who demanded 90 quid each!

'Best seats in the house, gov'nor, guaranteed.'

They were on the far right of the upper circle, which meant that the angle to the stage was severely shortened and we missed much of the front-of-stage action.

But it was wonderful. I loved it, and I think he did too. He said he did anyhow. He also said a lot about, 'you must come and see my house, you'll like it' and 'we must go out in my catamaran. Do you sail? Of course, after nine years in the States, and all that time in California, you must do. We'll have a ball.'

The telephone rang the next morning. 'Hi, it's Paul. Look, it's really my last day now, and I want you and Moya to see the facilities at the Grand. Why don't you come and have a swim and a sauna in the health club and then we can have a leisurely breakfast?'

We were ready by 9.00. Moya behaved beautifully, loving the water, and we had a good time. All the girls in the health club giggled as he passed, exchanging jolly nothings with him – he had obviously been there before, chatting them up. I felt that familiar twinge of jealousy, but smothered it. In the Gazebo for breakfast, we looked like the perfect young family and I could see everyone looking at each other and smiling approvingly. Paul liked it as much as I did, and Moya looked enchanting.

The only jarring note was from Paul, 'I know where you will be in ten years time,' he told me. I smiled, thinking he would say with him, or in luxury, or something similar.

'In Marbella, propping up a bar with a toy boy in tow.'

I laughed it off, but it really hurt. I didn't feel it was either fair or accurate, and it made the tears prick sharply behind my eyes. I wasn't going to show that he had hurt me, though, and smiled bravely at him. 'I think I'll prove you wrong. I never did like people much younger than me, anyway!'

He also said other hurtful things which I tried to pass off, like the fact that he didn't like long hair, he had never kissed a girl who smoked, and that I would 'sure have to shape up for California'.

'That was one of the reasons I left it,' I said sweetly. 'The hard work involved in keeping beautiful just got too much for me. I'm happy as I am in this country, and luckily, many people don't mind my shape either.'

After all this sparring, the meal continued in a strained fashion.

I drank the last of my black coffee, and had a cigarette, knowing as I did so that it was probably another nail in the coffin of the relationship. Moya chewed the last of her soldiers, and Paul read a newspaper, for all the world as if we had been married for five years and all this was perfectly normal. I'm not sure he didn't want me to see what could be possible, but also that it was something to do with me that it was not going to be. But I couldn't give up hope. I had had so many failures, mostly because I wouldn't want to touch them with a barge pole, that it did seem hard that when I did want someone they weren't interested. Or perhaps that is why I wanted him so badly? That and the way his hair fell into the sexy dip at the top of his neck, and his muscular body, and his twinkling eyes and his exuberance, which had stopped grating and had become something that inspired me.

I tried not to stare at him on the way home, sitting in the back of the car with Moya on my knee, but his strong hands on the wheel reminded me of when his hands were on my body and my breath caught in my throat at the thought that possibly it would never happen again. When he had made love to me the last time, in the uncomfortable single bed in Brighton, he had kept saying please love me, and I wanted to say 'I do, I do,' but because I knew by now that he was the sort of man who loses interest with a conquest, I kept quiet.

He had already said, half kindly, half criticizing, 'You wear your heart on your sleeve, Colette.' Not always, I wanted to say, but wisely didn't.

He was spending his last night in London, instead of in Sussex with me, which I thought made the whole thing pretty clear. When he left me at my house, he held me tightly round the waist as he had before, and looked into my eyes almost tenderly. Damn it, it *was* tenderly, but I couldn't trust myself to hold his gaze. Before my eyes filled with tears and I made another fool of myself, I twisted myself free.

'OK. Take care. Bye,' I said rather hoarsely, turning and walking into the house.

He never wrote.

I gave up running to catch the letters in the morning, and gave up asking Mummie if he had called whenever I got in.

Mummie's sharp eye and sense of humour helped a lot at this time. I was walking about with a face as long as a fiddle, and took to sitting in my room a lot, feeling deserted and rejected and all the other feelings that take over when you can't have someone. I would go over all the stupid things I had said, the way I had irritated him, and I would try to comfort myself with his appreciation of my clothes and my make-up – he liked all that. I asked Mummie what she thought of him, when he was safely away, and I could almost smile.

She didn't mince words, but I knew she wouldn't. 'Paul? He looked exactly like a baby chipmunk, with his little puffy cheeks, and a dent in his chin. I don't know what you ever saw in him. Insincere and too sure of himself, if you ask me. I got tired of the way he bounced along all the time. He never stopped – very exhausting!

'I felt he would just as soon be with me as with you, not in a sexual way, obviously, but because he really liked home life. He was in awe of you before he got to know you, dazzled by you. Then he lost interest – odd that he kept marching off on his own, I thought.'

There was more, and it was really helping. I began to enjoy her taking him apart, and each criticism made me laugh.

'I wish he had left Moya alone. He was so overpowering. He kept mauling her, too boisterously. I think she was a bit frightened of him – she didn't like it. Nor did I.

'He was worried that you wanted more money than he could afford, which was probably a bad sign for the future! But he could easily have done so, if all he said about his finances was true.'

'I know. I was trying to impress him, and perhaps I overdid the expensive clothes and the stories of smart places and smart people. I thought he'd like it,' I wailed, feebly.

'Never mind. It's for the best. Although he didn't mind your brother being retarded at all, which was nice. He was also genuinely mad about England. Mad about it. That was nice but, blimey, he thought a lot of himself. He wasn't nearly as good looking as he thought.'

I helped myself to another cigarette, feeling not a bit guilty any more. Stuff him – Mummie was right, and there are plenty of other people around. I curled my feet up under me on the sofa where I was sitting beside her and nodded hard.

'Mmmm. That's right. He did think he was marvellous. He wasn't bad, though, Mummie.'

'He never seemed very amorous, like young men are. Never, after the first couple of days, wanting to be alone with you. Odd, I thought. He never talked about his hobbies. I expect because his biggest hobby was himself!'

That was what I wanted to hear. It was a comfort to hear that he wasn't admired by her as much as by me.

'I didn't like him, really. He was a bit too perfect. His fingernails were too clean, his clothes too well coordinated. He smelt too good, too expensive.'

'Mmm, that was lovely though, wasn't it?'

'Yes, but with everything else, it made me feel he wasn't rugged enough. He probably combed the hairs on his chest!'

Life got back to normal, which meant badminton, taking Moya out and bringing her back, occasional visits to dentists and doctors, to Sainsbury's or for a walk to the beach. The phone rang at times, I answered ads and put some in and nothing very interesting came of them. The usual thing.

Then one day he did ring.

'Hello, Colette. How are you? I had a wonderful holiday. Thank you so much.'

Nothing about missing me, or about wanting to see me again. It was a short conversation, bubbling and friendly on his side of the Atlantic, slightly stilted and careful on mine. Valentine's Day was coming, and I had to send him a card. His voice had undone all my mother's good work, and I began missing him all over again.

He rang me when he got it, and we talked for half an hour or so. 'Be my Valentine for ever, Colette,' he said, and I thought I was hearing things. But in my heightened state I was trying to make more of things than they warranted, I knew that, so kept my voice calm.

'Are you coming to England again?'

'Not for another six months or so. I can't afford it.'

'Oh, I quit smoking. I wanted to tell you. For about six weeks now.'

I was the puppy now, pathetically trying to please. Perhaps that would make him like me more?

'Great, Colette. Glad to hear it.'

Not long after this, John, from Dana Point in California got in touch. The story you know, but the end of it was rather more dramatic than I said earlier, because then I hadn't introduced you to Paul, Mr Conceited.

One of the reasons I accepted his ticket to the States was that I had decided money might win over looks; another reason was that he lived in California, and once there, Mr Conceited was a whole lot easier to see than if I were stuck in England.

I called him before I left, and – I don't think it was just wishful thinking – he sounded very pleased I was coming. I called again after I had spent a lot of John's money on some clothes; in the back of my mind, I knew I was never going to Costa Rica with John and I boosted my confidence by the knowledge that, whatever happened, I would look pretty good when and if I got to see Paul.

'I'm here, in California. And I'm in the most awful mess.'

'What on earth have you been doing now? You do get yourself in some confusions, don't you?'

I explained – how he never stopped talking, what a mistake it had been to accept his invitation to come here, how ghastly he was, how short and boring and pushy and mean.

'You'd better come and see me.'

'Yes. Thank you. Carol's coming over tomorrow to help me get out of his house.'

'Well, call me at 11 the next morning if you can, and we'll sort something out.'

'I will. Oh, Paul, I'm scared. John's such a tight tense little man, with a real chip on his shoulder. He'll be mad.'

'Be careful, Colette, but it'll be all right if you are firm.'

Carol came round the next morning and I told John that I was going to spend the day with her. He was a bit jealous, and gave me the third degree about where we were going: 'Perhaps I could join you girls later in the day, if I have time. And if you want me to.'

We smiled weakly. 'Of course, John, but it'll be just girl talk. You'll be bored rigid. We haven't seen each other in a long time, so we have a lot to catch up on.'

We left smartly, driving off in her new red convertible – she had a good job in marketing, and it paid well.

'One thing I have to find out is whether I can cash in my return ticket, or whether the original purchaser can put a block on it,' I told her breathlessly.

She was really good to me that day. We rang British Caledonian, who put my mind at rest.

We had lunch at a restaurant near the beach, and as I toyed with my salad, I looked at her imploringly. 'What am I going to do? I can't be with him another day. I long to see Paul, and he seems to want to see me. I have spent so much of John's money on clothes to wear, he thinks, in Costa Rica, but there is absolutely no way I'm going to the end of the street with him, let alone on holiday. I haven't got much money, and I want to look my best for Paul. Oh Carol, what am I going to do? I ought to pay him back, but how can I? I wanted the clothes but I also was so beastly about the money because he was so mean.' Perhaps I should leave without them but Carol reminded me that they would be of no earthly use to him.

She was very supportive and positive. If it hadn't been for her, I would probably have gone with the little creep, I would never have seen Paul again and I would have been in court for murder.

'He doesn't own you. He didn't have to buy you the ticket and the clothes. It's a risk. He knew that, he must have done.'

'Yes, but he is such an overselling little twerp that he has convinced himself we are going to work and that we should get married and that he can satisfy any woman sexually – ugh,' I shuddered at the thought.

'Come and stay with me.'

'Thanks. I'd love to. But how am I going to get out of the house? And I want to see Paul so badly.'

'Haven't you talked about leaving?'

'Yes, but he won't listen. He keeps saying we should get married in Costa Rica.'

'Surely not. He must know you don't want to.'

'No. He does hear what I say, but he doesn't listen. He keeps saying "I'll take really good care of you. I'll take really good care of your daughter. Some guys wouldn't want her, you know." Oh God Carol. He'll make such a scene!'

Between us, we hatched a plan. We would go and have a drink at Delaney's and would call Paul from there. Then we would go to John's, I would pack while she talked to him, and then we would just walk out. Simple as that. I wished I felt convinced, but it was that or Costa Rica, and I couldn't bear that idea!

Paul wasn't in, and I left a message with his brother who told me Paul was down at the beach where he was just off to join him. 'I'm sure he will be back around 4 p.m. I'll tell him you rang, and he will get back in time for a call.'

I called again, and still he wasn't back. Of course, I thought jealously, he's down on the beach with some other woman, and can't be bothered to talk to me. I was so tense by now that if someone nudged me in the street accidentally I was convinced they were trying to push me into a waiting car to take me back to John.

I finally caught up with Paul at 7 p.m., by now panicking about getting back to John, who I know hadn't bargained for us to be out such a long time. If I hadn't been in such a state, I would have read the signs better. Paul obviously didn't have me on the top of his list.

'Tell him you want to leave. Don't discuss anything. Just state facts, and then go.'

It sounded so easy.

'I can't.'

'Yes, of course you can. Then, when you've done it, call me, and we can make arrangements.'

The thought of those arrangements carried me through that evening.

We went back to John's, Carol and I. He wasn't in when we arrived, which did nothing for my blood pressure (or hers, I suppose; we were both almost hysterical with nerves). When he arrived we were sitting round the kitchen table looking as though butter wouldn't melt in our mouths.

'Oh hello, John. Did you have a nice day?'

'Sure. How did you girls enjoy yourselves?'

'Oh, we went for a walk along the beach, had lunch there, a bit of mooching round the shops . . .'

As Carol talked, I excused myself quietly and rushed upstairs to pack.

I call it packing. It more closely resembled the sacking of a mediaeval city. I grabbed everything in sight, and shoved armfuls of clothes, make-up, scent, shoes, underwear into my suitcase. It has taken a bit of closing when I had left England – the paraphernalia of self-presentation is bulky – but now it yawned at me, exposing the teeth of its zip in a big mocking grin.

I pushed everything in on all sides, I sat on it, I bounced up and down. I pinched my fingers in the zip until they bled, I almost tore my shoes in half as they stuck awkwardly out one side of the case, I ripped precious silk underwear on the other, as I tugged it closed, speed being my only consideration. I lifted it with an effort when I had managed to almost pull the zip all the way, and left it at the top of the stairs poised for flight.

I walked calmly downstairs, and stood at the door. 'John. Things aren't working out between us. I'm leaving now.' It was out. It was easy, just like Paul had said. I stood there a little longer, looking at his fallen face, and felt sorry for him, but not sorry enough to stay.

There was no other reaction from him at all. Carol stood up, and I went to pick up my case, and walked into the street. He still sat there, in silence.

I felt rotten, as though I had kicked a kitten, but I knew if I returned to explain or excuse myself I was lost.

Carol turned the key in the ignition – the car growled into life and we drove off. I began to squeal with relief. 'I've done it. We've done it. I can't believe it was so easy. Oh God, Carol, I'm so relieved.'

We went back to her small studio apartment, and sat on her bed like two giggling schoolgirls, eating tortilla chips and drinking wine. The first thing I did was to write a note to John thanking him for everything, hoping to soften the blow. I unpacked my clothes, unhooking the delicate lace of my camiknickers from the teeth of the zip and unfolding my contorted shoes. I lay everything on the bed, piling it up neatly once more. We tried each other's clothes on, we smoked cigarettes, we exchanged gossip. It was the perfect aftermath to John and the perfect preliminary to Paul. I almost forgot about them both and luxuriated in being man-less for an evening.

Paul rang me the next day as he had promised. I told him the success of Operation Walkout and he was relieved.

'There, I told you it wouldn't be that bad. Poor devil, I should think it will take him a while to get over the shock. Still, what are we going to do with you now? I suggest you go down to the airport tomorrow. I'll arrange a ticket, and you can fly up here to spend a few days.'

'Can't you drive down here instead?' I asked.

'No, I can't, I'm sorry – I'm too busy at work to get away, and I want you to meet my family. See you tomorrow.'

I want you to meet my family, I repeated to myself, to meet my family. That must mean something, mustn't it? He couldn't want every casual girlfriend to meet his family, not when he had gone on and on about how important they were to him. I want you to meet my family. Oh, things were looking up.

The journey to Santa Barbara took an hour 45 minutes, in a neat little jet, a new service for executives. I wore my white Italian linen dress (one of the guilty purchases with John's credit card), and the weather was bracing, bright and breezy. I stood at the top of the steps when we arrived and couldn't see Paul at first. I concentrated on not getting my heel stuck in the ironwork of the steps, and when I looked up, there he was.

He looked very happy to see me, giving me an enormous cuddle and smiling from ear to ear. I was thrilled. We kissed quickly and cheerfully, and collected my luggage which he threw in the back of his car.

'I'm going to take you to the Alcantino Hotel for lunch.'

'I don't feel very hungry, Paul. I'd love a drink though.'

'Fine. I want to talk to you.'

We drove along chatting, as I looked around me. The Alcantino Hotel was a very smart one, old-fashioned and elegant. The carpet of the bar was emerald green, and there was some wicker furniture which looked airy and sophisticated. Some other chairs were reproduction Queen Anne, and although the mixture sounds odd, it worked.

We sat down, I on a chair, he on a sofa, separated by a glass table. Drinks were ordered and came almost at once, and I took a long cool swig and waited.

'I really had to see you, to tell you in person, Colette.'

I looked at him, straw still between my lips, wondering what was coming.

'I don't think it will work out between us, I don't think it ever will. You're super, but you belong in England and I belong here. I wish it were different, and I want us to have a good time while you're here. Can we do that? Would you like to meet my mother? She'd love you, and I'd like to introduce you.'

'Sure,' I said, my ears ringing. So it *hadn't* meant anything – he didn't care for me. All my excitement had been a waste of time. I was silent, dumbfounded, not knowing how to hide my disappointment. I should have known. I did know, but wouldn't listen.

'There isn't anyone else, Colette. Don't think that. I just don't think we are for each other, that's all.'

We soon drove back to his house, which was stylish, and I knew I would have loved living there if things had worked out differently. It was furnished in different colours of beige, highlighted with pale mauve and pale pink; black venetian blinds covered the windows, letting in strips of light that played on the large white sofa in the middle of the sitting room.

'I expect you want to put your things away.'

'Yes, please.' I was still monosyllabic, but feeling slightly stronger. I thought I would be put in the spare room, and was thus very startled to find him leading me into what was obviously his. He put the case on the bed and waved his arm at the cupboard – 'You can fit your things in here, I hope. Here's the bathroom. Make yourself comfortable. See you downstairs.' I sat on the enormous bed as he left, in a room that was very masculine, very like Paul. Colours were black and beige, and the counterpane was heavy and expensive.

We went to a movie that evening, ironically called *Blind Date*, which appealed to my sense of the ironic. I wore my tight khaki suit, determined to go down with all flags flying, and he held my hand reluctantly as I had to step over the puddles. In the cinema, we had popcorn and sodas, and when we sat down he would occasionally put his hand on my knee, or around my shoulders. My heart would leap each time he did this, but it was obviously a sort of habit, one that he found hard to break. It made for a very unsettling couple of hours, and I began to wish that he would stop raising my hopes in this way.

After we left, he didn't touch me at all, which was easier, but emphasized our new relationship.

'I'm really tired,' he told me, as we got in. 'I am going to bed.'

I had brought my passion-killer nightie, and now defiantly wore it, to show that I had got the message. I don't think he even noticed. He got in beside me, naked, and turned over to go to sleep.

'Tomorrow we'll go out to lunch with my mother, Colette. Sleep well,' he murmured, eyes closed.

Hah. As if I could. I felt embarrassed being there, and lay stiffly, afraid that any movement might be misinterpreted. I was humiliated, furious, unhappy. I waited for him to put an arm around me, to touch me somehow, so that I'd know he didn't mean what he had said, but it was plain he did. Then why put me next to him? It seemed a sophisticated form of sadism.

The next day, the alarm rang at about 6 a.m. and he leaned over me to put it off. I was half asleep, so almost responded to what looked like a change of heart (how foolish one's hopes are in such situations), but thank God I stayed where I was.

'I'll pick you up at about 1.00,' he told me after he had shaved and dressed and came back into the bedroom smelling of his usual expensive aftershave.

I got up a few hours later, dressed in my demurely pretty floral dress with its big white collar, and had a desultory snoop around. There was nothing very much. Lots of letters from various girls, a photograph album of his trip to England, with about ten pictures of me, which made me feel better . . .

The restaurant where he had arranged to meet his mother was lovely – French food, white lofty decor with palm trees and comfortable chairs.

His mother, you may remember, I had pictured as elegant, old-fashioned, rather grand in a quiet American way. I couldn't have been more wrong. She was delightful, but looked a young fifty-five, with short blonde hair, expensively cut. She wore a white jogging top, over pleated trousers that flattered her extremely nice figure. She was very attractive, although, in the Californian way, trying very hard to be young.

'She's gorgeous, Paul. You were right. She's such a lady, so pretty.'

He pretended for her sake that there was more between us than there was, which was puzzling, and was beginning to annoy me a little. I felt I was being used, and when she had a cigarette, I took one from her proffered packet with great pleasure. 'I'd love to come to Britain. Paul has told me so much about the country. It sounds absolutely divine. British clothes are so beautiful too – really original and stylish. We Americans are so stuffy, so unoriginal. I'd simply love to have a long day or six at the shops. Harrods, is it, and Marks and Spencers? Perhaps we could go together?'

Perhaps we could, I thought, but it is highly unlikely, Madam, with your son being so odd. I liked her very much though – she was open and friendly and wanted to know all about me and my child. So, of course, as a proud mother, I told her.

There was much talk about her coming to England, but although Paul had been all for it before, he seemed quieter and less keen now – I just kept quiet because my head was spinning with all the different signals I was getting. It was wishful thinking really – in the cold light of Littlehampton a year or so later, I can see that, but then I was so besotted by him, all I wanted to do was to stay with him, and make him learn to love me.

I went on to meet his sister-in-law at her house; she was nothing to look at, almost plain but extremely nice, and her children were adorable. I played all the *right* games with them, just to show Paul how wrong he had been with Moya, and to impress everybody, which I did! The kids loved me.

His brother was still at the office, and we swung by there on our way back to Paul's – he was ordinary-looking, wearing shorts and a T-shirt, and looking as if he had had a hard day. He reminded me of Paul in the way he laughed, but it was quite clear that Paul was the good-looking one and used to being treated that way. His brother was less bubbly and so, I thought, didn't have the insincerity that had put my mother off Paul. We drove off again in a bright, big blue Corvette, borrowed from a friend of his for the day, so he said. He did look handsome in California – the sun and the scenery suited him, and I wanted to stay there with him and fit into his life more than ever. But when we finally got back to his place, romance was the furthest thing from his mind. He fell asleep on the sofa, so I amused myself by watching an opera on the television – *Il Trovatore*, all anvils and caves and broken hearts. I loved it – I love opera, and watch and listen whenever I have the chance. It seemed very appropriate and I wept in the arias and hummed along with the rousing choruses.

'I'm going up to bed now,' said Paul, waking, and scratching his head. He stood up heavily and walked out of the room. I followed, and the same thing happened as the night before. He lay there naked, I lay beside him in my nightie, wishing the atmosphere would change and that I didn't feel so alone. About half an hour passed. I just wanted to leave, or die.

'I'm sending you home tomorrow, Colette,' he told me abruptly, his disembodied voice filling the room with gloom. 'I've booked you a flight back.'

Of course I didn't sleep a wink after that, but lay there, rigidly miserable. When he had gone to work. I went for a long walk on the beach by myself, to clear my head and work out how I was going to get my life together. The waves curled and slapped on the sand, little squirrels ran about, stopping and standing up on their hind legs, catching at a bit of wood or leaf and tearing it to pieces in their paws. The sky was very blue, and I was completely alone – but not as lonely as I had been in bed with Paul. Where did I go from here, I wondered? Back to England, obviously, but then what?

I rang Carol when I got back, and asked her to come and pick me up, but she was very busy and couldn't do so that day.

'But I haven't got a penny. What shall I do, Carol? I can't ask him for any money. He doesn't talk to me at all when we are alone, so what can I say to him?'

'Of course you can ask him. Just ask to borrow some money for a taxi. He won't mind. He's the one who's sending you away.'

He picked me up. 'I thought we'd stop by the shop and I could get you the T-shirts I promised you long ago. And then we could have a drink?'

'Yes. Yes, that would be nice. Paul – I wondered – could you lend me $20 for a taxi?' My voice sounded reedy and shaky even to my ears, and he looked at me, irritation showing in his face.

'Don't you have any money? OK, we'll get you some.'

The card with the T-shirts, which had obviously been put there a long time before his change of heart, said 'Love always, Paul,' which he didn't notice until it was too late. I looked quickly at it, and put it in my bag before he had the time to whisk it away or say anything to spoil my future recollections.

'Here's $100 – is that enough?'

'Oh no. Yes, I mean thank you very much. It's far too much. Are you sure? I'll get it back to you as soon as I can.'

'Don't worry about that. Keep it. Shall we go?'

We went to the Pacific Dance Company for a drink. It was rather embarrassing – I was dressed up to the nines, ready to go on a plane to leave Paul with a good memory of me, and every one else was casual. Someone finally came in in a leather outfit, which redressed the balance somewhat.

Then after a couple of gins, which made me feel worse, if anything, we went off to the airport.

'What are you going to do now, Colette?' he asked me, sounding rather concerned. There was nothing cheap about Paul – he was decent, as far as he could be, and he didn't behave tackily. Everywhere we went was smart, I never felt I couldn't spend as much money as I wanted, and when I needed sympathy or help, he offered it. He just couldn't offer me what I really wanted – him.

'I don't know. Get a job perhaps.'

'Are you wondering where it all went wrong?' he asked me, looking into my eyes. 'It's only fair to tell you how I feel. You are far too intense for me, too strong. I just don't love you, Colette. In England I was mad about you, but it didn't last. You don't know how many times I nearly called you, every day, but then something changed. You are a wonderful person, you're crazy, but life would never be boring with you. I think you're great, intelligent, smart, but I don't love you.'

Then I confessed that I had been married three times. 'You might be right. They didn't work out, and I may well be better off in the UK. I'm better there than in America.' I lied; some things about the States suit me very well, but I wanted to save a bit of face.

He went on and on about my good qualities, which didn't remove the sting from his often repeated sentence, 'I don't love you.' But I'm glad he told me – he could have just left me in mid-air wondering where on earth I'd gone wrong, whether I was really ghastly, boring, not as attractive as I once was . . .

We waited for the plane together for about an hour. I left him immediately they announced the flight, because there is never much gap between that and boarding. My heart was heavy, so heavy I could hardly lift my feet. I tried not to cry, but my eyes filled with tears. He gave me a hug, and looked embarrassed, sorry, relieved I was going – many things.

'If you're ever in England, be sure to look me up,' I said, trying to be jaunty.

'I will. Have a good trip. Look after yourself.'

I walked through the gate without a backward glance, towards the plane that was going to take me away from the one man I thought could make me happy. I wanted so much to stay with him, but he didn't want me, and that hurt.

It was a beautiful place, which made it even harder to leave. I could have been so happy there. The sky was blue, the air smelt fresh and sunny, the flowers were out. Everyone looked brown and busy and – well, Californian. Something I never would be again.

11

What Have I Learnt?

What have I learnt over the last couple of years in my man hunt?

I have learnt not to be discouraged – that there are a lot of men out there, a lot of warm, sincere men, with steady jobs, regular incomes, who want a happy, secure family life, and would love to marry me and look after Moya generously, caringly, conscientiously – the backbone of the country, but not the stuff that dreams are made of, mine anyway.

There are very few tall, good-looking, well off young men with outgoing personalities. They are either married or they don't need to advertise, because they are in such demand that women throw themselves at them.

But some of them do, perhaps once, on a whim, and that's what keeps me going. If you are prepared to take a chance on perhaps one in a hundred being a man you like, and one who likes you, then the dating game is an obvious, sensible way of meeting men. If you want someone special, someone out of the ordinary, then you have to try everything. If you're looking for Mr Perfect, that lengthens the odds to something like one in a thousand, and you really have to be determined to stick it out that long.

I am over halfway through now, and as I said, I have fallen in love two and a half times, apart from my three marriages (but they were based on very odd feelings and needs, half-romantic, half-mercenary, and don't really count).

The personal columns are a form of escapism, and as such are extremely addictive. There's always the chance that the next one will be the right one, and so you carry on and on and on. And I was lucky to begin with – my first two dates were extremely presentable, and so I thought that they were the shape of all things to come. They weren't – I've learnt that too.

You have endless scope for romantic fantasizing, which makes real life harder to come to terms with. And if Mr Right may be just around the corner, why stop here? Perhaps the next meeting will be with someone who fits the extremely ambitious bill you have concocted for yourself even more closely.

My motives have changed now – when I started it was because I wanted someone to make a home for Moya and me. Someone who would keep me in the style to which I was accustomed. I was used to having money, and being around people who were very rich. Now money is not so important. For a start I am older, so I am less attractive than I was, so it's getting harder and harder to find the right person. They have all the choice in the world too. But it is an artificial way of meeting people, and so it is hard to be yourself, although you know that is the only way you are going to find the right person.

I am always trying to please the man I'm with, and they are probably doing the same, so that doesn't make for a relaxed time. When you meet someone at a party, or in a lift or in any of the many other casual ways you are supposed to meet men, you don't have to give everything away, and prior knowledge of each other is limited. Someone may say 'Come and meet so and so. He's a merchant banker/taxidermist/farmer . . .' and he may know that you are a fashion model, a nuclear physicist or a housewife, but after that it's up to you what you tell them. The personal ads have to hit the right targets (and after a while you get better at aiming) and the telephone calls and letters before you meet have to tell you both a good deal about each other.

But people are rarely truthful. I am constantly amazed at men's inflated opinions of their attractions. I know attractiveness is subjective, but if you are 20 stone, there is no way you can get away with calling yourself slim. If you are 5 feet 7 inches, you can't say you are tall, or if you have acne and are bald you really can't describe yourself as 'considered attractive'. It's not fair to be dishonest – it raises one's hopes and, the higher they go, the harder they fall.

I have constantly been misled by descriptions such as these. I don't tell lies. I don't put 'solvent' when I mean broke; I don't say I have a career when I don't. It would just waste everybody's time.

I have never lied about Moya – I find men like the idea of a little daughter. It gives them a ready-made family, and she is small enough not to have too much of a problem accepting them as her new father. I think after she is five, in three years' time, it may become more difficult.

Also, I am now thirty-one, and many men are surprised if a

woman of my age has not had a child. They can't worry if I am able to have one, and many want to try for a family, however old they are. They have often lost their children by getting divorced and not getting custody, and miss them badly. So she has been more often a help than a hindrance with getting dates.

The men are most definitely out to impress, especially on the first, which might be their last, date with me. This is also the same for me – it's part and parcel of the blind process. Obviously a man will suggest dinner in a reputable restaurant, he is hardly likely to ask me to the local Wimpy bar, likewise I would put my best image forward and describe a suitably prestigious establishment. A merchant banker is hardly going to be impressed by putting forward the idea of fish and chips at the greasy joint in town, especially if he is driving over 50 miles each way for the privilege. He will also want to make a long night of it. I've always stayed the distance, not having the heart to say something cruel like 'I don't like your face' which in all honesty was the truth. Maybe I'm a fool but I would hate someone to deflate my ego in such an unkind manner. I strongly believe what goes around comes around.

Being on your best behaviour and trying to put your best foot forward causes unnecessary tension though this is the way it is for me even now. If one was less concerned on a date about pretences we might get to know one another a little more. So if you intend to do as I have, blind date, expect to see the best outward show. If they can't be bothered to make an effort then, despite what I've said in this paragraph, I feel that in the future, were there to be one, they may not bother about a great many other more important things.

Men don't know how to be romantic, I have found. Women seem to have to make all the effort, and men sit back and consider this normal. When people telephone me sometimes, I am hoarse at the end of the conversation, because it has been so stilted I have had to do most of the talking.

I get tired of the things I have to say. The questions, predictably, are all the same. 'What do you look like? How tall are you? What colour are your eyes? Your hair? Are you slim? What do you do? Why did you leave the States? Where are you living at the moment?'

People are very unreliable. Many men promise to call back and they don't. This has never bothered me very much; I have often been guilty of the same thing, but I understand it does bother other women, so if you are going to date this way, you must steel yourself for disappointment before you start. When you place an ad, you get a barrage of telephone calls, which soon whittle down to a manageable number – rather too manageable at times, like one or two, which is annoying when you start out with high hopes and a big response.

Men are the same the world over. They would like a woman to stay at home and look after the house, the baby and them. But they want the extra income of a working wife (who of course also has to look after the house, the baby and them). They don't want their wives to earn more than they do, though – a delicate balance of dependence in the guise of independence has to be struck. In America I have noticed women are expected to work, and do everything else well too – why have children, I wonder? Why leave them to be looked after by someone else, while you are slogging away at something high-powered all day, coming back home tired and irritable with no time to spend with the children anyway?

This is a personal opinion. In nature, the mother rears the young. I believe nature gets it right. I also think that a woman should have the option to work if she wants to, but that it is not possible to do both properly – and I want to be a proper wife and mother, to do the best I can for my husband and children.

Men also want a decorative, intelligent woman – but not too decorative, in case she is too attractive to other men, and not too intelligent, in case she knows more than they do about something. I can talk about many subjects, and have done a lot in my thirty-one years, often more than the men I meet. This does not go down very well at all – so I have to suppress myself quite often to avoid them getting annoyed or glassy-eyed.

A man might be old, ugly, bald and fat, but on the whole, he will still expect to catch a dolly bird of – well, he might accept thirty, at a pinch, but would of course prefer someone a bit younger if he can get away with it. Men of seventy want to start a family – surely they've left it a bit late, but I don't say so. I try not to hurt people's feelings. I know how nervewracking it is to either place or answer an advertisement, and so I let people down as lightly as possible. Putting in your own ads gives you a bit more control initially, but after the first phone call, it's down to whether you like each other or not, just like anything else.

At the initial stages rejection isn't personal. That is the most vital thing to remember. Like you, they have a vast choice of people – perhaps they don't like the way you do your 'y's, in your letters. Perhaps they aren't keen on brown hair. Perhaps their mother always told them not to trust people over 5 feet 2 inches.

Perhaps they were lying in the first place, or did it for a laugh – I have called in answer to a few letters to find a lot of giggling going on in the background. It could be anything, so if you are going to allow yourself to get discouraged at this stage, the personal columns are not for you.

I have had some plusses in my own life. I haven't been successful yet, but I get on a lot better with my mother than I did. We still argue, but she is no longer terrified that she is watching her small nest egg dwindle away with nothing to show for it. I wouldn't have met the people I have if I hadn't started this. I wouldn't have been on television on *Wogan*. I wouldn't have been interviewed in *The Independent* or the *Sunday Express* or on the radio. I would not have had a whole BBC radio programme on me and my hunt – it was truthful, but not palatable to the reviewers, most of whom thought the whole thing extraordinary, and some of whom were quite unnecessarily snide, I thought. I was upset to begin with but I soon got over it. I'm learning to take criticism and to believe in myself too, which I have never done before.

When I started my friends thought my behaviour idiosyncratic at best, tacky and embarrassing at worst. Now everyone thinks it's a bit of a lark, since they've seen my face in the newspapers and on the television, and heard my voice on the radio. Some of the most vociferous detractors have admitted that they are half thinking of using the personal columns themselves. Some now do!

My increased confidence has helped me meet men. I can talk to them on aeroplanes, in buses, on trains very easily. My first meetings are less frightening, and I am more certain of what I want, and of what I don't want.

I have found that the old maxim of 'treat 'em mean, keep 'em keen' is absolutely true. I use the technique myself, but am never able to when I am mad about someone. And that's usually when they haven't been that interested in me. Nothing like a bit of indifference to whet the appetite. When I like a man, I snag my stockings, break a heel, catch my skirt on the corner of a table and spill the drinks on it, get food on the front of my dress. When I couldn't care less, I am elegant, graceful, charming and magnetic – then they always call again, and I have to get rid of them!

When I haven't been out for weeks except to take Moya to her playgroup, or to go and have a game of badminton, I look forward to a blind date because it gets me out of the house. I have been to far more expensive restaurants, discos, bars than I would either be able to afford or to go to by myself. If that is all one wants, then the personal columns are the perfect way to meet men and have an uncomplicated evening or two out with them. It's an excellent way to meet people too, although this isn't my aim. Lots of married couples – more than they would admit, I'm quite sure – have met through the magazines, and good marriages have come out of the meetings.

It's been a hell of a laugh. I have had some real disasters, I have fallen for men and they haven't wanted me, but I have had some fun out of it too. Like Jemima, when it's been good, it's been very very good, when it's been bad it's been horrid. Every few dates there's been one I've half liked, so that has been encouraging. Had I met five rotters in a row, I might feel a bit differently about this, but I haven't. The men have all been polite. No one has been violent or unpleasant, but that has had a lot to do with my strict rules about never going up to their rooms on the first date, of meeting in public places, of always giving my mother the address, the times and where possible the telephone numbers. That's just common sense, and every woman who starts this should bear in mind that self-preservation is important, and common sense is the best weapon. Don't be too trusting – and never go anywhere without letting people know where you are. Don't let them pick you up by car. Where possible get them to meet you where people abound, so that other people can get a good look at them. If there ever should be any unpleasantness, or anything dangerous, then a description can be given. Use your sixth sense – it is never wrong. If there's something funny about a man on the telephone, if he lies, if his story is inconsistent, if he never confirms dates or cancels often and then is profusely apologetic more than once – anything that doesn't quite match up, or anything that sets alarm bells going – pay attention to it. You may be wrong, and you may miss a date, but if you aren't, what then? Doesn't bear thinking about.

I would of course have preferred another way of meeting men – like across a crowded room, or at work (not possible with Moya and my ideas about motherhood) or in a dizzy social scene – but in Littlehampton on my budget it isn't possible. I have never found it humiliating. If I wanted a car, a washing machine, a horse, I would look in the newspapers and magazines – the same principle applies. One has to be realistic. Romance rarely gets things done.

My experience in marketing in the States made my chosen method eminently logical. I just applied the principles to marketing myself, and got on with it. I studied the market, decided on the strategy, and applied it to the problem – it has provided me with months of entertainment (though that's not what I was looking for), and has taught me a lot on the way.

The art of handling the phone calls correctly is my biggest problem. Okay, I've mastered not confusing one with another and can more or less keep track of who likes doing what with my master list system kept by the phone but I still can't be short and sweet. I want to know a fair bit about the man before I go on a date, you would too, and it's difficult to get the answers without either being curt and questioning or long winded and boring. The length of calls ranges from 10 minutes to 6 hours, seriously 6 hours, I did insist on a coffee break after 3 hours at 1 a.m. before continuing. In general the average call, including arranging a meeting is 25 minutes. So if you have small children it can be a problem. I have tried finishing all my correspondence with 'If you like what you've seen and read then I would be pleased to hear from you, after 7 p.m. would be preferable'.

However, experience has shown that this is normally disregarded. I have also tried keeping sweets by the phone but this is not only bad for children, it also means that whenever the phone rings they expect a sweet. If I have one negative thought about this way of meeting men it's the length of time on the phone trying to sort the truths from the untruths. I should also bring your attention to the lonely men, most conversations begin in the usual fashion and then after an hour or the third shorter call I realize they just want to chat to a woman. There is no female company in their lives and they simply miss talking about everyday mundane subjects. Then for me the guilt sets in and I feel sorry for them so I spare them some time, they enjoy listening and call again! So at all costs avoid this, I'm trying to.

I like men, of course. I like being admired by them, and have been very used to their attentions. I was not a Goody Two-Shoes when I was young. I had a lot of boyfriends, and made sure that I wore sexy clothes that made them want me, but my experience of family life didn't make me yearn to be a wife and then a mother. A leather miniskirt was more important at the time.

I accepted the fact even then that life with a man tends to be better than life without one. The way other people treat you for a start is very different – as I get older it becomes more obvious that a woman's status is very dependent on having a husband. I should know, I've had three. And now I haven't got anybody, I miss the social security, the shared moments, the envious looks from women who are in the position I find myself in now. But I am learning that life without a man isn't the end of the world – I would just prefer life with one, for my sake and Moya's.

I could have married Rashid but I didn't think his parents would like me, he couldn't take me to Pakistan unless he married me – there were all sorts of reasons.

Out of the blue he called again.

'Collie, is that you?'

'Rashid? Hello.'

'I've been trying to contact you for years, but you have been out of the country every time. I want to see you again. Will you come up to London?'

'No, I can't. Come down to see me in Littlehampton. We could meet in Brighton.'

My mother used to hate him, another reason why life was a bit tricky all those years ago (and possibly one of the reasons I went out with him in the first place – I wasn't into being the dutiful daughter then, and most of the time with him hoping she was too drunk to notice and too preoccupied to care). Ignoring her disapproving face, I agreed to meet him in the bar of the Metropole Hotel in Brighton.

When he walked in, a bit late, I knew it was him at once, even though we hadn't met for fourteen years. He was better-looking than ever; being older seemed to suit him. He had always had class, and his clothes were stunning – Italian, well-cut, a straight wool jacket, gaberdine trousers, a silk shirt. He looked marvellous, and such a contrast to so many men I had seen recently. I began to wonder if it could really start again.

The old magic was still there. He told me he had been married but was now separated. I spoke about Moya and my life.

'Goodness, Collie. You *have* made a mess of your life, haven't you? You should have married me all that time ago. I've thought about you so much.'

We had dinner at an Italian restaurant. His manners were as perfect as ever. The atmosphere was great, the champagne kept flowing, as we celebrated his birthday and our reunion. I told him about the blind dates.

Reading between the lines, he looked hard at me: 'Sounds very much as though you have had some kind of a nervous breakdown, Colette. What *have* you been doing?' He was right. At times, all my life, I have felt near an emotional precipice, and I have sometimes wanted to throw myself over it. Moya is the only thing that has stopped me recently.

The old emotions were strong. I wanted him to take care of me, to make me forget all the disappointments and struggles of the past few years. But even that was different. I know now that you have, ultimately, to take care of yourself, but a little help eases the strain.

We went to the disco. 'Sorry sir. You have to be a resident to get in now. It's past midnight.'

'OK,' said Rashid. I recognized the gleam in his eyes, from old. He turned on his heel, went straight upstairs and checked in before the man had had a chance to close his mouth.

'Now will you let us in?' asked Rashid.

'Yes, of course sir.'

We danced for hours. We held hands, we kissed, we clung together. 'Please stay the night with me Colette. I want you to stay very, very much.'

'I can't. I'd be embarrassed.'

There was no fuss. He was too much of a gentleman for that. He walked me to my car and kissed me goodnight, tenderly. I was on cloud nine. Perhaps everything was going to fit into place. He called the next day, and we arranged for us to spend a few days in London together.

I met him at the Grosvenor House Hotel. He was late again, a recurrent fault. Suddenly another Pakistani guy rushed in and explained that Rashid had had trouble parking the car, and the traffic had been appalling. I didn't mind. I had enjoyed sitting there watching people, feeling that, for a change, I would be on a par with them, able to afford whatever I wanted.

We went off to the cinema, and during the film – the name of which I don't remember because we didn't see much of it – we held hands passionately, and kissed and whispered gentle words of love and lust in each other's ears. It was obvious that we would sleep together that night.

Over dinner later, he laughed at me. 'You never thought I would amount to much did you, Colette? It's funny that I have become rich, something you always said you wanted.' He had made his money by running discos in Dubai and now had a business importing and exporting to and from the Middle East.

We went back to the flat when we had finished some more bottles of champagne. It was one of those apartments that businessmen rent for short stays in London – apricot and green, smart but impersonal. Even the flowers on the table didn't smell of anything, and the whole place was thickly carpeted and curtained, and grandly utilitarian.

We fell on each other, hardly pausing to shut the door behind us. It was just the same. Sex was wonderful, our bodies were in harmony, we laughed and talked and teased each other, and then made love all over again.

So was this the answer to my search? Had I wasted my time? No. It was not the answer. The past cannot be resurrected that conveniently. The next day things were a little different. He was shifty about people seeing us together in the evening, and we had to pretend in a private gambling club that we didn't know each other, which I found insulting. I began to get angry with him – he was charming, but I felt used. Sex began to be tense, and I remembered all the other reasons I had decided to leave him fourteen years ago. He spent hundreds on an evening out – gambling and then dinner at Stringfellows with friends, several bottles of champagne (the bill was £600), and a slight contretemps with his friend and another man, which soured the evening and reminded me of the other, wheeling and dealing side of Rashid (the man demanded £700 which he insisted Rashid's friend owed him). Rashid sat back, stern-faced, and eventually, to shut him up, paid the money and proceeded to ignore him from then on.

I did enjoy myself, though. I wasn't part of the negotiations and I felt proud to be seen with this handsome dark-eyed, dark-skinned man, slim and tall and well-spoken. I tried to blot out the unpleasantness of the £700 incident, and concentrated on the champagne, the conversation, which was as interesting as ever it had been, but I had realized that there was to be nothing more.

I slipped out of the flat in the early hours of the morning, not wanting to explain or apologize, left a note thanking him for a lovely couple of days and went home quietly to Littlehampton. Another thing I have learnt is that, if it doesn't feel right, however much you want to persuade yourself it is perfect, it just isn't. I didn't hear from him again until a very smart card arrived at Christmas. I may see him again. I won't go out with him.

I also see Abdullah, my second husband, from time to time. We both know nothing will come of it, but he is rich, he likes me, I like him, we don't have to spend time getting to know each other. If he had been better-looking and not so closely connected to his country's royal family, things could have worked out differently. As it is, we re-met at Goodwood after a few years. He got me and my friends into the Royal Enclosure, and we had a lovely time together. He called again, took me out to dinner at the Dorchester, and routinely tried to get me into bed at the end of it. I said no, he protested a bit, then emptied the contents of his wallet into my handbag and drove me home. He is a gentleman. I know he cares deeply about me and the welfare of Moya, wanting only the best for us.

He finds me attractive, I find him physically unattractive. He knows that, and also knows that he isn't going to go to bed with me again.

We can still enjoy each other's company, and I see him every so often for dinner in town. We like each other – and it's such a pleasant relief being able to talk about the past, and not to repeat the answers to the usual questions, and to have a relationship without the promise of sex. I would not have been able to do that in my salad days – men weren't about being friends, they were about taking me out, and buying me things, and finding me attractive, and being made to work for my favours, which I rarely gave out.

Upon coming to the end of my story you must be under the impression that searching for Mr Right primarily through the personal columns has been one good time after another. This is not so. I have simply spared the reader the repetition of domestic routines which constitute my lifestyle.

Dates come and dates go, sometimes three in a week, sometimes three months without a single night out. The majority of the time I am at home learning French or Spanish, watching a video or TV, sewing on missing buttons or taking down hems, ironing – yes I do iron, funnily enough I don't mind it, writing to friends overseas, reading, partaking in one craft or another, and sorting out paperwork. Yes I must admit that many evenings are spent on the Man Hunt trail by phone or correspondence but by no means all. During the day, my search is down to a minimum, the post and some calls. My time is mainly taken up with being a good mother or at least trying to do everything I can to bring my daughter up in a safe, happy secure environment. We go shopping, rarely for my dating wardrobe, mainly humdrum grocery shopping or clothes for her. We play, I teach her, she goes to play school, swimming, dance lessons, friends come to tea and we go out to the beach, playgrounds and yes, McDonalds!

What I am really trying to say is that you are far more likely to find me in the evening curled up in front of the fire in my passion killer flannel nightie and candlewick dressing gown watching a TV documentary than ever you are in some fancy restaurant, done up to the nines with a would be Mr Right.

I have realized that I have a lot of things to offer men and a marriage, and I have realized that that is an honourable ambition: to make a marriage work and a family happy.

I am prepared to work much harder now, but I am not prepared to compromise any more. I have lowered my sights to Mr Almost Right, but I'm not going to settle for Mr Fairly OK, If You Ignore a Few Drawbacks. My expectations are more realistic I think, and I am involved with a musician at present. Nothing is settled. Nothing is promised. I am prepared to wait, watch and see how my life develops.

And in the meantime, I can fantasize about the Impossible Date, the Perfect Date, the Date to End All Dates. It may never happen.

It would begin with a bunch of twenty red roses, delivered to my door with a discreet card, on the day I was to meet him.

A car would appear to take me to London, possibly the Dorchester, to meet him for a pre-dinner drink. In the car would be a little gift of chocolates, the sort from Charbonnel et Walker with my name picked out in gold.

He would be on time, and look as if he had bothered with his appearance. He would be tall, dark and handsome, and his clothes would *fit* him. His manners would be perfect.

Cocktails at the Dorchester would be pleasant, not pushy; smart but not flash. He wouldn't have some revolting concoction with egg yolk and parasols, but would drink something like a vodka and tonic. We would talk sense, and he would be interested, interesting, and look appreciative.

I would begin to feel wonderful.

We would go to a musical, of course sitting in the best seats or a box, one with a decent view. There would be champagne in the interval in a private room. He would bring a corsage and his opera-glasses would be his own, which he would share with me as often as I needed them.

Then we would go for dinner, to Tante Claire in Royal Hospital Road. A surprise would be rolled up in the napkin – a little something, like a diamond (only kidding, but wouldn't it be nice). The meal would be effortless and wonderful, the wine perfect, the service (he would know the waiter and the owner) wonderful.

Tramp would be the next stop off. He wouldn't make a pass. We would dance together, very well, and drink a lot more champagne. We would return to a hotel – Blakes, perhaps – where he would have arranged separate rooms without asking. I would spend a dreamless night, and the next morning the car would be waiting to take me home. He would telephone as I walked in, and another date, this time somewhere abroad and exotic, would be arranged.

But if he were Mr Right, I would be just as happy for the date to be on Brighton beach, freezing cold, sharing a Pepsi, huddling next to him for warmth, and watching the stars together. My fate is in them, after all.

Postscript

To My Mummie

Thank you for financing my search for Mr Right.
Thank you for helping me through all the ups and downs of my search, for making me laugh at it all.
Thank you for being my personal assistant answering calls and writing letters.
Thank you for baby sitting and looking after Moya when I went on dates.
Thank you for providing a happy secure home for Moya to grow up in.
Thank you most of all for being a wonderful Grandma to Moya.

We love you